Understanding crime data
Haunted by the dark figure

6

CRIME AND JUSTICE

Series editor: Mike Maguire
University College of Wales, College of Cardiff

Crime and Justice is a series of short introductory texts on central topics in criminology. The books in this series are written for students by internationally renowned authors. Each book tackles a key area within criminology, providing a concise and up-to-date overview of the principal concepts, theories, methods and findings relating to the area. Taken as a whole, the *Crime and Justice* series will cover all the core components of an undergraduate criminology course.

Published titles

Understanding youth and crime
Sheila Brown

Understanding crime data
Clive Coleman and Jenny Moynihan

Understanding white collar crime
Hazel Croall

Understanding justice
An introduction to ideas, perspectives and controversies in modern penal theory
Barbara A. Hudson

Understanding crime prevention
Gordon Hughes

Understanding violent crime
Stephen Jones

Understanding criminology
Sandra Walklate

Understanding crime data
Haunted by the dark figure

Clive Coleman
Jenny Moynihan

Open University Press
Buckingham · Philadelphia

Open University Press
Celtic Court
22 Ballmoor
Buckingham
MK18 1XW

email: enquiries@openup.co.uk
world wide web: www.openup.co.uk

and
325 Chestnut Street
Philadelphia, PA 19106, USA

First published 1996
Reprinted 1998, 1999, 2000 2002

A catalogue record of this book is available from the British Library

ISBN 0 335 19519 9 (hb)   0 335 19518 0 (pb)

Library of Congress Cataloging-in-Publication Data
Coleman, Clive.
    Understanding crime data : haunted by the dark figure / Clive Coleman, Jenny Moynihan.
        p.   cm. — (Crime and justice)
    Includes bibliographical references and index.
    ISBN 0–335–19519–9 (hb).   ISBN 0–335–19518–0 (pbk.)
    1. Crime—Research. 2. Criminal statistics. 3. Victims of crimes surveys. 4.
    Criminology. I. Moynihan, Jenny, 1962– . II. Title. III. Series: Crime and justice (Buckingham, England)
    HV6024.5.C632 1996
    364′.0723—dc20   96–11903
                                                                                            CIP

Typeset by Type Study, Scarborough
Printed in Great Britain by Biddles Ltd, www.biddles.co.uk

Contents

Series editor's foreword

This is the second in a new series of textbooks on important areas of debate within the general fields of criminology, criminal justice and penology. The broad aim of the series is to provide relatively short and accessible texts, written by experienced lecturers and researchers, which will give under-graduates and postgraduates a solid grounding in the relevant area and, hopefully, a taste for the subject which will lead them to explore the literature further. Although aimed primarily at students new to the field, and although written as far as possible in plain language, the books do not give the false impression that they are dealing with a simple subject, easily mastered. On the contrary, all the authors aim to 'stretch' readers and to encourage them to approach criminological knowledge and theory in a critical and questioning frame of mind.

Clive Coleman and Jenny Moynihan's book covers the slippery subject of the sources, status and use of criminological data. How are such data produced? How 'reliable' are they? Do they really describe or imply what they appear to? As the authors make clear, such questions are fundamental to the whole criminological enterprise. They show how various forms of routinely collected statistical data (such as notifiable offences recorded by the police and records of court proceedings) still underpin widely accepted 'knowledge' about the nature and extent of crime and the characteristics of 'criminals'. They also discuss the impact of data from large-scale crime surveys, self-report studies and a miscellany of individual research projects, in challenging the 'official' picture of crime, in testing or supporting theories about the causes of crime, and in influencing and evaluating initiatives to prevent it. A particular strength of the book is that this broader context is kept constantly in view: although methodological issues are dealt with in a thorough and systematic fashion, the text never lapses into complex technical discussions for their own sake. Moreover, the authors have a lively, witty style and a taste for the concrete which produces colourful examples to illustrate and clarify the argument.

Other books in the *Crime and Justice* series cover penological theory (Barbara A. Hudson), criminological theory (Sandra Walklate), criminal justice and the penal system (Mike Maguire) and youth crime and justice (Sheila Brown and John Macmillan). All are central topics in the growing field of crime-related studies in universities, and each book should make an ideal foundation text for core courses or modules. As an aid to understanding, clear summaries are provided at regular intervals, and a glossary of key terms and concepts is a feature of every book. In addition, to help students expand their knowledge in specific areas, recommendations for further reading are given at the end of each chapter.

Finally, I must again record my gratitude to Roy Light and John Skelton for the original suggestion that I become involved in editing a series of this nature, as well as to Jacinta Evans, Joan Malherbe, Nick Evans and Pat Lee (past and present staff of Open University Press) for their help in bringing it to fruition. Most of all, I thank the authors,who have made my job as series editor both simple and pleasurable.

Mike Maguire
University of Wales, Cardiff

Preface

This book is intended to provide an accessible guide to crime data for those with little background in the subject. At the same time, we have tried to write a text which does not make those with a considerable knowledge of the field wince. We have, for example, minimized as far as possible the presentation of detailed figures and complicated tables, but we have not avoided some of the more difficult issues which arise in interpreting and using these data. Our focus is upon what particular types of quantitative data can tell us about crime and offenders. As we make clear, there are other important forms of data (and, as a result, certain aspects of crime) that we do not cover in detail. We also do not intend to discuss in any comprehensive way those data which are concerned with the detailed workings of the criminal justice system, such as those about sentencing and prisons.

In the town where one of us grew up, there was a café where, from time to time, the crockery would rise up from the tables and head for the nearest wall. People would sit for hours, hoping for a glimpse of the dark figure that was thought to be responsible, and wondering if they might witness it rearranging the furniture. The analysis of crime data has also been haunted by a dark figure – of unrecorded crime and offenders – with earlier attempts having to use various kinds of officially recorded data as the only available source of systematic quantitative information. In the first chapter, we discuss the way in which this was done by looking at the development of criminology as a discipline over the years, and the various ways in which it responded to the haunting presence of that dark figure. While its presence was frequently recognized, many were not too disturbed by it. For others, the dark figure threatened to rearrange the furniture of criminology in a fundamental way.

In the chapters which follow, we examine three different kinds of crime data. In Chapter 2, we look in detail at the official statistics of crime and offenders and how we might best understand them. We follow this with chapters on two ways of exploring (exorcizing?) the dark figure, which have been developed in the second half of the twentieth century: self-report studies and victimization surveys. In our view, although these methods have been successful in revealing aspects of that figure, ultimately there are issues about it that cannot be simply resolved by the use of such technical measuring instruments.

Having surveyed three main sources of numerical crime data, we then go on to discuss some key issues in their interpretation. In Chapter 5, we look at what the various forms of evidence seem to be telling us about certain characteristics of offenders, in respect of age, sex, race and social class. In Chapter 6 we first examine what the data can tell us about trends in crime over the last 60 years or so in England and Wales. We then go on to look at a related issue with considerable contemporary resonance: the relationship between crime and unemployment. Our choice of key issues is, of course, not definitive; our purpose is merely to present some examples to demonstrate what can and cannot be concluded from the available data. We conclude our discussion with a chapter which outlines a number of our personal observations about the field we have covered.

We cannot say, rather as Spike Milligan once did when receiving an award, that we did it all on our own. A number of our friends and colleagues have read and commented on parts of the text. We are very grateful to Keith Bottomley, Clive Norris, Dave Metcalf, David Dixon and Robert Harris. We are only sorry that we did not always have the space to respond to all their excellent suggestions. Jenny would also like to thank Diane McDonald for her support and Clive would like to thank his daughter Ellen, who waited so patiently while this book was being written for her room to be decorated. We are particularly grateful to our editor, Mike Maguire, who suggested this book in the first place and has been helpful and supportive throughout, having valiantly read all of it at some stage or other. Nevertheless, we must state, as authors seem compelled to do, that what is written here is entirely our own fault.

chapter one

Haunted by the dark figure: criminologists as ghostbusters?

This chapter introduces the following key concepts and terms, an entry for each of which is also to be found in the glossary at the end of the book: the governmental project; the Lombrosian project; the dark figure; the moral statisticians; positivism; triangulation; participant observation; life histories; social disorganization; the ecological fallacy; white-collar crime; deviant behaviour; Merton's anomie theory; self-report study; victimization survey; labelling perspective; aetiology; conflict theory; radical criminology; deviancy amplification; folk devil; moral panic; ethnomethodology; realist, institutionalist and radical perspectives on crime statistics; feminist criminology; left realists; situational crime prevention; rational choice perspectives; and epistemology.

The development of criminology, the iceberg and the dark figure

David Garland (1994) has argued that the discipline of criminology developed from, and continues to be influenced by, two rather different projects, the 'governmental' and the 'Lombrosian'. The first is constituted by 'the long series of empirical enquiries, which, since the eighteenth century, have sought to enhance the efficient and equitable administration of justice by charting the patterns of crime and monitoring the practice of police and prisons' (Garland 1994: 18). Such a project, which continues to this day and has come to be dominated by the state and state-sponsored agencies, collects and collates enormous quantities of information for a cluster of activities which are concerned with such things as policy, administration, management, monitoring and control. Such data occupy a central place in this project and contribute greatly to its claim to be a rational, evidence-based activity; in various forms they constitute a key subject matter for this book.

The second, the 'Lombrosian' project, has a different objective: to build a science of causes, an explanatory body of scientifically tested propositions about crime and criminals which, according to Garland (1994: 18), is 'based on the premise that criminals can somehow be differentiated from non-criminals'. Many readers will be familiar with Lombroso, and the broad outline of his conclusions, which are often paraded in criminology courses as examples of the funny things that people used to think in the olden days. Although the emphasis shifted (but not entirely) from the idea that the causes of crime were to be found mainly in the biological characteristics of individuals, the pursuit of Lombroso's ultimate objective of building that science of causes continued to drive much criminological work for years afterwards. In more recent times, although there has been considerable interest in 'the causes of crime', many criminologists have accepted that it is not possible to distinguish the criminal from the non-criminal by scientific methods in the way that earlier criminologists thought it could be done. However, let us see what the implications of that project were for data.

If the Lombrosian project was concerned with finding the differences between the criminal and the non-criminal, it could be thought that part of the task had already been done: samples of 'criminals' could be drawn from those populations produced by those agencies whose job it was to deal with offenders, with the prison in particular providing a convenient captive population. As Garland (1985) has argued, the development of the prison in the nineteenth century provided an institutional context within which the new science of the criminal could develop. The 'control' or comparison groups of 'non-criminals' required by the canons of good scientific procedure could equally, it was thought, be drawn from the general population, hopefully those without any record of criminal activity. Once these groups had been located, work could begin on discovering the differences between them which would eventually lead to that theory of the criminal.

It must be said that there were contrary voices, some of which said that it was wrong for any proper science to allow the state to define its subject matter, for that was a matter for the science itself. More frequently to be heard were those which said that, even if the state's formal definition of crime was acceptable for practical purposes, it was probably wrong for science to rely on other agencies to produce its data and its research subjects. Since such agencies' concerns were different from those of science, the use of data from such sources could be a risky enterprise. It was all very convenient and cheap to buy clothes off the peg, but these might not fit the requirements of those who would try to wear them. Such voices, as we shall see, became more and more audible during the twentieth century, so that in the end many clamoured for specially collected data that came from sources other than the official agencies. We shall examine the nature of the concerns about official data on crime and criminals in due course.

At this point, however, it is important to note that there are two rather different types of information that it is useful to distinguish. The first is the *official statistics on crime and criminals* produced by the state and its agencies. The second is the *data generated from research on samples derived from official sources* such as courts and prisons. Although these two types of data share something in common, the second clearly has an advantage in that the research itself can collect additional data, and do this in a way that reflects particular theoretical or other concerns (e.g., information on the physical or psychological characteristics of individuals). Those involved in the Lombrosian project would clearly prefer the second type of data to the first. For some critics, however, as we shall see, both types of data share the same fundamental flaw: such data come from only a sample of those items or persons which constitute the population in which we are interested. Not only does the sample not represent the 'actual extent' of crime and criminals, but it may not be representative of their nature.

One common way to speak of such problems has been through reference to the 'iceberg' of crime and criminals, with the suggestion that only the tip is visible, and a much larger element hidden from view. The attraction of this metaphor in the 1960s and 1970s, as we shall see, was perhaps that it conjured up a picture of the *Titanic* (traditional criminology) complacently going about its business with its gaze fixed upon the visible tip (official data) and about to be sunk by the huge unknown bulk beneath the water-line (unrecorded crime and undetected criminals). Every metaphor has its limitations. In this instance it is too solid, too homogeneous, failing as it does to convey the complexity of the realm of crime and criminals. For one thing, unlike crime, the composition of the hidden part of an iceberg is the same as the part that can be seen. For another, the relationship between the sizes of the two parts of an iceberg does not vary, following as it does a principle developed from the work of Archimedes, apparently after spending some time in the bath.

An even more popular way to talk about the problem of official data for both the governmental and Lombrosian projects is to refer to the dark figure of crime. Although not often recognized, the notion of the dark figure is ambiguous: it can refer to that vast *number* of unrecorded crimes and criminals (the conventional usage), or it can refer to our *picture* or *imagery* of the undetected offender and her/his offences. It can thus be used in a quantitative (numerical) or a qualitative (pictorial) sense, or in a way that combines both aspects. For many years, little was known about these dark figures, which have haunted the discipline of criminology throughout its short history. Few, if any, denied the presence of a dark figure in their midst; the differences came in the responses to its presence. For many years, little if anything was done about it, and researchers and others continued about their business as if, for practical purposes, it had no serious implications for their work. It was as if they were implicitly assuming that the dark figure had broadly similar features to those crimes and offenders which were already known. Eventually, however, some researchers found the presence of the dark figure too disturbing to ignore. They therefore set about trying to discern its size and characteristics. Some did so by the use of technical measuring instruments, while others had more of a bell, book and candle approach, driven as they were by a strong moral commitment to expose and if possible exorcize the hidden evil in our midst. It should not surprise us, therefore, if we find the dark figure taking a number of different forms as we look at the development of thinking about crime data. For some, as we shall see, the dark figure called into question some of the almost taken-for-granted beliefs about crime and the criminal.

Traditional perspectives on crime data

The first national crime statistics were published in France in 1827. Beirne (1993: 2, 71) has outlined the way in which these were brought about by a range of factors, which included the huge growth in the surveillance of the population by the state, the fears on the part of the middle classes of the 'dangerous classes', and the failure of the network of carceral institutions to deal with those classes effectively. The development of such data, also encouraged by certain intellectual trends, was thus inextricably tied up with the governmental project outlined above. These statistics recorded yearly for each *département* the number of known crimes against both persons and property; how many of these led to prosecutions; how many of those prosecuted were acquitted or convicted; and how those convicted were punished. Also recorded were the time of year of the offence, together with the age, sex, occupation and educational status of the accused. Beirne (1993: 74) also suggests that the French Ministry of Justice and a group of 'moral statisticians' thought that this information could eventually 'be used to perfect legislation in civil and moral matters'.

The moral statisticians

The moral statisticians were not called such in order to distinguish them from their less upright colleagues; instead, they were a group of statisticians who were interested in applying methods and quantitative techniques developed for the most part in the natural sciences to 'moral' (or social) phenomena. One of the most famous members of this group, Adolphe Quetelet, had worked in the field of 'celestial mechanics' (astronomy), and in his early work hoped to discover the sorts of laws and regularities which characterized the natural world in the realm of 'social facts': hence his conception of a 'social mechanics' (Beirne, 1993: 77). Quetelet recognized that this enterprise would not be as straightforward as that in the natural world. Not only were moral statistics more complex than their physical counterparts, but they might also be affected by the unpredictable operation of free will. Although this might lead one to expect great fluctuations in moral statistics as a result, Quetelet was pleased to find that crime statistics apparently displayed similar kinds of regular patterns to those found in data about the natural world.

Even during this period, however, any further analysis also had to come to terms with sightings of the dark figure. Beirne suggests that another moral statistician, de Candolle, was probably the first of them to recognize the possibly disturbing implications of this: 'It is purely specious to believe that the ratio of known to unknown crimes is constant' (quoted in Beirne, 1993: 106). Quetelet recognized not only the existence of this dark figure, but also some of the factors which determined its size. This depended not only on the seriousness of offences but also on the

> activity of justice in reaching the guilty, on the care which these latter will take in hiding themselves, and on the repugnance which wronged individuals will feel in complaining, or on the ignorance in which perhaps they will be concerning the wrong which has been done to them.
>
> (Quoted in Beirne, 1993: 80)

Wise words, but Quetelet's observations of the consistency in French crime rates between 1826 and 1829 led him to conclude that the ratio of known to unknown crimes was in practice relatively constant. In a later study of Belgian crime rates between 1833 and 1839 he also found a pretty constant ratio between crimes recorded and crimes prosecuted. These two conclusions led him to argue that, provided the operative causes remained constant, their effects (in the shape of their representation in the official statistics) would remain constant also (Beirne, 1993: 80). If true, this would mean that such data would still be a good guide to such matters as trends in crime over time, if not the absolute quantity. Quetelet's notion that the dark figure need not in practice disturb us very much was an assumption that was to be shared by many who were to follow. His pioneering analyses of the causes of crime, which included consideration of such items as age, sex, education, occupation and religion (Beirne, 1993: 83–8) and the work of Guerry (see below) clearly influenced the approach of others, including Émile Durkheim (1952; originally published in 1897) and his famous analysis of suicide rates.

An equally important figure in any discussion of the moral statisticians is A. M. Guerry, whose major work, *Statistique Morale*, was published in 1833. Although his work shared many of the same concerns as that of Quetelet and used the same sources, Guerry was also a pioneer of the cartographic approach (use of maps) in the study of crime. In doing so, Guerry was pioneering a tradition that was to establish an enduring place in the study of crime, from the work of the Chicago School, through to contemporary 'areal' and spatial analyses. In addition, Guerry argued that the totality of crime was more accurately indicated by the number of indictments than by the number of convictions, since the former were subject to less serious errors than the latter. For example, he claimed that indictments depended on the more reliable decisions of public prosecutors, whereas convictions depended on the whims of juries (Beirne, 1993: 116). This is a kind of recognition, but a very limited one, of a dark figure lurking in the shadows and of the fact that these were actually statistics of the *decisions of agencies* in the criminal justice system, which should really be examined as such before being put to use as measures of crime.

Similar developments were to follow in other countries. In Britain, Rawson, Fletcher and Glyde presented papers to the Statistical Society of London in the middle of the nineteenth century, using existing statistical materials to identify and interpret patterns in crime. Henry Mayhew's work at about the same time used a variety of methods, including surveys and official data to outline the features of, and suggest causes of, crime in the city of London (on these authors, see Morris, 1957). Garland (1994: 36) suggests that such studies, whether done by amateurs or (as increasingly occurred) by state officials, had the same 'concern with governance and the use of empirical data and scientific methods to improve government's grip on the population'. As he also notes, however, the notion that the study of crime could be split off from other aspects of social conditions and policy was unfamiliar to them. It was later in the century that the idea of a specialist discipline of criminology was to emerge, in this instance one based on the idea of a distinctive criminal type, the Lombrosian project.

The Lombrosian project

The new school of criminology of which Lombroso was the founder called itself 'positivist'. This term indicated a desire to emulate the methods, techniques and the kinds of astounding advances which had been made in the natural sciences during the nineteenth century, and thereby to press its claims to be superior to any alternatives. The term 'positivist' has since entered the vocabulary of textbook writers around the world, but it is by now more commonly a term of abuse than a source of pride or claim for superiority. It has, moreover, been used in so many ways, and often so vaguely, that we find that it more frequently now leads to confusion than enlightenment (see Giddens, 1974; Garland, 1994: 22–3).

We have already discussed some of the implications of the Lombrosian project for data. While official statistics alone could rarely provide the kind of data required, research was frequently done using samples from official sources. These were often compared with control or comparison groups (often rather crudely matched) of people who for practical purposes were assumed to be non-criminal. There was little practical recognition of the dark figure here. The Lombrosian project did not decline with the reputation of its founder, but continued to survive and prosper in the next century. Goring (1913) is commonly suggested to have published a convincing refutation of

Lombroso. However, while Goring denies the existence of an anthropologi-
cal criminal type, he concludes from his own work the existence of a
'physical, mental, and moral type of normal person who tends to be convicted
of crime' (quoted in Pick, 1989: 187). It was the statistically crude methods of
Lombroso that were the prime target of Goring's work (Pick, 1989: 186–7).
The work of finding the differences between criminals and non-criminals
continued throughout the twentieth century, supplemented by the disciplines
of psychiatry and psychology. The existence of the dark figure had generally
unrecognized but potentially devastating implications for this work, until
new methods could be developed to identify in a more satisfactory way those
engaging in criminal behaviour. Finally, as Garland (1994: 53) notes of
Britain, the 'scientific criminology which developed between the 1890s and
the Second World War was thus heavily dominated by a medico-psychologi-
cal approach, focussed upon the individual offender and tied into a
correctionalist penal-welfare policy'. What were mainly absent were the
successors to the kind of work produced by the moral statisticians and others
in the last century. This could not be said of the situation in the United States.

The Chicago School and environmental criminology

In the first half of the twentieth century, a group of sociologists at the
University of Chicago, who became known as the Chicago School, set about
the analysis of the city and the social and cultural forms that developed within
it. Their work (also frequently referred to as the 'ecological approach')
included studies of crime and mental illness, and often began by mapping
rates of these (as measured by official data) according to the various zones of
the city. Although these researchers frequently combined the use of official
data with data collected by other methods, such as participant observation
and life histories (the use of different methods and data in a piece of research
is often referred to as 'triangulation'), there is little doubt that the patterns
revealed by the official data had a decisive impact on the theoretical
framework developed. In the case of delinquency, data on where delinquents
lived revealed a concentration in those areas of the city characterized by low
rents and physical deterioration – the inner city (Shaw and McKay, 1942).
The rapid turnover in population in such areas, they argued, led to a
condition of social disorganization in which children were neither effectively
socialized nor controlled because of the absence of stable or common
standards and, in cities like Chicago in the early part of this century, even a
common language. In addition, in such neighbourhoods, delinquent traditions (later to be called 'subcultures') could become established and passed
on through the agencies of play groups and gangs.

Three points should be made about the enormous body of data generated
by this research tradition and the 'environmental criminology' that developed
from it (see Bottoms, 1994). The first is that, although the focus in the early

work was on the spatial distribution of *offenders*, much recent work has been concerned with plotting and explaining the spatial distribution of *offences*. The distinction between offence data and offender data is a key one throughout this book. Failure to be clear on this can be the source of much confusion. The second point is that the early work and much of what followed was based on data recorded by the police and courts. The whole edifice was constructed on the assumption that these data reflected some 'actual' distribution of crime and delinquency. Although the adequacy of such data was frequently questioned, the problem could not be tackled fully without comparable alternative measures. Since these were not developed until later (see Chapters 3 and 4), this kind of criticism was generally unsuccessful in restraining the ambitions of such studies and the theories built upon them. We are, of course, saying that this enterprise was haunted by the dark figure. Here there were at least two quantitative dark figures: one for offences and one for offenders. An authority in the field, with the benefit of the more recent research on this problem, has recently written: 'official crime and offender data often seem to reflect real differences between sub-areas of cities, but in any given case cannot be taken for granted and must be investigated' (Bottoms, 1994: 598). The third and final point is that more attention was probably given to a rather different potential problem with such data. This was called the 'ecological fallacy' (Robinson, 1950).

The term 'ecological fallacy' was coined to draw attention to the caution needed in dealing with aggregate data based on areas of the city. For example, in Britain in the 1960s, data suggested that areas with concentrations of minority ethnic population were also areas with high crime rates. It was tempting to conclude that it was the members of these groups who were responsible for the high crime rates of those areas. Such a conclusion at that time would have been an example of the ecological fallacy because, in fact, more detailed research suggested that the minority ethnic groups had, broadly speaking, lower offending rates (also measured by official data) than those of the native population (Lambert, 1970). The term 'ecological fallacy' has been used rather more broadly to refer to the trap into which we may fall when interpreting any aggregate data and attempting to draw inferences from them about patterns at the individual level. For example, if aggregate data (e.g., summary data for a whole country) show a correlation between rising unemployment and crime, it does not necessarily follow that unemployed persons are responsible for the increases in crime. It should be mentioned that in many instances aggregate data can often provide indications of relationships at the individual level; we cannot, however, be sure that we are on firm ground without further investigation, using more appropriate data.

The dark figure in a white collar

While the members of the Chicago School were busy plotting official data on to their maps of Chicago and other cities, a sociologist called Edwin

Sutherland thought he saw a dark figure which was very different from previously recorded sightings. This figure wore a white collar, and was to be seen from time to time in the offices and workplaces of the nation, including the buildings of the most respected corporations. Sutherland (1940) was drawing attention to the white-collar criminal and to white-collar crime: 'crimes committed by persons of respectability and high social status in the course of their occupations' (Sutherland and Cressey, 1960: 40). He claimed that not only were these very widespread, but a measure of them is not to be found in police recorded data. There were a number of reasons for this. Prosecution was often avoided because of the importance of the parties involved, the *apparently* trivial nature of the offences, and the problems in getting sufficient evidence. More significantly, other procedures were frequently used to deal with white-collar criminals, such as civil actions or those of special agencies, with conventional penalties used only as a last resort. This not only allowed some to argue that these were not 'really' crimes at all, but also resulted from and reinforced the absence of a strongly developed normative code surrounding this whole area. Sutherland, however, clearly believed that these white-collar criminals were the most damaging of all in terms of their effects. He substantiated his assertions by study of law violations of 70 of the largest corporations in the USA, concluding that 90 per cent of these were 'habitual white-collar criminals' (Sutherland, 1949). He did not feel it necessary to add the word 'allegedly'.

Sutherland's pioneering work has not been without its problems for subsequent work. Many have found the original definition of white-collar crime ambiguous; it does not, for example, distinguish offences committed against the organization from those committed on its behalf. For some commentators, some of the ambiguity surrounding the concept is an inherent feature of the whole area itself, and cannot be resolved by argument and a clarification of the definition of 'crime'. The contested nature of the concept points instead to ambiguities, the structure of power and conflicts of interest in the wider society which influence the way in which that society defines 'crime' (Aubert, 1952; Nelken, 1994). The importance of the concept also lies in what it suggested about the discipline of criminology, its definition of its subject matter, and its data. For Sutherland, conventional criminology had largely limited its attention to the crimes of the low-status, relatively powerless groups in society. The conventional definition of crime, which excluded anything about which there was ambiguity, made sure that only some crime and some offenders would be studied by criminologists. The result was a partial criminology, with theories that were not general but only applied to a part of the population in which we should be interested. Finally, criminologists could not confine themselves to the study of official data or samples from official sources as they had done in the past. Writing about half a century later, Nelken says:

Study of the distribution and frequency of white-collar crimes is made problematic by the fact (not in itself unimportant) that ... most white-collar crimes are not included in the official statistics which serve as the basis for debates about 'the crime problem'. The usual difficulties of interpreting the statistics of crime are greatly magnified here.

(Nelken, 1994: 355–6)

The implications of Sutherland's work were therefore momentous; not only were there vast dark figures of offences and offenders which required different data sources and research techniques to do them justice, but also our image of the 'typical' crime and criminal and our explanations of them needed drastic revision.

Sellin's dictum

At about the same period another famous criminologist was pointing out that '[t]he value of criminal statistics as a basis for the measurement of criminality in geographic areas decreases as the procedures take us farther away from the offense itself' (Sellin, 1951: 494) – a clear reference to the view that the statistics produced at each subsequent stage in the criminal justice process are of declining value as a measure of crime and criminals. This statement, which is often referred to as 'Sellin's dictum', represented a commonly held view among researchers and textbook writers. The same author had also argued that the criminologist should study violations of 'conduct norms' rather than merely that behaviour defined by legislatures as crime (Sellin, 1938). This was one version of the argument that the subject matter of science should be defined by scientists for scientific purposes rather than by the state. This clearly made any attempt at measurement far more complex; not only were ready-made statistics unavailable, but conduct norms could vary substantially between groups, without the 'authoritative resolution' (Matza, 1969) provided by the state. This was yet another indication that the definition of crime itself could be contested for various reasons, with each definition having its own implications for the size and nature of any dark figure. Similar considerations lay behind the work of other sociologists, who were beginning to speak of a subject matter rather broader than crime, that of 'deviant behaviour'.

Merton's anomie

One of the most influential and enduring attempts to explain variations in the rates of deviant behaviour between societies, and between groups in the same society, was Merton's theory of anomie, first developed in 1938 but subsequently developed by Merton himself and others over many years (see Adler and Laufer, 1995). Just as Durkheim (1952; originally published in

1897) before him had attempted to demonstrate how suicide rates could be explained sociologically, Merton tried to show how rates of deviant behaviour could be explained by reference to aspects of the social and cultural structures of societies and the location of individuals and groups in relation to them. Unlike Durkheim, however, Merton gave relatively little attention to the statistics to be explained. Merton had by the 1950s recognized the work of Sutherland and others on white-collar crime, and also cited one of the earliest self-report studies, which attempted to measure offences and offenders independently of official records (see Chapter 3). Having done so, however, he did not think that these studies had serious implications for his analysis, in which the lower classes were still seen as the major recruits to the world of vice, rackets and crime:

> But whatever the differential rates of deviant behaviour in the several social strata, and we know from many sources that the official crime statistics uniformly showing higher rates in the lower strata are far from complete or reliable, it appears from our analysis that the greatest pressures toward deviation are exerted upon the lower strata.
>
> (Merton, 1957: 144)

Merton's approach was typical of the period: it acknowledged the existence of the dark figure, but did not see the need to worry too much about its possible implications; after all, crime statistics, our theories and our common sense all seemed to concur about crime and the criminal. Elsewhere Merton noted other problems with such data, again with a familiar ring: they are 'social book-keeping data' and are unlikely to be in a form relevant for sociological research; in addition, they are unreliable because 'successive layers of error intervene between the actual event and the recorded event' (Merton, 1956: 31). Other highly influential work of the 1950s showed a similar notion of where the problem (for both policy and explanation) lay – in the lower classes, particularly among young males living in deprived city areas, who were seen to be candidates for recruitment into delinquent subcultures (see, for example, Cohen, 1955; Cloward and Ohlin, 1960). Such sociological work as existed in Britain at this time seemed to reflect many of the same concerns (see, for example, the earlier studies in the collection by Carson and Wiles, 1971).

The dark figure as a woman

There were other occasional dissenting voices. While Sutherland had seen the dark figure wearing collar and tie, Otto Pollak claimed he had seen the dark figure frequently wearing a dress (1961; originally published in 1950). Here was someone prepared to question the taken-for-granted view from official data that men far outnumber women in terms of criminal behaviour. According to Pollak, offences committed by women were less likely to be reported, and if reported less likely to be detected, and even if detected women would be likely to be treated more leniently by the police and courts. The production of this dark figure was due to a number of factors: that women are more likely to instigate crimes than commit them; that women are more able to exercise deceitfulness because, among other things, they are more able to simulate or conceal things such as sexual arousal (perhaps he had heard that old joke about it 'sticking out a mile' among men); that the victims of typical women's crimes (e.g., those in the family) are less likely to report them; and finally, that men will typically act chivalrously towards women in a number of contexts, thereby affecting the probability of official action and recording. It may not surprise you to hear that Pollak has received a rough ride from the critics (for an example, see Smart, 1976: 46–53). However, what is most significant here is the way in which he attempted to build an argument that official data suffered not only from *omissions* (which everybody accepted) but also from *systematic bias*. While Sutherland saw this in terms of class bias, Pollak questioned the accuracy of official data in a different way. While there were objections to some of his assumptions, few if any alternative data were available at that time that could help in such debates about the nature and extent of women's crimes.

Changing times, changing perspectives

During the 1960s a substantial body of work developed which questioned some of the traditional approaches to crime data, their uses and limitations, and what we could conclude from them. The occasional critical lone voices of the past came to be replaced by a chorus of alternative views. As we show below, the overall sound was not particularly harmonious, for they were singing to a number of different tunes. Two main sources of these views can be identified: the development of new forms of crime data, and the impact of various new theoretical perspectives on the study of crime and deviance.

New forms of crime data

The development of new ways of quantifying the extent, nature and distribution of crime and offenders falls into two types, the *self-report study* and the *victimization survey*. The former involves asking people directly about their involvement in rule-breaking behaviour. We discuss these studies extensively in Chapter 3. As we show there, although there were isolated examples in the 1940s and the 1950s, they did not appear in any quantity until the 1960s. Not only did these studies suggest that offending was far more widespread than had been indicated by official data, but some of the early studies also came up with findings which suggested that some of the traditional views about offenders (such as about their class origin) might be seriously mistaken. These studies appeared to have important things to say about the dark figure of *offenders*, both quantitatively and qualitatively.

The second new method developed was the victimization survey, now frequently referred to simply as the 'crime survey'. This was a rather later development than the self-report study. Large experimental surveys were carried out in the USA in the late 1960s, but exploratory studies were not conducted in Britain until the 1970s, and the regular national sweeps of the British Crime Survey did not begin until the 1980s. These studies involve asking samples of the public to recall crimes committed against them during a recent period. They appeared to provide, for the first time, a way of quantifying the extent and nature of the dark figure of *offences*. Although these expectations were to prove somewhat optimistic, there is little doubt that these surveys and associated developments such as local crime surveys have had a major impact on the ways in which crime is discussed. We explore these issues in Chapter 4.

New theoretical perspectives

We now turn to the new ways of thinking about crime, which were to have a resounding impact on thinking about crime data. In Britain, for example, a whole group of sociologists of deviance were much influenced by such ideas and sought to distance themselves from the governmental and Lombrosian projects which they thought were still dominant in the orthodox criminology practised in that country at the time (Cohen, 1981). The first to mention is the *labelling perspective*, a body of ideas originating in the USA which attempted to change the way in which deviance was conceptualized and studied. Briefly stated, this perspective drew attention to the nature, origins, application and consequences of deviancy labels (Plummer, 1979). Put another way, it was concerned with the previously neglected topics of the social definition of deviance and social reactions to it. This represented a considerable change in focus from previous perspectives on deviance, which were mainly interested in the causes of deviant behaviour (aetiology). When applied to the area of crime, this perspective suggested that laws (the key element in the definition of crime) have *origins* which should be investigated, whereas traditional approaches had tended to take the laws as given. Laws were the product of power and interest-group activity, and study of this and its implications for the definition of the subject matter should be considered as central issues. It was urging that politics should be brought to the centre stage of criminology. Such ideas were to be taken up and developed, first by conflict theory (e.g., Quinney, 1970) and later by the emerging Marxist-inspired radical criminology of the 1970s (e.g., Taylor *et al.*, 1973; 1975). Such perspectives urged the structural analysis of power, the state and the way in which the law reflects their mode of operation. These cast the official statistics, and the definitions of crime built into them, in a new light.

The labelling perspective also urged that the *application* of deviancy labels should be a prime focus for investigation. It argued that a number of agencies were involved in the process of conferring such labels upon a variety of acts and actors, and an important research question should be how this is accomplished. How important, for example, are the nature and seriousness of the act *vis-à-vis* such aspects as the class, race, gender, demeanour and age of the actor in the probability of a deviant label being applied? Such agencies are involved in the routine production of statistics, and it was possible to see such statistics as *socially constructed*, rather than as measures of deviant behaviour or persons. This viewpoint therefore argued for the need to investigate the organizational processing of deviance. At two levels, therefore, the labelling perspective was arguing that crime and the criminal were *social constructs*, and the process of their construction must be a matter of concern for sociologists and criminologists. It could be that systematic bias was operating at both levels, in definitions of crime enshrined in the law, and in the official statistics produced by the criminal justice system. The implications for researchers who wanted to use those statistics and for the dark figure were obvious.

The other preoccupations of the labelling perspective were with the nature and consequences of labelling. The first point is that labels are often composed of bundles of characteristics, the composition of which has its own history. These labels carry implications for those who apply them, for those in the wider society, and for those to whom they are applied. A simple example is that labels often carry stereotypes about a particular type of offence or offender. Secondly, such bundles may have important consequences, not only for those who are labelled, but also for a range of others. In some circumstances a process of *deviancy amplification* might result from the labelling of certain individuals or groups (see, for example, Young, 1971). Often implicated in this process were the mass media, inflating concern about a particular problem and carrying powerful messages about it, including the production, maintenance and transmission of stereotypes. Such processes may begin on the flimsiest basis in official data, but may in the end produce the very data that confirm the initial fears. In what was a distinctively British development of the labelling perspective, there arrived the concepts of the folk devil and moral panic (Cohen, 1973). These concepts were used in an important study of the concern about 'mugging' in the 1970s, which suggested that this was a moral panic, based on an imported label and without any firm statistical base, but which nevertheless carried important messages about law and order, race, crime and the condition of Britain, and served as a kind of scapegoat which drew attention away from the real problems facing British society at that time (Hall *et al.*, 1978; for a critique of their use of statistical data and the concept of moral panic, see Waddington, 1986).

The concepts of the folk devil and moral panic can be seen as diametrically opposed to the dark figures of crime and the criminal. Whereas the first two mentioned are seen as suffering from over-exposure, over-dramatization and various kinds of adverse distortion, the latter two are characterized by under-exposure, under-recording and often a lack of sensitization on the part of the public. The first two are front-stage in the drama of crime and justice, the latter two back-stage. The link can further be seen in the idea that folk devils and moral panics can often have the effect of concentrating the attention and efforts of those concerned with law and order on certain targets, rather than upon others (such as the crimes of the powerful). In a world where audience attention span, journalists' time, column inches, police resources and so on are finite, this may be a powerful structuring principle upon perceptions of, and activities directed towards, 'the crime problem'.

Other theoretical influences can be mentioned. Jack Douglas (1967) published an important critique of the way in which Durkheim and other sociologists had studied suicide; their studies had mainly been done by using official statistics. He made two main points. The first was that suicide statistics are socially constructed, based as they are on the activities of friends, relatives, coroners and other officials. The second was that, in any case, such statistics can tell us little about actual suicides as meaningful social actions. In fact meanings are often read into those statistics by the researcher from a preconceived theoretical framework or from 'common sense'. Douglas was but one example of a number of sociologists who stressed the need to provide an interpretative understanding of actions that gave full weight to the point of view of the actor. From this perspective, aggregate statistics, remote from the social meanings of the events in question, were of little value. Instead, close familiarity with the social world under study and qualitative data were frequently to be preferred.

A further influence came from that school of sociology called *ethnomethodology*. This took as its focus the way in which people (whether as officials, researchers or others) use practical reasoning, stocks of knowledge, language and so on in accomplishing a range of activities, including the production of official reports and statistics. One who was clearly influenced by the ethnomethodological programme was Cicourel, who co-authored a key article which argued that 'rates [of officially recorded deviant behaviour] can be viewed as indices of organizational processes rather than as indices of the incidence of certain forms of behaviour' (Kitsuse and Cicourel, 1963: 137). He followed this up with a study of the official handling of juveniles which argued that:

> Unless we seek an independent study of the discourse that precedes reports by the police and probation, or unless we elicit information from these officials about their decisions and their use of terms in the writing of reports, we cannot understand the meaning of aggregated information like official records and statistics.
>
> (Cicourel 1976: xii)

Others had come to similar-sounding conclusions, although not necessarily from the same theoretical perspective. Wilkins (1964: 148) had suggested that official data relate to counts made at different 'decision gates' in the criminal justice system, rather than to crime. Wheeler (1967: 318) had claimed that crime statistics could be seen as the product of a three-way process of interaction between offenders, members of the public and law enforcement agents. Black (1970: 734) studied what he termed 'the production of crime rates', in which he took up a strategy which 'makes official records an end rather than a means of study. . . . From this standpoint crime statistics are not treated as inaccurate or unreliable'. This kind of approach – to make crime statistics the *topic* in their own right, rather than a *resource* with which to study crime – was also the approach adopted in a study of the production of crime statistics in a northern English city (Bottomley and Coleman, 1981).

Realist, institutionalist and radical perspectives on crime statistics

All of this seemed to suggest that there were now two basic approaches to crime statistics: the 'realist' and the 'institutionalist' (Biderman and Reiss, 1967). The first, the traditional approach, was primarily concerned with the accuracy and 'completeness with which data represented the "real crime that takes place"' (Biderman and Reiss, 1967: 2), while the second urged the study of official data as outcomes of social and institutional processes. To these is frequently added a third: the 'radical' position which attempts to go a little further than the institutionalist approach:

> Whilst not denying the importance of organizational processes and everyday interactions, the radical position emphasizes that such processes and interactions are the product of wider social structural arrangements, particularly those relating to class conflicts. Therefore, official crime statistics are themselves products of these wider structural arrangements and should be treated as such.
>
> (Jupp, 1989: 48)

Such a classification is initially helpful. The first encompasses most traditional approaches, with their concern for accuracy, reliability, and completeness, and self-report and victim surveys can be seen initially as attempts to fill gaps in the official data by progressively revealing the dark figures of offenders and offences, respectively. The second is usually taken to include those we have considered who saw data as socially constructed products. The third includes those with a broader, structural and radical view of the whole area.

   In practice, things are not quite so simple. For example, we have already seen how those in the broad 'institutionalist' camp came from a variety of theoretical positions, each with its own set of assumptions and questions.

Few were prepared to go all the way with the ethnomethodologists (but see Atkinson, 1978, on suicide for an example of one who was). Hindess (1973: 24), for example, was horrified by what he saw as the implications of their work for knowledge – an alarming relativism, with all of us cast adrift in a sea of floating representations, without any fixed or necessary connection with any underlying 'reality': 'since any categorisation, even the sociologist's, is the result of human judgement and argument, we can never do more than compare one judgement with another and neither to the "real-world events" to which they refer'. Neither were many happy to follow the labelling perspective to what some saw as its logical conclusion. An interesting attempt to do so was provided by Ditton (1979: 20) who suggested that 'the reaction is constitutive of the criminal or deviant act . . . Accordingly, the idea of a "dark figure" of offences committed without a reaction is an unnecessary absurdity'. Ditton (1979: 20) also drew upon a much older view – that it is improper to call something a crime or offender without due process: 'No "crime" has been committed (in law and logic) until a court finds – i.e. creates for all intents and purposes – guilty intent'. He concluded that the dark figure was a myth.

A myth? This was bad news for those who had spent most of their working lives looking for the dark figure. Ghostbusters without ghosts – this would not do at all. Such versions of the institutionalist position were not only unwelcome news for those who were committed to the measurement of crime in order to explain, control or prevent it, but also unattractive for some of those of a radical persuasion, who wanted to test out the idea that crime statistics (and the system that produces them) were flawed by a systematic bias against the less powerful groups in society. How could this be done in a convincing way without some baseline of crime or offenders against which to measure the degree of bias in the official system and its statistics? Although some of the ideas covered above are understandable in terms of their theoretical underpinnings, they are not attractive for those with a need to know about crime and criminals for practical and other purposes. For various reasons, then, we find many writers adapting what they could from two or three of these basic positions. Steve Box (1981), for example, came to a view that was in fact a mixture of ideas from all three: realist (belief in a dark figure, to some extent accessible by victimization and self-report studies but ultimately unknown and probably unmeasurable in any precise way because of practical problems); institutionalist (official crime figures as socially constructed); radical (bias against the powerless in the system that records crime and in the definition of crime in law).

Recent developments

We now turn to developments since the 1970s which have had a major impact on discussions of crime data and the dark figure. These are not separate or self-contained, but in certain respects interconnected: feminist criminology, the new focus on victims, and the 'rediscovery of the offence' (Bottoms 1994: 592). The treatment can be brief, since most of the issues are followed up elsewhere.

A recognizable body of work that we can call 'feminist criminology', even though there are important differences among those who are often grouped under this label, began to emerge in the 1970s. Although much of the early work was concerned with criticizing the way in which criminology had neglected women and gender in their studies, or had studied them in unsatisfactory ways (see, for example, Smart, 1976), a number of other themes emerged in the attention given to women and crime. One of these was an argument that women's offending rates were rising more rapidly than men's, that women were switching to more aggressive, 'masculine' patterns of offending, and that this was due in some way to the influence of the modern women's movement (see Simon, 1975). Such an argument faced a number of difficulties, not least of which was the nature of the overall trends in the officially recorded data. Not only were these not entirely clear, but the whole enterprise was haunted by the dark figure. As Smart (1979) pointed out, the relatively small numbers involved in figures of female crime could be influenced by changes in recording practices, policing and other policies to produce spurious 'trends'.

A second linked issue which began to receive increasing attention was the ratio of women's crime to men's (or of women offenders to men offenders – the two are often not clearly distinguished), which had been raised by Pollak. Unlike Pollak, however, recent discussions have had the benefit of alternative sources of data collection such as self-report studies. While these did reveal hidden female crime, in this instance the evidence did not radically challenge our ideas about the dark figure in the way that Pollak thought that it would. We discuss this issue in Chapter 5. Instead, a dark figure was sighted elsewhere, often in the private and seemingly cosy world of the home, and was frequently a man. The feminists played a key role in drawing attention to 'those offences committed mainly by men against women and children in which they use power or force' (Heidensohn, 1989: 105). These include offences such as domestic violence, physical and sexual abuse of children, rape, sexual assault and harassment. With some help from the victim surveys of the 1980s, they were able to suggest that such offences, which are difficult to measure by any method, had low reporting rates to the police, and yet often did considerable and lasting harm to their victims.

The second development is the new focus on victims:

> Studying victims has become one of the growth industries of criminology. Since the 1980s there has been an extraordinarily rapid increase in national and local victim surveys and in studies of the impact of crime, of victim needs and services. Academic research has been

mirrored and encouraged by the growth of dynamic and influential groups set up to help victims and to promote their interests.

(Zedner, 1994: 1207)

We have already mentioned the growth of victimization surveys, which we discuss in Chapter 4. These were at first regarded as a excellent way of revealing the dark figure, particularly that of offences. At last an independent indicator of trends in (at least some) offences over time was now possible, so that criminologists would feel a little more confident when asked if the rises in crime indicated by official data were 'real'. It soon became apparent that there were certain offences that the national surveys did not reach. More focused local surveys, often conducted by the emerging group of 'left realists' (see, for example, Jones *et al.*, 1986), were seen as a way of filling some of the gaps, but some offences could not be reached at all. The emphasis on the dark figure of crime, however, soon came to appear as a very narrow interpretation of the potential of these studies, which opened up a whole range of questions and provided a range of new data that had not previously been available on a systematic basis. We find, then, a growing interest in such topics as the characteristics, attitudes and perceptions of victims, the impact of crime upon them and their reactions to it, and ways of changing policy and services in order to respond to these. We find studies of the patterns of victimization to rank alongside those of patterns of offences and offenders. Such topics as the fear of crime and repeat victimization have become established in the literature of criminology. Indeed, we find a whole new set of issues for theory, research and policy, and a whole new data base to go with them.

The third development is the shift in focus from offenders to offences, which Bottoms (1994) suggests began to occur in the 1970s. Much criminological work until then had focused on the *offender*, with data being collected on physiological and psychological characteristics from Lombroso onwards, and on the social background and characteristics of offenders for the main sociological theories. The change in focus was indicated by, for example, the work of the Home Office Research Unit on the role of opportunity in the explanation of where and why *offences* are committed (Mayhew *et al.*, 1976). Other work followed on what was called 'situational crime prevention' (see Clarke, 1980), particularly through changes in environmental design. All of this constituted a significant change in the direction of the 'governmental project' referred to earlier. Rather later came the development of 'rational choice perspectives', which were intended to deal with some awkward issues in situational crime prevention, and also claimed to be offence- rather than offender-based (Cornish and Clarke, 1986). All of this work required detailed information on patterns of offences – their nature, their distribution in time and space, the physical circumstances in which they were committed and so on, rather than details about the background, characteristics and psychological state of the offender. While some information of this sort was available in police recorded data, the dark figure was too disturbing to ignore any longer, and a powerful impetus was given to alternative sources of information on offences that would include aspects of that elusive figure, such as victim surveys (including some on businesses) and the records of organizations other than the police to which victims might turn in cases of crimes, especially those less likely to be officially reported.

Conclusions

In this preliminary sketch of the major developments in perspectives on crime data over nearly two centuries, it should be clear that the dark figure has been a haunting presence. It might be thought that, with the advent of self-report and victim surveys in recent years, we have been getting closer and closer to a 'total picture' of crime and criminals, with the dark figure progressively exposed for what it is. This is not our view. Crimes and dark figures are not simply 'out there' waiting to be counted by the application of a simple rule to unambiguous events in a laboratory setting by neutral observers. Instead, any crime rate is produced in the sense that people with particular interests, concerns and objectives use a set of definitions, rules and procedures (on which there may not be agreement) in a complex environment to arrive at that product. As we shall see, self-report and victim studies, although they try to avoid some of the problems of official statistics, do not avoid the problems involved in converting people's reports of complex events into numerical data.

As Maguire (1994) suggests, crime itself is a social construct, and statistics that relate to it are socially constructed. He goes on to suggest the following metaphor, which is a rather more helpful one than the iceberg or the traditional dark figure:

> There is a tendency to present the accumulation of data about unreported crime as the gradual unveiling of more and more of the 'complete picture', the 'true total' of offences committed, when a more appropriate metaphor might be the constant repainting of a canvas of indeterminate size, with new areas highlighted and depicted in greater detail.
>
> (Maguire, 1994: 239)

This is fair enough, but it could be added that there are differences in *styles* of painting, which approximate to differences in epistemology (views about the methods for gaining, or grounds for claiming, knowledge about the social world) held by social scientists. We are thinking of the broad distinction between realist and other forms of art; between representational and non-representational art; between art where the attention is focused upon the final picture and the message given, and others where the attention is focused on how the picture was produced. We are thinking of the way in which interests, values and ideologies shape the topics chosen as subjects and the manner of their portrayal (in socialist realism, for example). Jock Young (1992: 58) has suggested that the dark figure 'expands and contracts with the values that we bring to our study'. As in any good horror film, the nature of the spectre that haunts us often reflects those things that concern us most. There can be no surer indication that the study of crime data cannot ultimately be divorced from moral and political debate, and from debates about what counts as knowledge, both in the social sciences and in the wider society.

Summary

Early analyses of crime often depended upon various forms of official data. Although there was an awareness of the existence of the dark figure of unrecorded crimes and criminals, most users of those data concluded that the dark figure did not pose serious problems for coming to conclusions about trends and causes of crime. There were some exceptions, such as the work of Sutherland on white-collar crime, which suggested that the use of official data resulted in a partial criminology. Various developments from the 1960s onwards have led to changes in thinking and research. New ways of measuring crime and offenders were developed: the self-report and victimization survey. In addition, new theoretical perspectives questioned the narrow traditional concern with the reliability and completeness of official data as measures of crime (the realist perspective). Instead, official data were seen by some as products of social and organizational processes (institutionalist perspective), and by others as also representing outcomes of wider structural processes in the political and economic structure of society (radical perspective). More recently, feminist writers have drawn attention to issues about women and crime, there has been a new focus on victims, and more attention has been given to offences, as opposed to the traditional focus on offenders. The chapter concludes by suggesting that the analysis of crime data is not simply a technical matter but raises important questions about how we represent aspects of the social world in which we live.

Further reading

There are few references which encompass all of the ground covered in this chapter. As with subsequent chapters, useful items for further reading should be clear from the references cited in the text. Garland (1994) and Beirne (1993) are very helpful when looking at the earlier periods discussed. Bottomley and Coleman (1981: Chapters 1

chapter two

Official statistics:
the authorized version?

This chapter introduces or discusses the following key concepts or terms, which are also to be found in the glossary at the end of the book: official statistics; notifiable offences; cleared-up offences; indictable offences; summary offences; 'triable either way' offences; 'known' offenders; the Offenders Index; standard list offences; 'no crimes'; clear-up rate; TICs (offences 'taken into consideration'); 'prison write-offs'; primary and secondary clear-ups; principal offence rule; discovery of crime; reporting of crime; recording of crime; 'cuffing'; classification of offences; 'offence mix'; and 'gate arrests'.

This chapter is concerned with those statistical data on crime and offenders which have their origins in the records which the police and other criminal justice agencies are obliged to keep. These are often called 'official statistics', in that they are compiled by officials, working for official agencies, and published by the state. In 1611 King James of Scotland and England had published what was known as the Authorized Version of the Bible; this was a translation produced by those given the authority to do so by the most powerful in the land. Similarly, official statistics are compiled and presented by those who have been given the authority to identify and count crimes and offenders by the state. In a sense, therefore, they can be seen as the authorized version of crime and criminals.

We begin by outlining the major types of these official data on crime, offenders and criminal justice. Although many countries have broadly equivalent data, we concentrate mainly on England and Wales. We then look in more detail at the annual publication which is most commonly taken as providing the key information on crime and offenders (our concern in this book): *Criminal Statistics*. We examine the main contents of this to see what kind of information is included and excluded, and the various rules and principles that influence the way in which the data are compiled and presented. This is followed by a consideration of the way in which such statistics can be viewed as social products, in accordance with the institutionalist perspective outlined in the previous chapter. Having done this, we then look at the picture of some major aspects of crime and offenders painted by those statistics, and the kinds of conclusions that we might draw from them.

Main sources of official data

The following publications are the main sources of data on the criminal justice system in England and Wales and appear each year:

- *Criminal Statistics* (HMSO)
- *Judicial Statistics* (HMSO)
- *Probation Statistics* (Home Office)
- *Prison Statistics* (HMSO)

Similar material is available for Scotland, such as *Recorded Crime in Scotland* and *Prison Statistics, Scotland*, published by the Scottish Office; for Northern Ireland, there is *A Commentary on Northern Ireland Crime Statistics*, published by the Northern Ireland Office.

Next, there are the *Home Office Statistical Bulletins* (HOSB). These include a half-yearly issue, giving the latest basic figures on recorded offences, called *Notifiable Offences*; annual bulletins, such as *Statistics of Drugs Seizures and Offenders Dealt With, United Kingdom* and *Motoring Offences, England and Wales*; and occasional bulletins, such as one on violent crime in the year 1984 (HOSB 29/86) and one on offences of rape in 1977–87 (HOSB 4/89).

Other valuable sources of statistical information on crime and offenders, which begin to move us from the realm of official statistics as defined at the outset of this chapter into officially sponsored research of various kinds, are the series of *Home Office Research Studies*, which include reports from sweeps of the British Crime Survey, and their *Research and Planning Unit Papers*, including, for example, one entitled *Rape: From Recording to Conviction* (Grace *et al.*, 1992). Most recently, the Home Office has begun to publish a series of papers entitled *Research Findings*, which present brief accounts of results of its own research, including ones on the British Crime Survey (see, for example, Mott and Mirrlees-Black, 1993), and the *Digest* of information on crime and criminal justice, the third edition of which was published in 1995 (Barclay, 1995a).

This far from comprehensive account should nevertheless demonstrate the scale on which such data are compiled and made available to those outside the organizations which produce them. What may not be so obvious is the way in which the quality, quantity and scope of such information has increased over recent years. Part of the reason for this seems to lie in the politicization of crime and criminal justice and the demands for more openness and accountability in this and other spheres of the public sector. These trends have brought with them requirements for more detailed records in many areas, especially where concerns have emerged about such matters as miscarriages of justice, discrimination of various kinds, and 'value for money'. So, for example, Section 95 of the Criminal Justice Act 1991 requires the Home Secretary to publish yearly information which will

> (a) enable persons engaged in the administration of criminal justice to become aware of the financial implications of their decisions; or
> (b) facilitate the performance by such persons of their duty to avoid discriminating against any persons on the grounds of race or sex or any other improper ground.
>
> (Home Office 1994a: 247)

As a result, a number of publications on such topics have appeared, to some of which we refer later in this book.

Criminal statistics

As already indicated, the volume *Criminal Statistics England and Wales* is published annually, together with volumes of supplementary information. The statistics contained in these volumes are of great significance, not only for those who study crime or work in the criminal justice system, but also for politicians, the mass media and the general public, for whom these are the major source of authorized information about the extent and trends in crime. The principal contents of the main volume are described below; we go on subsequently to explain some of the terminology and the rules governing the assembly of the statistics. We are using the latest volume available to us at the time of writing, relating to 1993 (Home Office, 1994a).

Principal contents

- *Notifiable offences recorded by the police.* The figures given under this heading are the official statistics normally used to chart trends in crime. A key point to note is that only some offences are *notifiable* (see below for explanations of key terms), in the sense that police forces are required to produce statistical returns for them to the Home Office; these returns then form the basis for the published statistics. Information is therefore given for different offence groupings of these (including trends over time, and data for different police force areas), *but not for other offences*. Some comparisons are made between these data and those from the British Crime Survey. This section also includes information on the proportion of offences '*cleared up*' by the police. This information is followed by special chapters on each of two categories of notifiable offences: offences recorded by the police in which firearms were reported to have been used or stolen, and homicide. These two groupings benefit from a far more detailed treatment of the circumstances surrounding such offences than is the case with other notifiable offences.

- *Offenders found guilty or cautioned.* Such offenders are often referred to as 'known' offenders. It should be noted that we have now moved from offence- to offender-based data. Statistics on those found guilty and cautioned are presented by offence group, in numerical terms relative to the general population, and by police force area, with separate tables for what are called *indictable* and *summary offences*. In general, the only information given on the offender is sex and age group.
- *Court proceedings.* Information is given for persons appearing at magistrates courts and the Crown Court. Some of the tables are broken down according to the type of offence. Once more, we are only provided with information about the age group and sex of the person involved.
- *Sentencing.* Again these are very much criminal justice statistics, with a wealth of information on sentences meted out. The tables often include breakdowns according to offence type, and by the sex and age group of the offender.
- *Use of police bail and court remand.* Some information is presented on offence types of those affected by these procedures.
- *Previous convictions: studies based on the Offenders Index.* The Index is a large data base which details the criminal records of all those convicted of a *standard list offence* in England and Wales between 1963 and the present. Each of these records holds details of court appearances, offences and disposals for each individual. This is potentially a valuable resource for researchers to study criminal careers, and a chapter in *Criminal Statistics* presents findings of some studies already undertaken.

Key definitions, rules and procedures

Indictable, summary, notifiable and standard list offences

Indictable offences are those that are triable by a judge and jury at the Crown Court. Examples of 'indictable only' offences are murder, manslaughter, rape and robbery. Summary offences, on the other hand, are those which, if they get to the stage of court proceedings, are triable only at a magistrates court. A large proportion of these, however, are motoring offences, in many of which fixed-penalty proceedings (e.g., parking fines) may be used. A third category is made up of 'triable either way' offences, which, as the name implies, can be treated in either way, such as theft from shops (for further details on this and other aspects of the criminal justice system in England and Wales, see Barclay, 1995b).

Notifiable offences, for which figures are provided in *Criminal Statistics*, include most indictable and 'triable either way' offences. In addition, a few summary offences are notifiable, such as unauthorized taking of a motor vehicle. Each notifiable offence has its own classification number (for a full list, see Home Office, 1994a: Appendix 3). It is sometimes assumed that notifiable offences constitute the most serious offences, thus providing some kind of rationale for the provision of statistics for these offences alone, but this is by no means necessarily the case. In fact, many minor offences are included; all thefts are included, even though the property stolen may be some sweets or a bottle of milk from a doorstep. By contrast, no statistics are provided on the incidence of most summary *offences*, although some information is given about *persons processed* for such offences in the statistics about offenders.

Finally, we come to standard list offences, which are those included in the Offenders Index referred to above. These include all indictable and 'triable either way' offences, together with a number of more serious summary offences, such as assault on a police officer (for details, see Home Office, 1994a: Appendices 4 and 5). Although there is considerable overlap between this list and that of notifiable offences, the key point is that while the constituents of the latter can and do change somewhat over the years, the standard list remains unchanged, thus facilitating comparisons over time using the Offenders Index.

Counting crimes

This issue has caused some consternation over the years, for different methods of counting can produce very different results. While there were inconsistencies in the methods used for counting crimes from certain sorts of incident in the past (e.g., where there was the repetition of a certain act over a period of time), an attempt was made to establish clearer rules about counting after the recommendations of the Perks Committee in 1967. These have since been revised and the most recent rules, effective from 1 January 1980, can be summarized as follows.

- In offences of violence against the person or sexual offences with more than one victim: one offence per victim.
- With other offences, where several offences are committed 'in one incident': only the most serious is counted.
- If there is 'a continuous series of offences, where there is some special relationship, knowledge or position that exists between the offender and the person or property offended against which enables the offender to repeat the offences, only one offence is counted for each continuous offence' (Home Office 1994a: 222).

Although these rules appear to have made practices more consistent than in the past, there is still room for ambiguity and discretion in decisions about how to count crime which may bring about variations in the figures, as we show below. Just as important is the point that these counting rules are artificial conventions, and others might be equally if not more defensible, depending upon the purpose of the exercise. These rules are not entirely consistent with those used for the British Crime Survey, making comparisons more difficult. Walker (1995: 10) makes the point that one result of these rules is to 'overrepresent' offences of violence (the notifiable ones, at least) as compared with thefts. Maguire (1994: 249) makes a different point: 'If the rule were changed, for example, to allow all cheque frauds to be counted separately, the overall picture of crime might look significantly different'. The important lesson is that these are not simply technical matters, but may have a significant impact on the overall totals and picture of crime created. It is also possible to envisage a number of radically different ways to represent crime, based on such criteria as seriousness of the act (Sellin and Wolfgang, 1968), the impact on the victim, or the 'social harm' created (Sutherland, 1949; Box 1981; 1983) (all of which are not unproblematic concepts in themselves), which might alter the resulting picture of the 'crime problem'.

The impact of legislation
It is certainly true that the welter of legislation since the mid-1960s or so has brought about great changes in the criminal justice system. *Criminal Statistics* currently has an appendix detailing procedures and legislation affecting the statistics. Many of the changes have affected the penalties available for offenders, and these need to be appreciated when using the data on such matters as sentencing. Rather fewer changes have involved the definition of offences, but it should always be remembered that the definition of crime is not to be taken as given, but is a conglomeration of legislative and judicial decisions, going back through the years. New offences can be created, such as those under the Race Relations Acts of 1965, 1968 and 1976. Some offences may likewise be abolished, as were homosexual acts in private between consenting males over 21 years of age by the Sexual Offences Act 1967. Nigel Walker (1971) has argued that the anticipation of such legislation led to a dramatic reduction in police operations in this area, and thus in statistics of 'indecency between males', in the years leading up to the Act.

Few changes are so dramatic. Monica Walker (1995: 7) discusses the impact of a number of recent changes in legislation, and notes how the many minor alterations in the classification of offences brought about by the Criminal Law Act of 1977 mean that the figures before that date are not strictly comparable with those after it. Another good example she provides is that of the Criminal Justice Act 1982, which resulted in gross indecency with a child and trafficking in controlled drugs becoming notifiable offences from the beginning of 1983. Such changes need to be appreciated in order to understand trends in the statistics over time.

Changes in the classification of a crime as a result of later
investigation or proceedings
The initial recording and classification of an event into one of the offence
types is initially made by the police on the information then available. As is
well known, however, additional information may come to light which casts
doubt on these initial decisions, and offenders may be charged or convicted of
a different offence from that initially recorded. Generally speaking, however,
no changes are made to these initial classifications of crime, with two major
exceptions.

First, in the case of homicide, information is given on offences initially recorded as homicide *and* offences currently (i.e. at the time of preparation of
the statistics for publication) recorded as homicide. The second set of data
therefore takes into account subsequent police and court decisions and is pro-
visional until all proceedings are complete. Second, if additional information
comes to light that makes the police feel able to decide that an incident that
was initially recorded by them as a crime was not a crime after all, provision
exists for them to 'write it off' as a 'no crime'. No information is, however,
given for these in *Criminal Statistics*, with figures for them deducted from the
totals in the returns made to the Home Office by police forces.

'Cleared-up' offences
Figures for these offences are frequently calculated as a percentage of all recorded notifiable offences to yield a clear-up rate. This percentage figure is
often called the 'detection rate' by journalists and others, and is often used to
make judgements about the efficiency of police forces, although this is to
some extent a dubious practice (a point to which we return). There are a
number of circumstances under which a crime may be counted as cleared up:

- someone has been charged or summonsed (but not necessarily found guilty
  of that or any other offence);
- someone has been cautioned;
- the offence has been admitted and has been, or could be, 'taken into consideration' by a court (these are often referred to as TICs);
- there is enough evidence to charge a person but the case is not proceeded
  with because of, for example, the death or serious illness of the offender,
  complainant or essential witness;
- the offender is below the age of criminal responsibility;
- the victim is unable or unwilling to give evidence;
- the crime has been admitted by someone already serving a custodial sentence for another offence (these are often referred to as 'prison write-offs').

Only since 1985 has information been available in *Criminal Statistics* to
show the breakdown in the broad methods for clearing up crime. It has
become customary to distinguish between primary and secondary clear-ups.

Before 1994, the first category covered those cleared by means of charge, summons or caution and the second by the remainder of the methods listed above. However, it now appears that the definition adopted by the Audit Commission is likely to be used, in which secondary clear-ups only include offences 'taken into consideration' which have not previously been recorded by the police, and 'those which involve attributing an offence to someone already charged or convicted of another offence' (HOSB 5/95: 24).

Counting offenders and their offences

As previously suggested, the offender data are best regarded as criminal justice statistics, recording as they do decisions which have been made about individuals in the criminal justice system. They are in essence indices of organizational processes and should be studied as such (Kitsuse and Cicourel, 1963). They do however, appear to give a limited amount of information about the characteristics of those who are processed and their offences. A number of points should be borne in mind when looking at these statistics in this way.

First, offenders may be processed for more than one offence on each occasion, but this is not shown in these statistics. Instead, only one offence is shown, generally the one for which the most serious penalty has been or can be given. This overall principle is sometimes referred to as the *principal offence rule* and results in a heavy emphasis on indictable offences (for which more severe penalties are usually available) in these statistics (for details, see Home Office, 1994a: 224–6). Second, the statistics for persons proceeded against show the number of persons dealt with during the year. While someone who is dealt with for more than one offence *at the same time* will appear only once in the statistics, another repeat offender, if dealt with on more than one occasion during the year, will appear more than once. As Monica Walker (1995: 30) points out, this affects certain sorts of calculations which are often made using these data, such as the ratio of male to female offenders, since males are more likely to be repeat offenders. If Snow White had used similar methods to calculate the ratio of Dwarfs to Princesses as she kissed them goodbye in the morning, she would have come up with a result in excess of 7: 1 because one of them had a habit of running round to the back of the house to come through for yet another kiss. Finally, these statistics do not include offenders who have received informal warnings, and the written warnings, cautions and fixed penalties for motoring offences.

These brief points about the offender data should reveal some of their main limitations. The statistics are not generally a good guide to the range of offending behaviour, with only one offence identified for each time a person is processed. In addition, the recording mechanisms are heavily weighted towards indictable offences, with many summary offences receiving pretty short shrift. To this should be added the point that the information about the characteristics of offenders is usually limited to sex and age.

An overview

Our discussion of the contents of *Criminal Statistics England and Wales* (more detailed information is available in the *Supplementary Tables*) leads to some basic points about these data. First, there is the distinction between offence- and offender-based data. The former are confined in their coverage to notifiable offences. Second, there is the point that, in spite of all the detail evident, very limited information about the nature of offences and the circumstances in which they were committed is available, except in the cases of homicide and offences involving firearms. Homicide, for example, has details of the method of killing, relationship of victim to principal suspect, age and sex of victim, and outcome of cases. Criminologists can therefore find a good deal more material here on these admittedly less frequent offences than on the others. Third, although there is a great deal of information about what happened to people processed by the criminal justice system, there is little information on their characteristics except their sex and age group. It is easier to find more detailed information from prison records (see Walmsley *et al.*, 1992), but such groups may not be a good guide to generalization about offenders overall. What this and the previous point mean is that it is often necessary to conduct special research studies to find out more about offences and offenders. The fourth point is that it is not easy to understand these statistics without some knowledge of the system which produces them. We have already illustrated this by considering some basic rules, procedures and definitions, without knowledge of which it is difficult to interpret these data. We go on, in the next section, to expand this knowledge by looking at the production of these statistics as a social process.

Before doing this, however, we should like to stress that it is too easy to get bogged down in the more detailed and technical aspects of the official statistics, while losing sight of the kinds of broader questions which were raised in Chapter 1. For example, we must not lose sight of the dark figure – those events and persons which are very much akin to those recorded in the figures of notifiable crimes, but which never find their way into these official records. There are also those kinds of offences which tend to be dealt with by agencies other than the police and the orthodox criminal justice system. Mike Maguire (1994: 248) points to tax and benefit fraud, some of which is dealt with by the Inland Revenue, Customs and Excise, and the Department of Social Security. While these agencies may keep their own records of cases dealt with, they do not keep figures of the numbers of offences (many of them repetitive). This, of course, leads us back to the discussion of white-collar and corporate crime in Chapter 1, which drew attention to the idea that some misdeeds and their perpetrators have relative immunity from the processes of orthodox criminal justice and the records they produce. Finally, we reiterate the point that it is possible to visualize other ways of defining crime, and ways of counting and representing it, which lead to different pictures of crime and the dark figure.

The social construction of official statistics

Having looked at the main rules and definitions which apply to the compilation of official data, we shall now examine the production of these statistics as a social process. At the outset, it is worth re-emphasizing the point that the very definitions of crime are themselves the result of wider social processes, sometimes ancient, sometimes recent, which reflect religious, political and other considerations, and which provide the framework in which the statistics are created. In no sense, therefore, should these and the associated rules that we have considered be taken for granted. The study of development and change in criminal categories and their relation to wider social processes should be part of any comprehensive criminology (for a recent example, which looks at gambling legislation, see Dixon, 1991). Having said that, it is then helpful to divide the remaining parts of the process into four main stages: discovery, reporting, recording and 'clearing up'.

Discovery

In some ways this term is misleading, for it may be taken to imply that all crimes are simply 'out there' and easily recognizable to anyone. In practice, not only do people differ in their knowledge of what constitutes crime, but there are occasions where there is no victim in the usual sense to discover the offence, and others where the victim is left unaware that a crime has been committed. We know relatively little about this area, but we can say something about who first became aware of those incidents which eventually find their way into the official statistics of crime. Studies in Britain indicate that between 77 and 96 per cent of these are initially discovered by members of the public in various guises (Bottomley and Pease, 1986: 34). One study found that only 14 per cent were initially discovered by the police, while 57 per cent were by personal victims, 23 per cent by representatives of victimized organizations, and 3 per cent by witnesses (Bottomley and Coleman, 1981: 43–8). This pattern does not necessarily apply to all offences. The police role in 'discovery' is far more pronounced in many non-notifiable offences, particularly those without a clear victim who has an interest in bringing the incident to the attention of the police (e.g., some of the offences relating to drugs, prostitution, drunkenness, and public order). Here the police have a far more dominant role in the identification of offences and offenders for possible further action.

Reporting

The agent who initially discovered the event is very often also the one who reports it to the police. The information of the previous section should therefore make clear that we need to take into account the role of such agents as victims, witnesses, store detectives, caretakers, security staff, managers of private and public organizations, and others in the production of crime statistics. Just to take one example, it is now well known that many stores and shops tend only to report cases of shoplifting where a suspect has been apprehended, but that policies and practices show some variability. In view of the probable extent of shoplifting, such policies and practices are likely to have a very large impact on figures of recorded crime.

Successive sweeps of the British Crime Survey (BCS) have asked respondents whether they had reported an offence to the police, and if not, why not. Only some offences in the official statistics can be compared with the more limited range in the BCS. For those that could be compared, it was estimated in the 1994 sweep (figures refer to 1993) that 41 per cent of BCS 'crimes' overall were reported to the police (Mayhew *et al.*, 1994). However, it was clear, as in other years, that the proportion of different offences apparently reported varied widely, ranging from 32 per cent of instances of vandalism to 97 per cent of motor vehicle thefts. These differences need explanation, and it is often suggested that the seriousness of the offence is the main factor influencing reporting. This certainly seems to be borne out by burglary, in which 87 per cent of instances where loss was experienced were reported, whereas only 53 per cent were reported in cases of attempts and no loss of property. This should not be over-generalized as an explanation. Some cases of physical and sexual abuse, for example, come to light, if they ever do, only after considerable periods of time.

The BCS produces its own figures on reasons for not reporting a crime; those most often given by respondents in the 1992 sweep, for example, were that the offence was too trivial (55 per cent), the police could not do anything (25 per cent), or that it was dealt with privately (12 per cent) (Mayhew *et al.*, 1993). What these global results do not reveal is the way in which crime is such a varied category, with a range of reasons for reporting or not, which are often embedded in particular circumstances and sets of relationships, associated experiences of harm, and assessments about what could usefully be done about it. So statements about seriousness should be supplemented by an analysis of the social and psychological context, in which such aspects as embarrassment, the nature of any relationship to the offender, expectations of police reaction or performance, the implications of any insurance policies held, and fears about any possible consequences of reporting (such as reprisals, incrimination, or simply involvement in criminal justice proceedings) should be considered. Just to give one example, Malcolm Young (1991: 368) writes of the small shopkeeper who avoids reporting offences of shop theft to the police in order to avoid having to close the shop at a later date if required to attend any court proceedings.

Recording

The mere fact that an incident is reported to the police (even one which, on the surface at least, appears to qualify as a crime) does not ensure that it will be recorded as a crime. One further step is therefore necessary before it becomes a statistical unit. Information about this stage is again available from the BCS. In the 1994 sweep, for example, there is the kind of varied pattern according to offence type shown in other years, such that only 38 per cent of thefts and robberies from the person that have been reported to the police (according to the BCS), 29 per cent of attempted motor vehicle thefts, but 77 per cent of burglaries with loss and 95 per cent of motor thefts, appear to have been *recorded* as such. Overall it was estimated that only 60 per cent of the type of offences covered by the BCS and apparently reported to the police were recorded by them (Mayhew *et al.*, 1994).

The authors of the report of the earlier 1992 sweep suggested a number of reasons for such 'shortfalls', such as the police not always accepting victims' accounts, their view that a report was mistaken or 'disingenuous', their feeling that there was insufficient evidence for a crime to be said to exist, their view that some items were too trivial to justify formal action, especially if the complainants wanted no further police action, were unlikely to provide evidence, or the incident had somehow been 'satisfactorily resolved' (Mayhew *et al.*, 1993: 16). These are, however, largely speculations and it is important to appreciate that the very large shortfalls in some instances also raise questions about the BCS findings, and should be subject to research to find out more about their explanations. Finally, it is now also possible to discern broad changes in police recording practice over the years since 1981, the year of the first BCS estimates. From a comparison of these with the broadly equivalent official data over the period 1981–91, it appears that police recording of acquisitive crimes reported to them decreased, while recording of offences of violence and vandalism increased significantly (Mayhew *et al.*, 1993: Table A2.6). More impressionistic accounts have suggested that there has been a broad decline in the practice known as 'cuffing' (the deliberate non-recording of offences for various reasons by police officers) over a much longer period (Young 1991: 323–5).

Although it may be broadly true that 'reported offences that fall by the wayside in the police recording process may not be especially serious' (Mayhew *et al.*, 1989: 12), it seems to us that this is an area, like that of reporting, which is ripe for investigation. Not only are these significant topics of enquiry in their own right (for they are a key stage in the mobilization of the criminal justice process), but they have important implications for the data produced by the police and by the BCS. The *classification* of the offence is also an important element here; one reason for the discrepancies between official and BCS data may be that some offences were classified under different categories in the two sets of figures. The influences on decisions whether and how to record may be grouped according to three broad levels.

- *The social and political context.* It is worth noting that crime data are produced in a broader economic, political and social context, from which the recording process is not immune. For example, Malcolm Young (1991: 323) suggests that in the 1950s and early 1960s, when crime was not a political issue, there was little incentive for the police to record large numbers of crimes. No extra finance would have been available from local budgets as a result. In fact, because the efficiency of police forces was largely judged on the basis of clear-up rates, there was little reason or incentive to record as crimes minor offences for which there was little prospect of their being cleared up. All of this was gradually to change in the following decades, as there was a dawning realization that claims for resources could ultimately be mounted on the back of a burgeoning crime rate in a society in which crime had increasingly become a political issue. A number of studies have been conducted in the USA which illustrate the impact of political pressures, often at a local level, on crime recording (see the summary in O'Brien, 1985). Many of these studies were concerned with offences in the areas of drugs, prostitution and gambling; most of these offences are non-notifiable in England and Wales, but the data on those persons processed for them are very sensitive to police activity. Other social changes leading to increased recording could be mentioned, such as the growth of technology, allowing rapid response to scenes and improved contact with the station. Under these circumstances, incidents are less likely to be resolved informally and more likely to be formally recorded, and at an earlier stage.
- *The organizational context.* Research in the USA has shown how crime recording can be responsive to organizational factors, such as changes in working practices and personnel (McLeary *et al.*, 1982), and to the degree of 'professionalization' of a police department, higher levels of which may result in a greater use of record-keeping generally and corresponding increases in crime rates (and lower clear-up rates!) (Skogan, 1976; 1978). In England, Farrington and Dowds's (1985) study suggested that between two-thirds and three-quarters of the difference between the higher crime rate of Nottinghamshire and that of two similar counties in 1981 was due to a greater tendency for the police in Nottinghamshire to record thefts of items of little value, offences originating in admissions, and multiple, continuous or series offences as separate crimes. A report by the Inspectorate of

Constabulary in 1994 found 'institutionalised anomalies' and different recording practices across seven divisions of the North West London Metropolitan police area which made it difficult to assess the effectiveness of operational performance on crime, especially burglary (*Guardian*, 14 December 1994). One of these anomalies was that in the past some forces had classified many attempted break-ins as criminal damage rather than burglary. New guidelines were issued to eradicate these anomalies, which had produced significant variations in the politically sensitive burglary figures.

- *The situational context.* Decisions to record are ultimately made in particular situations, within the broader context mentioned in the previous two sections. Again we have some evidence from the USA about the factors here. The main influences seem to have been the seriousness of the offence, the complainant's preference, the relational distance between complainant and suspect, and deference to the police on the part of the complainant (Black, 1970). Pepinsky (1976) found that officers were very much affected by whether the dispatcher named an offence when the officer was first dispatched to an incident. Maxfield *et al.* (1980) suggested that levels of recording were affected by the total demand for police service at the time – but this applied to property and minor crimes only. Block and Block (1980) found that the recording of robberies was much more likely if the incident was serious, if the robbery was completed, and if a gun was used. Not surprisingly, similar results have been obtained for arrests (a type of offender-based data). Smith and Visher (1981) found that arrest decisions were also related to the presence of a bystander, race of the suspect, and an antagonistic demeanour on the part of the suspect, when controlling for a range of factors, including seriousness of the offence.

No doubt many of these factors affecting recording apply in the British context, but we do not have the kinds of studies to be sure. We do have a number of valuable, but rather impressionistic accounts of 'cuffing' and the reasons for it (Bottomley and Coleman, 1981; Young, 1991), such as a preference for doing something else, to avoid work, to improve detection rates, or a feeling that to record might be counter-productive in some way, although such decisions are more safely made in those cases where there is unlikely to be any 'comeback'. Such decisions are not always uncontroversial, as police practice in cases of domestic violence, particularly in the past, illustrates. We also have other studies of crime recording and writing off incidents as 'no crime' (McCabe and Sutcliffe, 1978; Bottomley and Coleman, 1981) which reveal some of the reasoning employed. Finally, we have the fascinating account given by a former police officer of the various practical techniques adopted to count and record crime during his service, which included 'the rituals of "cuffing", "creating", "keepy-backs juggling", "fiddling", and "bending"' (Young, 1991: 377).

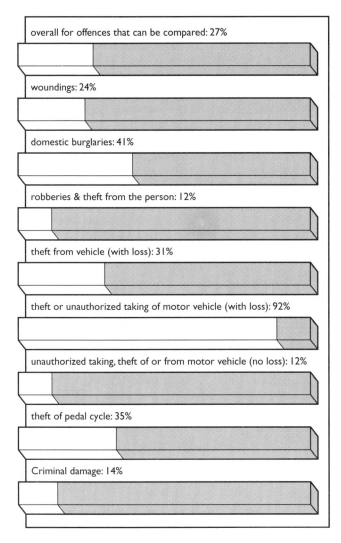

overall for offences that can be compared: 27%

woundings: 24%

domestic burglaries: 41%

robberies & theft from the person: 12%

theft from vehicle (with loss): 31%

theft or unauthorized taking of motor vehicle (with loss): 92%

unauthorized taking, theft of or from motor vehicle (no loss): 12%

theft of pedal cycle: 35%

Criminal damage: 14%

Figure 2.1 Estimates of percentages of BCS offences recorded by the police: England and Wales, 1993
Source: Home Office (1994a: 27)

Having looked at those three stages in the production of crime data, BCS data can now help us to estimate the proportions of certain 'offences' which end up as recorded crimes. The figures can give some indication of the combined effects of reporting and recording decisions on the resultant statistics. Estimates relating to 1993 of the percentages of BCS offences which were subsequently recorded as crimes are shown in Figure 2.1. Leaving aside any qualifications about these figures (see Chapter 4), it can be seen that, from a 'realist' perspective, different offence groups have very different 'dark figures' of offences. The use of the same kinds of data over time also gives us a different perspective on trends in crime. For example, over the 1981–93 period, officially recorded crime rose by 111 per cent whereas BCS crimes rose by only 77 per cent (Home Office, 1994a: 27–8). However, this long-term pattern conceals a reverse trend during 1991–93, when BCS 'crime' rose by 18 per cent, whereas comparable recorded crime rose by only 7 per cent, apparently owing to a fall in reporting.

Clearing up crime and the identification of offenders

Clear-up rates and official offender data must also be understood in terms of the context in which they are produced. It is now fairly well known that few crimes are cleared up in the style of classic detective fiction. Many are solved by a suspect being at the scene when the police arrive, or by the provision of information by members of the public (Bottomley and Coleman, 1981; Burrows and Tarling, 1982). Although the lion's share of clear-ups is produced by charge or summons, a significant number are produced through methods such as TICs and 'prison write-offs', which involve offenders already processed for other offences (Home Office, 1994a: Table 2.12). The use of 'secondary' methods of clearing up crime has created some controversy in recent years, such as when Constable Ron Walker went public in alleging that Kent detectives had bloated their detection rates by persuading convicted offenders to admit to crimes that they had not committed (*Observer*, 13 July 1986).

Clear-up rates vary widely between different types of offence (see HOSB 5/95: Figure 10), reflecting the nature of the detection problem facing the police on arrival (e.g., with offences against the person the offender is often well known to the victim, thus producing high clear-up rates). These rates also vary a good deal between police forces, and although often used to compare effectiveness between them, it should be remembered that the rates are influenced by such things as the policing problems faced in particular areas, including the 'offence mix', and practice and policy over the use of 'secondary' clear-ups, which are known to differ between forces (Walker, 1992; Bottomley and Coleman, 1995). For example, some forces have dedicated squads to deal with 'prison write-offs'. Other forces do not have such squads, but may respond to letters from prisoners requesting a visit. These forces might sometimes find their clear-up rates adversely affected as a result, and coming under media and political pressure. If so, the use or threat of 'gate arrests' (the arrest of persons on release from prison) may be used as a way of encouraging prisoners to 'wipe the slate clean' before release. Word soon gets around and more letters are likely to be received. Finally, another key issue concerns the way in which clear-up rates have fallen over recent years – from 35 per cent to 25 per cent between 1985 and 1993, for example (Home Office, 1994a: Table

2.12). The reasons for this are complex and clearly require illumination to avoid such statistics being used in a naïve way as simple indicators of police effectiveness.

Turning briefly to offender data, it is clear that these must be viewed in a similar way. Here the various policies and strategies adopted, together with the styles of suspicion, and methods of investigation, detecting and clearing up crime have an influence on records of offenders. This is true from stop and search right through to 'secondary' methods of clearing up crime. To the extent that methods used encourage concentration on 'known' offenders, or on those thought to resemble them for various reasons, or on those not so protected by such institutions as privacy (Stinchcombe, 1963) and so on, the records will be bloated with those sorts of persons. The old idea that offender data were merely the product of police stereotypes and operational strategies has, however, been found to be too simplistic (Mawby, 1979; Bottomley and Coleman, 1976; 1981). There are too many inputs from others for that, especially in the case of most notifiable offences. Although there is insufficient room here for a full discussion of the perspective that sees suspect and convicted populations as socially constructed (see McConville *et al.*, 1991), we discuss what official data and alternative measures suggest about some of the characteristics of offenders in later chapters. Here, it is time to move on to consider the picture presented by official data, and what kinds of conclusions we might be able to draw from them, in the light of the foregoing discussion.

Offence data: What picture? What conclusions?

Geographical distribution

Criminal Statistics consistently shows that predominantly rural police force areas tend to have the lowest number of recorded crimes per head of population, whereas metropolitan areas and those with conurbations the highest. In 1993, for example, the lowest rates (per 100,000 population) were recorded for Dyfed and Powys (5200) and Suffolk (6700), and the highest for Humberside (16,000), Nottinghamshire (15,000), Northumbria (14,800) and West Yorkshire (14,400) (Home Office, 1994a: 29). These findings broadly concur with the traditional finding of a positive relationship between urbanization and recorded crime rates, but the fit is by no means perfect (e.g., the most urbanized areas do not have the very highest rates of crime). Our foregoing discussion suggests that some of the differences between areas may be due to variations in reporting and recording practice (Farrington and Dowds, 1985).

Offence types

A simplified breakdown of the 5,526,000 crimes recorded in 1993 into broad offence groupings gives the picture shown in Figure 2.2. A number of points

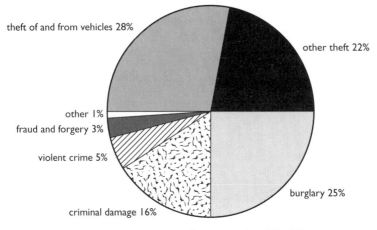

theft of and from vehicles 28%

other theft 22%

other 1%
fraud and forgery 3%

violent crime 5%

burglary 25%

criminal damage 16%

Total notifiable offences recorded: 5,526,000

Figure 2.2 Notifiable offences recorded by the police by offence type: England and Wales, 1993
Source: Home Office (1994a: Figure 2.1)

can be made about this rough and ready breakdown, which does not correspond exactly with the official broad groupings, in which vehicle crime is not an overall category and violent crime is broken down into violence against the person, sexual offences and robbery.

- *Theft of and from motor vehicles.* What is perhaps most striking is the considerable part played by this category in the overall picture. It should be remembered that theft of a vehicle is an offence that is generally more likely to be reported and recorded, but many of the other types of vehicle crime are not. There is little doubt that vehicle crime has been a major growth area over recent decades, showing to a considerable extent how crime develops in accordance with available opportunities.
- *Other theft.* Thefts accounted for half of all notifiable offences recorded. Next to vehicles, the figures indicate that shops were the second most favoured target, providing one in ten of recorded thefts. However, it must be remembered that very many similar events go unrecorded in official data. No figures on shop thefts are available from the BCS to help us here, but it is likely that such offences would constitute a big proportion of any attempt to reveal a dark figure which did include this offence. The BCS data do indicate, however, that thefts from the person also have a very large dark figure.
- *Burglary.* Offences in this category made up a further quarter of the total. A quarter of domestic burglaries in that year involved no property actually

being stolen, indicating that many may have been attempts (Home Office, 1994a: 32). Looking at broad trends over time, it appears from victimization data from the General Household Survey and the BCS that some of the increase in recorded figures of burglary since the 1970s has been due to increased rates of reporting and recording (Home Office, 1994a: 33).

- *Criminal damage.* Contributing 16 per cent of the total, this is an offence which, according to BCS data, has one of the largest dark figures of unrecorded instances, with only 14 per cent estimated as recorded in 1993 (see above). In addition, while recorded offences more than doubled between 1981 and 1993, the BCS figures indicate a rise of only 25 per cent (Home Office, 1994a: 34).
- *Violent crime.* This is the most complex category; it can be divided into violence against the person, sexual offences and robbery. Even within these, there is considerable diversity. To take the first, less than a tenth (17,999) of the violence against the person recorded in 1993 (205,102) was of the more serious types, involving taking or 'endangering' life. The whole category is dominated by 'other wounding etc.' which is a group mainly made up from assaults, often involving simple fights rather than the use of weapons.

Sexual offences (31,284 recorded in 1993), over half of which were indecent assaults on a female, include rape (the next most frequently recorded at 4589) and indecent assault on a male (3340). The steady recorded increases in these sorts of offences over the years, together with the recognition that there is a sizeable dark figure here, raises questions about changes in offending behaviour *vis-à-vis* such aspects as improved police procedures and the possibly greater willingness of victims to come forward. BCS data are of relatively little help with these offences.

Finally, there is robbery, which made up just 1 per cent of the total of all recorded crime. This includes those controversial offences known as muggings, although, as the commentary in *Criminal Statistics* makes clear, 'of these there are some types of incident which could reasonably be classified either as robbery or as theft from the person' (Home Office, 1994a: 32). This reminds us not to think of the categories in too rigid a way, and of the opportunities for some discretion and practical reasoning in the assignment of incidents to them.

The fact that violent crime overall constitutes 5 per cent of the total is often taken as a measure of the relative size of 'the problem', which 'should be kept in proportion'. Apart from all the incidents which never find their way into these statistics (for example, the BCS estimates that only 24 per cent of 'woundings' are actually recorded, and this leaves aside the many 'common assaults' which are not in any case notifiable), this view exemplifies the overriding concern with the *quantity* of crime, rather than with its nature and impact. As Maguire and Corbett (1987) show, such offences and the fear of them commonly have a far greater impact on their victims than do thefts. This points again to the idea that there are other ways of measuring crime than simple numerical counts.

- *Fraud and forgery.* A related point could be made about these categories, which constituted only 3 per cent of the official picture. This category has a claim to be the Bashful of the world of criminal statistics, dwarfed as it is by at least three factors. As Maguire (1994: 252) points out, the counting rules (discussed earlier) for these offences, many of which are of the continuous series type, effectively 'downsize' their relative contribution. Futhermore, a point also mentioned earlier, many of those that do come to light are dealt with administratively by other agencies. Also, such figures do not take into account the size of the sums involved in some of these cases. Maguire cites the key work of Levi (1993) to illustrate this last factor, to point out the sheer size of the sums involved in the major recent alleged fraud cases in Britain (Barlow Clowes, Guinness, Maxwell, BCCI, and Polly Peck) compared with the amounts stolen in thefts and burglaries. A similar kind of reasoning to that noted with the previous offence grouping appears in the *Criminal Statistics* commentary: 'In view of the public concern about major financial frauds, it should be noted that such offences constitute only a small proportion of the total frauds recorded, the majority of which involve relatively minor sums' (Home Office, 1994a: 34).
- *Other crimes.* The largest contributor here was trafficking in controlled drugs, which weighed in with 14,800 recorded in 1993. According to Monica Walker (1995: 19), '[t]his offence may well be the largest component of the "dark figure" of unknown offences (although fraud offences may be a large component)'. There are a number of favourites for the biggest dark figure, and the contest between them is, in our view, unlikely ever to be fully resolved.

Offender data: What picture? What conclusions?

In this short section we confine ourselves to a few key points. The first is that statistics on offenders, rather than on events, are our main guide to offences which are not notifiable, such as those relating to drunkenness and motor vehicle licences, and TV licence evasion. These statistics, of course, are very much subject to the activities of the police and other agencies, such as TV licence inspectors and local authorities (Walker 1995: 20). Figures for motoring *offences* (in the form of police action taken) are also available in *Home Office Bulletins* and *Supplementary Tables*. The obvious point to make here is that changes in the figures of cases dealt with by the courts over the years should be interpreted in the light of the more widespread use of other methods of dealing with such offences in recent times, such as the extended use of fixed penalties since 1986.

The second point is that these official data give a picture of the typical offender as male and young. Other data, including that on prisoners (Walmsley *et al.*, 1992), suggest that officially defined offenders are also skewed in terms of such attributes as race and class, and also suffer from various forms of disadvantage. As Walker (1995: 34) comments, '[t]here is no reason to suppose that these offenders are representative of all offenders in the community in respect of gender, age or race'. We therefore explore these issues in a later chapter, with the help of alternative types of data wherever they are available.

The third point is that while the number of recorded offences increased substantially during the 1983–93 period (from 3,247,000 to 5,526,300), the number of persons found guilty or cautioned overall did not. In fact there was something of a decline in the overall number during the 1980s. Drugs offenders were the major exception to this, increasing steadily over the whole period. Walker (1995: 35) has suggested three explanations which might account for the overall decline in the 1980s. First, there were reductions in offender rates for males aged 10–16 and females aged 10–13, probably due in part to an increase in the use of diversion from the criminal justice system (see also Farrington and Burrows, 1993, on the decline in 'known' shoplifters in the second half of the 1980s), and the reclassification of a number of indictable offences as summary under the Criminal Justice Act 1988. Second, the Police and Criminal Evidence Act 1984 (PACE) tightened up procedures for the detention and questioning of suspects. Third, drawing on the research of Fowles (1993), she suggests that the new Crown Prosecution Service (introduced, like PACE, in 1986) 'resulted in a weeding out of weak cases' (in our view, an over-simplification), with the result that fewer reached trial stage. Whatever the precise reasons, these trends appear to be telling us more about the system than about the behaviour of offenders.

Finally, we should like to make another reference to the wealth of data contained in the Offenders Index. Whereas the other forms of data we have considered so far give us counts of events and persons which have clicked their way through the turnstiles of the criminal justice system during a year, the Index can give us more of a *developmental* picture of offenders over time. Of the cohort born in 1953, for example, just under 35 per cent of men and 8 per cent of women had been convicted of a standard list offence by the age of 35 (see Home Office, 1994a: Chapter 9; Tarling, 1993). Plenty of other details can be found in these sources. A drawback of the Index is that it excludes information on cautioning, which has been increasingly used as a way of dealing with offenders outside the courts over recent years. This has the effect of reducing the conviction rates (based on court convictions) of offenders born more recently and consequently makes comparisons across generations more difficult.

Conclusion

In conclusion, we return to the three basic approaches to official statistics outlined in Chapter 1. We hope that we have shown the limitations of these official data for those who approach them from a traditional realist perspective (i.e. with a concern to discover the 'real' amount of crime that takes place). Some of their hopes have been maintained with a few isolated offences, such as vehicle theft and homicide. Even with the latter, some recent discoveries of alleged murder victims of long ago and the sheer number of 'missing persons' may cast doubts on this view. Little wonder, then, that many from this viewpoint have turned to victimization surveys and self-report studies for alternative measures of at least some offences and offenders. At the same time, the argument is to be heard that 'official statistics are valid indicators of serious crimes as defined by the citizenry' (Gove *et al.*, 1985: 451), and many criminologists still use official statistics, in the absence of anything better, or in combination with other forms of data (triangulation).

The institutionalist perspective, on the other hand, reconceives official data as products that are socially constructed. We hope that it is clear that this viewpoint also helps us to understand some important aspects of the processes of law enforcement and criminal justice, including the role of the public. Although realists can learn much of value to their enterprise from this perspective, it is hardly surprising that some of them become ultimately irritated by it, focusing as it does on the myriad of complex social interactions in the production of crimes and offenders. Some versions of this perspective seem to have very few, if any, answers to traditional realist questions about crime and offenders. Quite right, too – those questions are not their focus. Expecting these researchers to answer such questions is a bit like phoning Stephen Hawking to ask him the time, on the understanding that he is, after all, an expert on the subject.

Finally, there is the radical perspective, broadly conceived. This viewpoint questions some basic elements of the way in which the official picture of crime is produced. It often questions the definition of crime itself, the structures of law, the way in which crime is represented, and the operation of the system charged with processing those who are criminalized. It often has visions of how things could be different, including the definition of crime and the values and operation of criminal justice. It often maintains that the official portrait of crime carries important ideological messages about where the problems in society lie, messages which in themselves may have real consequences. Its values, its special techniques, and its distinctive style of painting gives it the potential to produce a picture of crime which is different from the official one, and which relates crime to wider questions about the structure of society and its culture. Whatever the merits and limitations of any particular version, there is a place for questioning basic values and assumptions and discussion of what might replace them. Without such insights, discussions of crime data would be that much poorer.

Summary

The main sources of official statistics on crime and offenders are outlined, with a particular focus upon *Criminal Statistics England and Wales*. Key definitions, rules and procedures employed in the assembly of these statistics are explained, such as those governing the counting of offences and the circumstances under which they can be regarded as 'cleared up'. The statistics of recorded offences relate only to 'notifiable' offences, while those of offenders show only the 'principal offence'. Only very limited information is available in most instances about the nature of crimes and the characteristics of offenders. These data are then considered as being socially constructed, by dividing their production into four main stages and discussing each in turn: discovery, reporting, recording of crime, and the clearing up of crime and the associated identification of offenders. Official data for 1993 are then considered to see what broad conclusions, if any, we can draw from them about such aspects as the geographical distribution of crime, the breakdown into different offence types, the characteristics of offenders and trends in their overall numbers over recent years. The chapter concludes by considering some of the implications of the discussion for the three perspectives on crime statistics outlined in Chapter 1.

Further reading

We have avoided extensive discussion of detailed statistical data in this chapter – this would take up too much space and would quickly date. The most recent official statistics that can be obtained would therefore be a useful supplement, such as *Criminal Statistics* or *Home Office Statistical Bulletin: Notifiable Offences* for readers interested in England and Wales. Much can still be learned from the general text by Bottomley and Pease (1986), even though much of the illustrative material is now rather dated. It includes coverage of the data on later stages of criminal justice, such as sentencing and imprisonment. Another comprehensive general text is Walker (1995), which contains some recent articles on the various types of data. For more in-depth material on the social processes that lie behind official statistics, Bottomley and Coleman (1981), Farrington and Dowds (1985) and Young (1991: Chapter 5) could be consulted. Finally, we regret that we did not have the space to look at official statistics from other countries. O'Brien (1985), for example, includes a concise discussion of the *Uniform Crime Reports*, the official crime statistics of the USA.

chapter three

Self-report studies:
true confessions?

This chapter introduces or discusses the following terms and concepts, which are also to be found in the glossary at the end of the book: delinquency; epidemiology; incidence; frequency; prevalence; cross-sectional research design; longitudinal design; validity; conflict theory; strain theory; cultural deviance theory; control theory; predictive validity; reverse record check; panel effect; reliability; reference period; bounding techniques; telescoping error; annual prevalence rate; general offending rate; ever variety measures; last year variety measures; and test–retest procedure.

Although people have been confessing sins for centuries, it is only comparatively recently that this kind of material has been employed in the service of the discipline called criminology. Self-report studies involve asking people directly about their involvement in criminal and other forms of rule-breaking behaviour, usually by means of a self-completed questionnaire or an interview. You may be sceptical about the kind of information obtained in this way; quite right, too – a sceptical approach is usually advisable in matters criminological. Let us, therefore, look carefully at the development of these studies, the purposes for which they might be used, the various ways in which they have been carried out and the quality of the information they yield. By the end of the chapter, we should be in a position to assess the overall strengths and weaknesses of such studies, to indicate some main findings and their implications for criminology. Let us, first of all, consider the matter of the purposes, or objectives, of these studies.

The question of objectives

Different objectives have different implications for the design of self-report studies, the instruments they employ and the use of their findings. Let us take some examples of objectives to illustrate. First, as Hindelang *et al.* (1981: 88) suggest, one of the goals of much of this research seems to have been to 'construct a measure of delinquency identical to the measure of delinquency explicit in official definitions and implicit in official procedures, but without the omissions, mistakes and biases of official measurement'. Although such a quest is suggested by the way research is often discussed by researchers, in practice, as we show below, a much wider range of behaviours has often been measured by such studies. This gap between what studies appeared or claimed to be doing and what they actually did has been the source of much confusion. This confusion has been encouraged by the fact that the term 'delinquency' is used in more than one sense; some use the term in a limited way to refer to violations of the law, while others use it more loosely to refer to a whole range of juvenile misconduct. In addition, in the USA, the term 'status offences' is used to refer to acts which are offences only if committed by persons within a certain age category, so that research studies often include acts which would not be offences if committed by adults.

A second objective, often leading on from the first, may be to explore the epidemiology (the nature, extent and distribution) of delinquency and crime in a population. This involves selecting a representative sample of the given population so that the findings can be generalized to that population. Any kind of bias in the sample selected and the response rates of different groups should be avoided beforehand and compensated for afterwards wherever possible. If, for example, (as seems to be the case) the more delinquent individuals are less likely to be sampled, and less likely to respond, this affects the inferences that can be made from the data. The researcher must also be clear about whether the interest is primarily in offences or offenders, for it is sometimes easy to confuse the two. An interest in offences may mean a great deal of trouble is taken in trying to arrive at fairly precise estimates of the number of offences over a given period (commonly referred to as the *incidence*, but a better term is *frequency* of offences). Identifying the number or proportion of offenders in a population (often referred to as the *prevalence*) is a different enterprise.

A third objective may be to test theories of delinquency or deviance. Theories may differ in their definition of what they are trying to explain, and this may not correspond with the definition given by the first objective above. They may instead be interested in a broader category of behaviour, or indeed a narrower one; again, it is important that there is correspondence between the theoretical definition and what is actually measured. Here a major concern is with identifying causal factors, and not simply with the distribution of delinquency as with the previous objective. Traditionally, the main concern was with identifying non-delinquents on the one hand, and individuals who could be classified as delinquent on the other. For research with this objective, the attempt to arrive at precise estimates of the frequency of acts in a given time period could be to some extent overlooked, and often largely was. As a result, some studies were happy to identify as a delinquent anyone who confessed to ever having engaged in any of the acts asked about in these studies (called the cumulative, or 'ever' prevalence). Once the two groups had been identified, the task was then to explain patterns in the data by reference to other variables or factors.

According to the canons of causal analysis, correlation is not enough; we must also, among other things, try to determine whether the factor or variable suggested by theory preceded delinquency. If it did not, it cannot be seen to be causal in this case. Some argue that the problem of causal order is difficult to resolve using the cross-sectional design, in which all the measurements are taken at one point in time. Better, they argue, to use a longitudinal design in which, for example, a group is followed over a number of years so that data can be collected at a number of different points in time and the order in which events occurred can be seen. Such studies are relatively rare in criminology; they take a long time, can be expensive and some have doubts about their superiority (see, for example, Gottfredson and Hirschi, 1987). We shall nevertheless encounter some in this chapter.

The material in this section may seem rather technical, not to say dull. The important point is that different objectives, of which we have identified three, must be made clear by both producers and consumers of self-report studies. They have important consequences for the way data are collected and analysed. If this is not understood, various confusions are likely to occur.

The career of the self-report study

The 1940s: a star is born?

An early flurry of relatively unsystematic but mildly titillating self-report studies can be detected in the mid-1940s. Porterfield (1946: 38), in a comparative study of convicted youth and students, found the latter freely reporting similar delinquencies to those of the former, including one 'successful pastor' who admitted committing 28 of the 55 offences listed in the schedule presented to the respondents. The admission of a murder by one of the students 'strains credulity', according to Hindelang et al. (1979: 996), but who was to know? At this time, perhaps many did not know what to make of the reports of the pastor's peccadilloes and the murderous student. Wallerstein and Wyle (1947) similarly found large quantities of self-reported criminality among the apparently respectable in another US study. Finally, there was the study of Murphy et al. (1946), in which a large sample of boys in the USA were followed through their adolescent years. Of the minimum of 6416 infractions over a five year period reported by the boys, only ½ per cent of these overall resulted in official action. Only 11 per cent of serious offences were prosecuted. The offences of 'official' offenders were, however, more frequent and serious overall than those of the 'unofficial' group.

There is little doubt that these studies created considerable interest at the time, and were noted by many sociologists and criminologists (e.g., Merton, 1957: 144). It was perhaps felt to be unwise to jump to too many conclusions when basic issues about the quality of these data had not been confronted. However, it was clear from what might be called this exploratory or exposé phase of self-report studies that more systematic and rigorous work along these lines might produce interesting returns. It was to be a few more years before this happened.

The 1950s: the youngster shows promise

Perhaps the major breakthrough came in the mid-1950s with Nye's (1958) study of family relationships and delinquent behaviour, and his other studies, notably with James Short (Nye and Short, 1957; Short and Nye, 1957; Nye *et al.*, 1958). All of these employed self-report techniques to measure delinquency, and it is worth spending time on what may seem to be ancient studies because of the influence they were to have on later research. The basic research instrument was an anonymous delinquency check-list, administered to a variety of populations. The full list included 23 items, of which seven were used in a scale constructed for a variety of statistical tests: driving a car without a licence/permit; skipping school; defying parents' authority to their faces; taking little things worth up to $2; buying/drinking beer, wine or liquor; purposely damaging or destroying public or private property belonging to others; having sexual relations with someone of the opposite sex. A moment's reflection may indicate that these were not very serious items and not all were crimes (what's your score – how many of these did you engage in during your youth?). The full list included a few more serious items – taking things worth over $50 (a fairly substantial sum in the USA of the 1950s), and using or selling narcotic drugs, for example, but most of the others were of similar relative triviality. Many of these items were to reappear in later studies.

Respondents were asked to respond to each item in a variety of pre-determined categories concerning frequency. The top category was often 'over five' or 'over six' times. These truncated scales have the obvious disadvantage that they do not allow any precise count of the frequency of acts, and they may end up treating individuals with very different actual frequencies as being, for all intents and purposes, the same. For example, we would be unable to distinguish young people who had had illicit sex nine times (the top category for this item) from those who had had it 90 times (an important and absorbing issue not only for science but also for young males; we return to the general issue of exaggeration later!). Most of the items, however, presented respondents with four grades of frequency, of the 'very often' to 'never' variety. This, of course, has similar disadvantages, and the added one that much is left to the subjective interpretation and standards of individuals. Finally, another feature of the full check-list was the overlap between some of the items: for example, fist fight and gang fight are listed as separate items. This allows the possibility of counting the same act more than once. Again, similar features were to characterize many later studies.

The sample and the details of each study varied somewhat according to the objectives of each; one was concerned with testing a particular theoretical perspective on delinquency (Nye, 1958), two with more methodological issues (Nye and Short, 1957; Short and Nye, 1957) and a fourth with examining the relationship between socio-economic status and delinquent behaviour (Nye *et al.*, 1958). The last mentioned article makes quite clear some of its own limitations: that the measure of delinquency did not include some of the more serious types; that the samples were from high schools in rural areas and small towns and cities, with no large city or non-Caucasian samples included, so that generalizations about such populations had to wait until further research. Nevertheless, the authors conclude that in these samples measures of socio-economic status and self-reported delinquency for girls and boys were not highly correlated, contrary to what might have been expected from popular theories of the time. By contrast, in another sample of boys from a state training school (for 'official' delinquents), 50 per cent of them came from the lowest socio-economic category, which constituted only 13 per cent of the high school population (Short and Nye, 1957). The authors suggested that these results had implications for theories which assume a concentration of delinquency in the 'lower class', and for researchers drawing research data from 'official' sources.

The 1960s: the young upstart questions the beliefs of the elders

The 1960s witnessed self-report studies in increasing numbers. Dentler and Monroe (1961), for example, studied self-reports of early adolescent theft among junior high school students from suburban and rural areas using anonymous questionnaires. They concluded that there was no relationship between the occupational level of parents (for this is how the 'class' of the child is usually measured in these studies) and this type of deviance in their data. Erickson and Empey's (1963) study used small samples (white males 15–17 years of age) with a heavy preponderance of officially defined delinquents, and is interesting from a methodological point of view; it used detailed interviews, which were found to be helpful with those with literacy problems and to improve the overall understanding of the questions. In this study a correlation was discovered between status and delinquency, but this was only because of the lower contribution of the upper-status group, which constituted 16 per cent of the sample but contributed only 9 per cent of the total violations confessed (Empey and Erickson, 1966). Although some other studies were interested in the quality of the method and its data (Clark and Tifft, 1966), most concentrated on the issue of social class and delinquency

(Reiss and Rhodes, 1961; Clark and Wenninger, 1962; Akers, 1964; Voss, 1966; Gold, 1966, for example). All the studies mentioned so far were conducted in the USA, but some work on this topic was now being done in Scandinavia (e.g., Christie *et al.*, 1965) and there was an overdue study in England (McDonald, 1969).

Perhaps the study during this decade which was most sensitive to the problems of quality of the data was that by Gold (1966; 1970) of boys and girls between the ages of 13 and 16 in a large industrial city in the USA. Gold used personal interviews rather than the traditional questionnaire because this enabled him to discover other related offences and to get detailed descriptions of possible delinquent acts. This seemed to be important, for many initial admissions were subsequently found to be 'non-chargeable' items. In addition, there seemed to be some signs of systematic bias in this source of over-reporting: for example, trivial property destruction was most often admitted by wealthier boys, a feature which might help, to some extent at least, to account for the tendency for studies to find a weak or negligible relationship between class and delinquency. A common argument against the interview was, of course, that it was likely to lead to more concealment than the anonymous questionnaire. For this reason, Gold not only gave respondents assurances of confidentiality, but also interviewed a group of friends of the respondents in order to gather independent information on acts which had been witnessed by these informants, or described to them by the perpetrator. He then checked this information against the original self-reports. From this check, Gold concluded that 72 per cent of his original sample were 'truth tellers' and only 17 per cent were 'outright concealers'. Interestingly, the more delinquent were not necessarily the concealers. As Gold accepts, this check does not tell us anything about the answers of 'loners' (those committing acts alone and not communicating details to others) and there is still a possibility of exaggeration. However, in view of the serious attempts made to improve data quality, his findings are of special interest.

But it was Gold's findings on social status (measured by the prestige of father's occupation) that were of most interest at that time. He estimated that whereas five times as many of the lowest-status boys as of the highest-status boys had an official record, the ratio of low-status to high-status delinquents would be reduced to about $1.5:1$ if the self-reports were taken as the indicator of delinquency. However, he also notes that three to four times as many low-status boys were to be found at the highest level on both his frequency and seriousness scales, indicating that perhaps, after all, official records were not such a bad indicator of the social status of persistent and serious offenders, even if not of their numbers.

Gold's careful and detailed study is still worth our attention for its findings and for the way in which it raises, implicitly or explicitly, some of the key issues which were to continue to be important in this area of study for years to come: the relative merits of interviews versus anonymous questionnaires; that different population samples may produce different results, and limit conclusions which may be drawn from them; that conclusions may also differ according to whether the focus is on persistent and serious offenders or on a much bigger group which includes those who have been involved in a small number of less serious acts; and finally, the issue of validity (how can we be sure that these instruments are measuring what they are intended to measure?).

Gold's study also shows the emerging concern with another possible social correlate of delinquency, race, which had been largely neglected in the earlier self-report studies. Another example of a study demonstrating this concern looked at differences by race among a sample of male students, aged 13–18, in a central lower-class, high-delinquency area of a city (Chambliss and Nagasawa, 1969). Three times as many black youths were found to have been arrested as whites, whereas the percentage confessing high-delinquency involvement was found to be the same for the two groups. The authors conclude that the discrepancy between the two measures might be accounted for by bias of official agencies, self-fulfilling over-scrutiny of black youths, and the less respectful demeanour exhibited by them, resulting in higher proportions being arrested.

We do not fully discuss the issues of race and class here; this is reserved for a later chapter. However, we hope that what we have said will give some impression of why self-report studies aroused so much interest during this period, and why they were being conducted increasingly frequently. It was clear that the studies were throwing up a number of challenges to widely accepted 'facts' about delinquency, which had been the starting point for many theories of it (see Chapter 1). Underlying this, there was the appearance of a number of key discrepancies between self-report and official measures of delinquency. If these discrepancies could not be resolved in some way, it appeared that criminology had no firm foundation upon which to build generalizations and theories. All criminologists could accept that official statistics suffered from various sins of omission; what was more disturbing was the idea that the statistics might suffer from bias to such as extent that social class, and perhaps race too, could no longer be key tools in the criminologist's explanatory tool-bag. Self-report studies therefore gave a powerful stimulus to the development of theories that did not take class as the key explanatory variable (such as control theory), and to research investigating the possibility that there were various forms of bias in the way in which people were handled by the criminal justice system that might result in biased statistics. The latter research topic dovetailed neatly, of course, with the concerns of the labelling perspective and the various forms of conflict theory which became influential in the late 1960s (see, for example, Chambliss, 1969; Quinney, 1970). What these perspectives suggested was that the application of the criminal law was very much a function of the class and power structures of the wider society, rather than simply an impartial response to the law-breaking behaviour of individuals.

The 1970s: settling down to a steady job?

Attention to the relationship between social class (or, more precisely, the occupational status or prestige of parents) and the self-reported deviant behaviour of young people was to continue throughout the next decade (see the discussions in Tittle *et al.*, 1978, and Chapter 5 of this volume, for example). Added to this, and following the lead of the pioneer studies mentioned above (Gold, 1970; Chambliss and Nagasawa, 1969), there was increasing interest in the relationship between race and self-reported delinquency (Williams and Gold, 1972; Berger and Simon, 1974; Forslund, 1975; Jensen and Eve, 1976).

Another 'social correlate' which also began to receive increasing attention from self-report studies in this decade was gender. Again, following some first tentative steps in the 1960s (Wise, 1967), a number of studies looked at the relative contribution of males and females to delinquency (Jensen and Eve, 1976; Weiss, 1976; Cernkovich and Giordano, 1979; Hindelang *et al.*, 1979; Johnson, 1979). Here again there appeared to be the possibility of discrepancies between official data and self-reports. Steven Box (1981: 84), summarizing the studies available to him at the end of the decade and concluding that the overall ratio of male to female contributions was much smaller than that indicated by official statistics, stated tentatively that 'just as we have to be suspicious about theories based on a major class difference in delinquency so too do we need to be suspicious of those premised on the view that delinquency is primarily a male preserve'. There could be no clearer indication that some criminologists had been taking seriously the challenge to traditionally accepted beliefs about the distribution of delinquency and were not slow to draw out the implications for explanations of it.

On the other hand, at the end of the same decade, Hindelang *et al.* (1979) were claiming that the notion of discrepancy between self-report and official measures of delinquency on such matters as class, race and gender was 'an illusion'. Their argument was that studies in the past had employed items of low seriousness and high frequency in their measures in order to capture enough delinquent acts among their samples of officially non-delinquent youth. Not only were these items likely to elicit behaviour largely outside that which would in practice interest the police, but such trivial items would swamp any serious items in the kinds of global omnibus scales typically used in research, thereby concealing important differences in the relationships between social correlates and different types of delinquency, especially the more serious and less frequent. After a review of the main relevant studies, they concluded that the relationship between serious crime and these social correlates had simply not yet been investigated adequately, and the inclusion of more serious items, together with much bigger sample sizes or much more efficient survey designs, would be necessary in order to do so (Hindelang *et al.*, 1979: 1002). In their view, therefore, the main reason for the apparent discrepancies was that 'self-report instruments typically tap a domain of behaviour virtually outside the domain of official data' (Hindelang *et al.*, 1979: 1009). Their important study in Seattle (Hindelang *et al.*, 1981), of which more later, was to follow in the next decade and was intended to test out their various claims in detail.

While research into social correlates continued to develop in these ways, a second major strand in self-report research was the use of the method in the testing of theories of delinquency. A pioneering study in this respect had been published at the end of the previous decade: Hirschi's (1969) systematic testing of strain, cultural deviance and control theories of delinquency. Hirschi used an anonymous questionnaire with a sample from a big city population in California. The measure of delinquency incorporated six items, taking two of these from Short and Nye (1957) and four from Dentler and Monroe (1961); there was a deliberate attempt to choose items that would elicit violations of law rather than trivial deviations, although Hirschi himself and his colleagues were later to question whether this attempt had been entirely successful (Hindelang *et al.*, 1981: 90). Nevertheless, the study remains important, not least for two of its major conclusions.

The first conclusion from the data was that there was a very small relationship between socio-economic status and delinquency, one that could easily disappear through changes in sampling or in definitions of the key variables. Here Hirschi was keen to suggest the continuity with much previous research with similar findings. The second major conclusion from his study was that the data systematically favoured control theory as an explanation over its competitors; there is little doubt that this study was a major stimulus in the relatively successful career that the theory was to enjoy in subsequent years. At the time, this study appeared to deliver a devastating blow to those theories which had dominated the field in the 1950s and 1960s. What was just as important, however, was the way in which the self-report method gradually came to be accepted as a way, if not *the* way, to measure delinquency in the testing of theory. During the 1970s, therefore, we find a number of studies testing theories of delinquency using self-reports, sometimes in combination with official data of some sort (see, for example, Thomas and Hyman, 1978; Johnson, 1979).

In Britain, too, we find a few studies using the method, even if many writers seemed to view such studies as the last gasps of positivism, which many thought was a Jolly Bad Thing. It was therefore mainly from the bastions of 'traditional criminology' that a few examples emerged. There was a Home Office study of vandalism, conducted in Liverpool (Gladstone, 1978). There was a study of the causal factors in juvenile theft, conducted among London boys (Belson, 1975), which found that all of the 1425 boys, aged 13–16, admitted some form of stealing. Finally, perhaps most importantly, is the Cambridge Study in Delinquent Development, so called because it has been conducted by criminologists from the Cambridge Institute of Criminology; the original research site was a working-class area of London. This is a longitudinal study of 411 males who were first contacted in 1961–2 at the age of 8 or 9. Data were collected from and about these individuals at a number of ages, most recently in their thirties. Self-reports were collected on ten offences at each occasion, and information was also collected on these and other offences for which the individuals had been found guilty from the Criminal Record Office in London. At the same time, the researchers attempted to measure many variables that had been suggested as causes or correlates of crime (West, 1969; 1982; West and Farrington, 1973; 1977).

This study allows the comparison of self-reported crime and officially recorded crime for the same group of individuals over a long period of time, spanning much of the period that we are discussing. It also provides data on adults, something which has been very much lacking in most self-report studies and limited the inferences that can be drawn from them. It is difficult to do it full justice here, but a few examples may help to indicate the kind of data provided. The cumulative prevalence of self-reported offending, for example (the proportion of individuals who admitted ever engaging in one or more of the offences), was very high by age 32, with only 4 per cent of the sample denying all ten offences at all ages. In comparison, one-third of the sample had been *convicted* of at least one of the offences by that age. Nearly 70 per cent admitted at least one of the six theft items, including nearly 50 per cent admitting shoplifting (Farrington, 1989: 406). Other findings add to our knowledge of such topics as age and offending, continuity, versatility and specialization in offending and the relationship between official and self-report data. In addition, it is also valuable in any consideration of the validity of self-report data and its use in longitudinal studies. We shall therefore return to it on future occasions.

The awareness shown by the Cambridge study of methodological issues brings us neatly to this topic. There were a few discussions and relevant studies which took such issues seriously during this decade. Farrington (1973), for example, using data from the Cambridge study, showed that self-reports had *predictive validity*: that self-reported delinquency at one age significantly predicted future official convictions, independently of other predictive factors. A few others did studies explicitly concerned with the quality of the method (see Hardt and Peterson-Hardt 1977), but the situation at the end of the decade has been described thus:

> Sufficient work has been done in this area that it is now customary in delinquency research to preface one's work with a brief summary of the previous research on the reliability and validity of self-report measures. These summaries generally reach the optimistic conclusion

that research has shown the self-report method to be reliable and valid . . .

(Hindelang et al., 1981: 212–13)

As they go on to suggest, however, the situation was never so simple; there are some situations where such a view is reasonable, but others where it is not. We return to such questions later in this chapter, when we shall have the benefit of later research.

The 1980s and beyond: maturity or mid-life crisis?

The first major study to note is the one done in Seattle by Hindelang *et al.* (1981), which deliberately set out to answer some of the nagging questions which had been surrounding self-report methodology for some time. First, there is the question of validity. This research suggests that self-report studies are entirely appropriate for white, in-school, not seriously delinquent populations, yielding results of acceptable validity. Unfortunately, the method produces the least valid results among those who are black, male and officially delinquent. This group was less likely than others to report to researchers offences already known to the police; the rate of non-reporting of officially recorded offences for black males was three times that for white males (the validity check here is often called the 'reverse record check'), with the result that they are less likely to appear as delinquent as they should in comparison with other groups in a sample. This differential validity problem, suggest the authors, means that black groups should be separated out in any analysis of such data and has serious implications for attempts to assess the distribution of delinquency according to race (Hindelang *et al.*, 1981: 213–14).

The second major issue tackled by them was the method of administration of the self-report study, which we have mentioned previously. The researchers set out to test the effects of using four different conditions of administration on the amount of delinquency reported and on the reliability and validity of the reports: anonymous questionnaire; anonymous interview; non-anonymous questionnaire; non-anonymous interview (Hindelang *et al.*, 1981: 28). Their conclusion from their data was that: 'Interviews rarely provide measurably better results than questionnaires (except that the latter consistently produce more missing data), and anonymity does not improve the quality of the data by any test we have been able to devise' (Hindelang *et al.*, 1981: 214). They go on to suggest, however, that the in-depth interview was useful in establishing the nature of reported incidents, although their data were not systematic enough to allow estimates to be made of the impact of this. Other researchers have found the interview preferable for similar reasons, as we have seen (Erickson and Empey, 1963; Gold, 1966). This point, and the one about higher rates of missing data with the use of questionnaires, seem to give interviews the edge, provided that expense is no problem.

A second major study published in the 1980s was the National Youth Survey. This was a longitudinal survey, based on households rather than schools, of youths aged 11–17 chosen to be representative of the US population between those ages (in order to be able to make generalizations about that wider population). The household basis was chosen to avoid some of the problems of missing cases in school populations. The study made important contributions to the debate about the social correlates of delinquency (Elliott and Ageton, 1980), but also went on to test an integrated theoretical causal model of delinquency and drug use (Elliott *et al.*, 1985). Finally, the research provided an opportunity to review many of the methodological issues of self-report studies (Huizinga and Elliott, 1986; Elliott and Huizinga, 1989), and for this reason we shall return to it in the next section. Here, however, it is worth noting that, unlike many earlier studies, these researchers found significant race and class differences in self-reported delinquency. They attribute this to the extended frequency range they employed in their response sets to the self-report items, in contrast to the truncated frequency scales employed by many earlier studies. When they rescored their findings according to the measures employed by earlier studies, they found that the class and race differences all but disappeared (Elliott and Ageton, 1980: 103). It was clear to them that blacks and lower class youths were more often likely to be among high-frequency offenders, and many previous studies had been unable to detect this because of their measuring techniques.

Despite the expense, and the time taken to get results when a cohort is followed over a long period of time, longitudinal self-report studies seemed to be appearing more frequently in this recent period. The Cambridge Study in Delinquent Development continued to produce publications (see, for example, West, 1982; Farrington, 1989). In the USA a Philadelphia cohort born in 1958 was being tracked over time to look at the development of their offending careers (Wolfgang *et al.*, 1987). An earlier Philadelphia cohort had been studied, but was confined to males and official sources of data only (Wolfgang *et al.*, 1972). Furthermore, a volume on self-report research published at the end of the 1980s devoted a whole section to the consideration of the methodology involved, and longitudinal studies contemplated, under way or completed in Europe and North America (Klein, 1989). Such studies have their own special problems to face. Farrington (1989), for example, found that the questions he had asked at age 14 were not always appropriate at later ages. Not only were the respondents older and likely to favour different types of offence, but also times had simply changed. Nostalgia alone could not prevent him from removing references to taking purple hearts and smoking reefers. The number of drugs listed in the question about this grows at each age until at age 32 it has become one of the longest in the schedule. Another example of a possible problem with longitudinal research concerns the possibility of what is called a 'panel effect'. Thornberry (1989) suggests from his data that interviewing the same group of people a number of times over a period leads to a decline in their admission rates, which is due to the fact of being reinterviewed.

In Britain, Riley and Shaw (1985) did a cross-sectional national study of teenagers and their families, using structured household interviews to investigate the relationship between parental supervision and juvenile delinquency. Campbell (1986) did an exploratory self-report study of fighting by females. Other data about self-reported offending have come from certain questions which have been included about this in the British Crime Survey. Such material is of special interest because it includes information on adults. If done on a regular and systematic basis, the surveys can provide estimates of crime trends over time to complement those from the reports of victims. Existing published work does not always seem to allow this at present. The number of offences included was much smaller in 1984 than in 1982, making comparisons difficult (see Mayhew and Elliott, 1990). The findings do, however, provide interesting material on offending, age and gender, as we show in a later chapter. Using material from the same surveys, on drink-driving, Riley (1984; 1985) found 22 per cent of men and 9 per cent of women admitting driving recently knowing they were over the legal alcohol limit, with a significant decline in this on moving from younger to older age groups. A final example from these surveys concerns the prevalence of drug use. Mott and Mirrlees-Black (1993) report from the 1992 British Crime Survey that 17 per cent of those aged between 12 and 59 admitted ever taking any of 12 drugs listed without a doctor's prescription (ever, or cumulative prevalence), and 6 per cent said they had in 1991. As many as 24 per cent of those aged 16 to 29 said they had taken cannabis at some time, while 3 per cent of this group had ever used cocaine.

The final and most recent development to which we wish to draw attention is the work conducted in connection with the international study of self-reported delinquency (ISRD). This seems to have grown out of a conference held in the Netherlands in 1988 (a selection of the papers given is contained in Klein, 1989). A programme of research has been developed in order to investigate self-reported delinquency among 14–21-year-olds in a variety of countries, with all studies adopting a common format in certain respects so that comparisons can be made between them. Such studies bring their own particular problems. For example, there is the fact that different countries have different definitions of crime and delinquency, questions may have to be altered substantially in the way that they are expressed because of local language differences, and delinquency items suitable for one context may be entirely unsuitable for another (for a fuller discussion, see Junger-Tas, 1989; Moffitt, 1989).

The first results of this enterprise have now been published (Junger-Tas *et al.*, 1994), including a contribution from the English and Welsh component (Bowling *et al.*, 1994). The latter is based on a standard instrument developed for the ISRD to survey 14–21-year-olds, but it also sampled some respondents up to the age of 25 and included extra offences such as serious motoring offences, insurance, tax and benefit fraud, and credit card and cheque fraud. It is good to see studies including older age groups and including offences that may be more favoured by them and, perhaps, by white-collar respondents. These features have often been lacking in previous studies. Some alterations to certain questions were also necessary to make them fit the definitions of offences in this country. Although the research encounter (based on households) began with an interview, self-completion booklets were used for drug use and self-reported offending. As might be expected from past research, this resulted in non-completion of the booklets which 'was higher than it might have been' (Bowling *et al.*, 1994: 45). Furthermore, non-completion rates were higher for respondents from minority ethnic groups than for whites, possibly resulting in a sample skewed towards low offenders, especially for the minority groups. Finally, in the analysis of self-reported offending and demographic characteristics presented, simple prevalence rates are mainly used, categorizing respondents as offenders if they admit to one offence or many, thus treating serious and minor, one-time and frequent offenders, as pretty much the same. As we have seen from past research, this is also likely to limit the conclusions we can draw from the findings presented so far about gender, socio-economic status and minority ethnic groups.

We have now completed our overall survey of the development of self-report studies over the last 50 years. It may be apparent that the self-confidence which once characterized the method has been eroded somewhat in the light of the increasingly sophisticated research which pointed up the weak as well as the strong aspects. It is clear, however, that the method is here to stay, more widely used in the USA perhaps, but definitely part of the scene in Europe also. The latest phase of international recognition is something that any footballer or rock band would enjoy. Having come so far, let us try to summarize the lessons which seem to have been taught by this research, beginning with methodological aspects.

Madness in their method? Methodological issues

Most discussions of methodology, however hard they try, seem unable to avoid the terms 'validity' and 'reliability'. We have already defined the first term in our own way. To remind you, here is someone else's definition: 'the evidence that the test measures what it was intended to measure or that it represents what it appears to represent' (Huizinga and Elliott, 1986: 308).

The 'test' in this instance is the self-report instrument; 'what it was intended to measure' may, of course, vary somewhat according to your objectives. The same authors define reliability as 'the level of precision of an instrument. In this context, the level of precision refers to the extent to which the measuring instrument would produce identical scores if it were used to make multiple measures of the same object' (Huizinga and Elliott, 1986: 295). Without making things too complicated, they are both measures of the quality of data of any kind; the more they are present, the more we can have confidence in the methods used and the data produced. Let us look at the various methodological issues raised by self-report studies before coming to a conclusion about these aspects. Most of these issues should by now be familiar.

Too many trivial items?

Too many studies have concentrated on less serious offences, as well as including 'adolescent-status offences and bad manners', as Box (1981: 74) put it, together with other items which elicit some acts unlikely to produce a formal response from the criminal justice system. This makes comparisons with official statistics and relevance to many theories tenuous. There have been some improvements in this respect in recent years, although Weitekamp (1989: 338) claimed that the most widely known instruments to date were still largely composed of trivial items, with Hindelang *et al.* (1981) and Elliott *et al.* (1985) including only four or five items of greater seriousness than Short and Nye (1957). The second Philadelphia cohort study (Wolfgang *et al.*, 1987) included white-collar, occupational crimes and murder (Weitekamp, 1989: 338), although there must be doubts about the validity of responses on the most serious of offences. A related point concerns the capacity for some apparently 'valid' items to produce high rates of trivial acts; we have already seen an example of this in Gold's (1966) research, but this was also a particular problem with the minor assault item in the National Youth Survey where the vast majority of initial responses were 'trivial', indicating the need to be careful about the wording of items and to have follow-up questions about the exact nature of incidents (Elliott and Huizinga, 1989: 157–61). In most studies, however, we are left in the dark about the extent of such trivial responses.

How do we choose the items to be included?

Since there are so many items which could be included, we have to be selective. Our selection should be 'representative', but of what? For example, different populations (age groups, genders, classes, cultures) are likely to favour different patterns of offence. This is a particular problem when we are comparing different categories and their relative contributions to crime; our check-list may be biased towards the offences favoured by one group.

Many use the offence patterns revealed by official statistics as a guide (see, for example, Huizinga and Elliott, 1986: 311), but this runs the risk of reproducing any biases in those statistics which self-reports were intended to avoid. There seems to be no ideal solution, but there has been more awareness of this issue as researchers have moved beyond the traditional focus on the delinquency of lower-class urban adolescent males. Certainly, studies of adults need to include a different range of items from those used on adolescents.

Overlap between items?

We have seen how this can result in double or triple counting of the same act for any respondent. This is a particular defect where any attempt is being made to measure and compare the frequency of offences, since it will lead to inflation of the figures for some offences. It may not be so serious if testing of theory is the objective, where precise figures may not be required.

How specific should the items be?

Many studies have used a range of fairly general items that cater for a range of offences under different circumstances. This allows a wide coverage with relatively few items. Researchers who have used more specific items, on the other hand, have found that admission rates increase accordingly, the greater specificity apparently helping recall of incidents (Hindelang *et al.*, 1981). Unfortunately, the more specific the items, the more of them are needed to produce anything like the same coverage in terms of the range of offences (and however many there are, there are always likely to be offences or circumstances that are not covered). And the more items there are, the more problems like subject fatigue appear, and the quality of the data suffers accordingly. Again, there seems to be no ideal solution, with different considerations pulling us in different directions. A major consideration in answering this question in practice should be the objectives and circumstances of the particular research project.

What frequency response categories for the items?

Many studies in the past have used rather vague categories or truncated scales for measuring frequency. These can result in imprecise frequency counts and an inability to distinguish very persistent offenders. Open-ended questions have been advocated for epidemiological analysis to elicit more exact information about frequency (Elliott and Huizinga, 1989: 176), although it is evident that persistent offenders may have difficulty in recalling precise numbers of acts and may need the help of an interviewer. For the testing of theory, precise numerical frequencies may not be required, but any scale should allow us to distinguish persistent offenders. On reliability tests, Elliott and Huizinga (1989: 175) found no clear evidence favouring open-ended or fixed categories. Again the objectives of the research should be paramount.

What reference period should be employed?

This refers to the period about which respondents are asked to recall delinquent acts. Many studies have used fairly long periods, such as Short and Nye (1957) who asked about the period since the beginning of 'grade school', while others have asked how many acts of particular kinds have 'ever' been committed. Long reference periods should have the advantage of maximizing the chances of detecting involvement in delinquency in a sample, perhaps keeping down the size of sample necessary (see below), but they have disadvantages. For example, it is difficult to compare the results with published official statistics and crime surveys, which employ shorter and specific time periods. Furthermore, such periods, especially over a long time, appear to result in data loss; in the Cambridge Study in Delinquent Development, for example, over all eight offences an average of 46 per cent of those who had previously admitted an offence denied it at age 32, leading Farrington (1989: 416–17) to conclude that although 'ever' questions may be a useful supplement, they are not a substitute for repeated self-reports over a long period of time, rather than just at the end if it. The National Youth Survey data suggested serious levels of under-reporting for periods of two and three years, as compared with a one-year reference period (Elliott and Huizinga, 1989: 166). Experience on this project also suggested that although in some respects a 12-month reference period was too long, a shorter period increased the amount of telescoping error (inaccurate placing of incidents inside or outside the reference period), and pushed up costs considerably (theirs was a longitudinal survey attempting coverage of a much longer period); these considerations lead them to advocate the compromise of a 12 month reference period, supplemented by bounding techniques (using anchor points with some relevance for the subjects: for example, 'have you done X since last Christmas?') in order to reduce telescoping (Elliott and Huizinga, 1989: 168–9). This seems a good general guide, although choices in particular cases will be influenced by specific objectives.

What kinds of scales?

As we have seen, some researchers such as Short and Nye combined certain items into a general scale to represent the category of delinquency. Others preferred to take one particular type of delinquency (for example, Dentler and Monroe, 1961), perhaps taking the view that delinquency is a multi-faceted phenomenon and differences should be recognized in our research. More recently, a number of researchers (such as Hindelang *et al.*, 1981; Elliott *et al.*, 1985) have developed subscales of particular types. Certainly there are important patterns relating to particular types of offence which may be concealed by the use of omnibus general scales. We have already seen how the combination of serious and non-serious items into one scale may lead to high-frequency non-serious items concealing relationships between social correlates and the more serious offences. But analysis also needs to be offence-specific at times in order to unravel the reasons behind particular findings. Elliott and Huizinga (1989: 179), for example, found that their general assault scale produced no significant race differences overall, but there were significant differences for different types of offence which, because they were in different directions, cancelled each other out in the overall statistical picture.

What kinds of samples?

We have seen that, in the early self-report studies, samples were often drawn from groups of rural or small town adolescents. Although we should not be too harsh on those pioneers, it must be said that these samples limited the conclusions that could be drawn from them. Samples should always be as representative as possible of the population about which we wish to generalize. So, for example, if we wish to find out about the distribution of offending among young people in England and Wales, we should try our best to produce a sample which is a microcosm of that population (see the brief discussion of this in Bowling *et al.*, 1994). Many early studies took their samples from school settings (with the attendant problems of those who, for various reasons, were not in school, often those most likely to be delinquent). More recent studies, trying to make population estimates, and trying to go beyond the usual focus on children up to the last age of compulsory education, have tended to use household samples instead. Even these will tend to leave out a number of people such as 'students, nurses, the homeless, and those in residential care, Young Offenders Institutions and prisons' (Bowling *et al.*, 1994: 46). This, of course, means that at least some of the most serious and persistent offenders may be missing, but Bowling *et al.* (1994: 46) suggest that as the last two groups constitute no more than 0.25 per cent of the population targeted, it seems doubtful 'that the inclusion of these groups would influence the overall findings'. This view should perhaps be qualified according to the objectives of research, for these groups are likely to contribute to delinquency in terms of frequency and seriousness out of all proportion to their size in relation to the target population. We might be unwise to assume that the standard self-report sample can provide enough data on chronic offenders (Cernkovich *et al.*, 1985). Similarly, if the theory we wish to test is about persistent offenders in run-down city neighbourhoods, our samples should reflect this. There has been a tendency to generalize from the samples of the early studies, which were very limited in their age range, geographical location, and other respects.

A final point concerns sample size. We have already seen how there has been some recognition that studies should focus more on serious offences. This means that samples have to be much larger in size or more sophisticated in design to capture sufficient numbers of serious offences to make analysis of them meaningful, especially where the reference period is relatively short.

Is non-response a problem?

This issue is clearly related to the last. Hirschi (1969) eventually obtained data from 73.5 per cent of his original sample, with absence of permission from parents the largest source of loss. All the indications were that the more delinquent were less likely to be in the final sample. Hindelang *et al.* (1981) found that contact with sample groups was easier with the non-delinquent groups (the two delinquent groups were as defined by police or courts), with rates of non-location ranging from 1.3 per cent for white non-delinquents of high socio-economic status to 48.5 per cent for black court delinquents. However, in a finding out of line with most other research, police delinquents were the *most* likely groups to agree to participate in the research once contacted (Hindelang *et al.*, 1981: 33–4), with rates of agreement to participate in a narrower range between 41.1 and 83.8 per cent of those located. It can be seen that rates of attrition can be quite high, and can be selective. Junger-Tas (1989: 22) reports a sliding scale of response rates, more or less according to the degree of contact with the criminal justice system, ranging from 60 per cent for those with no contact, to 34 per cent for those with recorded police contacts. She also cites research that indicates that the older the respondents, the higher the non-response rate (Junger-Tas, 1989: 21). Reuband (1989: 90), on the other hand, reports response rates of 68 and 70 per cent in two representative samples of the West German population over the age of 18, in interviews conducted by professional survey organizations. An interview study of men from Stockholm experienced a non-response rate of 31 per cent, this being larger among those with the most registered offences (Sarnecki, 1989: 122).

Our conclusion must be that non-response is not random, but results in the under-representation of certain key groups. Researchers must take every possible step to reduce this, with follow-up visits and so on. When such attempts have been completed, a number of researchers have then followed the practice of weighting their sample so that it corresponds as closely as possible to the population from which it was drawn on key variables such as gender, race and official delinquency record (Hirschi, 1969; Hindelang *et al.*, 1981). As O'Brien (1985: 72) comments, this does not guarantee representativeness on other variables. It seems as though the method, when used in general population samples, has most problems with groups likely to be the most delinquent, although satisfactory results have been reported with high-delinquency groups within an institutional setting (Erickson and Empey,

1963). Not only this, but there are also some indications that response rates may be more of a problem with adult populations than with the traditional adolescent ones.

What method of administration?

We have already considered this issue in some detail. Our conclusion is that the confidential interview seems to be the method of preference where time and resources allow. Not only does it allow the researcher to explore initial answers and determine important details about such matters as the nature of incidents (whether they would be likely to be recorded by the police if known, their degree of seriousness, for example), but it also seems to result in less data loss of various kinds (uncompleted questionnaires, for example).

Confusion over measures?

Difficulties are created where there are inconsistencies in the use of terms, and comparisons between studies are hazardous where different measures have been applied. Although many writers talk about 'the distribution of delinquency', the findings are often expressed in terms of an *offender*-based measure. This has usually been the '*ever*', or *cumulative, prevalence rate*, which refers to the proportion of a sample who report ever having engaged in one or more delinquency items. For various reasons, we have seen that many recent studies have expressed findings in terms of an *annual prevalence rate*, which refers to the proportion of people reporting offending in a population during a year. By contrast, a measure such as the *general offending rate* is more sensitive to the frequency of offending, measuring as it does the number of offences or acts (per person or per 100,000 persons, for example) over a particular time period. The term *incidence* has often been used in this context, but this can be confusing since this term, borrowed from medical epidemiology, refers to the proportion of a population at risk who become infected with a disease during the year. It therefore seems preferable to use the other term. To complicate the picture further, some researchers have used *ever variety* or *last year variety* measures (the range of different offences engaged in during the period) (Hindelang *et al.*, 1981). Finally, it must be recognized that self-reports are what we might call person offences (they are offences linked to particular individuals, but others may have been involved in the same offence). They are not, therefore, strictly speaking, crime events in the way that crimes recorded by the police and offences reported by victims are, because others may self-report the same incident. Although this may seem a quibble, it is one difficulty in making direct comparisons between self-report results and the other forms of crime data (Elliott and Huizinga, 1989: 180–81).

Having looked at a number of issues and problems, many of which have a bearing on the reliability and validity of the findings of self-report studies, we now return to those concepts as a conclusion to our assessment. Although other measures of reliability have been used, it seems to us that one of the best is the test–retest procedure, in which an instrument is administered to a sample, then administered to the same group at some later time and the results compared to see how closely they correspond: the more they correspond, the more reliable the method or results are thought to be. Encouraging results have been obtained in the past for periods of between less than one hour and two months, although results are only moderate after this (Huizinga and Elliott, 1986: 300). However, Hindelang *et al.* (1981) found lower reliability for black males with only a police record than for other groups. Huizinga and Elliott (1986: 303), however, did not find a systematic difference on this or other characteristics of the respondent, such as sex, class and place of residence. Instead, it was those reporting few acts who were able to recall them more reliably later, and the more serious acts which were most reliably recalled, as might be expected. But a consistent response is not necessarily a valid one, so it is to this issue that we now turn.

One of the problems here is the absence of any widely accepted alternative measures of delinquency or crime by which we can judge the validity of self-reports. Most tests involve the use of official records – precisely that data whose alleged deficiencies led to the development of self-report studies. Sometimes self-reports of official contacts are used. Other unofficial sources involve friends, teachers, victims, and direct observation (Hindelang *et al.*, 1981: 98). Three strategies have generally been used: 'known group' studies, to see if self-reports can distinguish between groups known to be different in terms of official delinquency; correlational studies of the association between self-reports and other indicators; and record checks, which try to see how far self-reports and official delinquencies match. Huizinga and Elliott (1986) review the evidence of each of these very thoroughly in turn, and conclude on the basis of the third type of study:

> official record checks indicate that some, and usually the majority of officially known individuals will report the majority of their known offences, including their serious offences. However, these record checks also indicate sizable levels of underreporting, especially among blacks, and in general the rate of underreporting was larger for more serious offences.
>
> (Huizinga and Elliott, 1986: 323)

It must be remembered that checks against official records can at best only tell us something about self-reports of offences that have already come to the attention of the authorities. It might be argued that people will be more able and inclined to report these than other derelictions which have not been officially registered. However, the reasons for the 'underreporting' by blacks are still not firmly known, and deliberate concealment is not necessarily the answer. This finding is also not necessarily replicated elsewhere. A study in the Netherlands found that self-report measures were markedly less valid (measured by a record check) for Turks and Moroccans than for Surinamese (and indigenous Dutch) boys (Junger, 1989). That said, the implications should be clear enough, casting some doubts upon the use of self-reports for some groups and for more serious offences.

Conclusion

Opinions differ on the contribution of self-report studies to the criminological enterprise. Thornberry (1989: 348), from a US perspective, thinks that '[t]he introduction of the self-report method has had a greater impact on theory and research than any other single innovation and it has lead to fundamental shifts in how delinquent behaviour is described and explained'. In Britain, however, Bottomley and Pease (1986: 21) suggested in the mid-1980s that '[p]erhaps because of the particular difficulties and disadvantages of self-report studies, recent years have witnessed an increasing reliance on and preference for victim surveys, despite their necessarily partial coverage of crime'. In our view there were differences in contexts and objectives which might partly explain the difference in usage between the two countries. Whereas in the USA the tradition of research into the causes of crime focusing on offenders had continued, in Britain this had to some extent been eclipsed by the focus on situational crime prevention, victimology and 'left realism'. These concentrated on crime and its impact rather than on the offender, and many of the issues they raised could be best tackled by victim surveys rather than by self-report studies. By contrast, the victim survey is almost mute on the offender.

There is little doubt that self-report studies have contributed much in documenting some of the omissions in official data and raising the possibility of various forms of bias in those data, and in the agencies that produce them. They have made clear that offending behaviour is far more widespread in the population than was once supposed, and that the 'offender' cannot be so clearly distinguished as a minority with certain key characteristics as was once thought. Perhaps a number of misleading impressions were created by the early studies, but there are signs that more recent research is more attuned to such key matters as the seriousness and frequency of offending. Progress in methodology has been evident so that, if researchers learn from past experience, we can have more confidence in their findings. Self-report methods have become standard in the testing of theories of delinquency and have made major contributions in that field. They have shown how important it is to be clear about what is being explained. Significant contributions have been made to the debates about the social correlates of delinquent behaviour.

Some progress has also been made in making estimates about the extent of delinquency in certain age groups in the general population.

Fundamental objections to the whole enterprise can, of course, be raised, such as the view that it is improper to regard those persons and acts which have not been duly processed by the authorities as criminal, or that, because of various practical and philosophical difficulties, crime cannot be measured in this way at all. We understand those objections, but to take either to its logical extreme leads to a very stunted criminology that has very little to say on topics of key concern for all those with an interest in crime. All forms of crime data are deficient in their various ways, but self-report data, if the methodological lessons are heeded, can be used as one of a number of sources of data about crime and offenders. If used in conjunction, a composite picture can be built up. Unfortunately, much of our knowledge about the strengths and weaknesses of the method is derived from experience in the USA, which may not be fully replicated in other countries. However, this experience suggests that the method yields satisfactory results with juveniles who are not seriously delinquent. There do seem to be problems in eliciting enough good data from persistent and serious offenders (although acceptable results may be obtained for these in an institutional setting), and from those from certain minority ethnic groups. We do not yet have enough experience with general adult samples to be entirely confident about the findings with those groups.

Steven Box (1971; 1981), who did much to make us aware of self-report studies and their implications in his well-known textbook, was nevertheless very much aware of the overall limitations of much of this research so far. Not only had this whole area been obsessed with the study of juvenile delinquency (rather than adult crime – a deficiency that is only now beginning to be corrected), but it has also avoided definitional controversy over what crime is. In his view the adoption of a legalistic definition of crime is a political decision, since law is a conglomeration of political decisions. A more scientific approach for him would be to define crime on the basis of 'objective' and avoidable harm, injury and loss. If we did so, it would be clear that our most serious criminals are nestling in the higher echelons of our most powerful corporations (Box, 1981: 85). Even violations of current law by corporate and government officials are ignored by self-report studies. Although it is unlikely that self-report studies would get very far with such subjects, and Box's views on the definition of crime would need a lengthy discussion to deal with properly, his basic point is a key one: the actual coverage of self-report studies has continued to render invisible whole areas of criminal and associated activity; 'this is ironic, considering that the purpose of such studies was to make good the deficiencies of the official statistics' (Box, 1981: 87). Similarly, it could be added that such studies have not contributed to our knowledge of other areas of hidden crime, such as domestic violence and child abuse. Although self-report studies have a part to play, other forms of data are clearly required if we are to avoid a partial criminology.

Summary

The development of self-report studies is traced from their origins in the USA in the 1940s, through to the recent developments in international comparative work. The early studies aroused considerable interest, as they appeared to provide alternative measures to official data, and produced findings on such aspects as class and race which seemed to question some key assumptions derived from those official data and traditional theories. Much of this tradition of research has been characterized by a number of limitations, including too much concentration on trivial misbehaviour, too much concentration on adolescent populations, often less than satisfactory samples, and problems in obtaining valid data from some serious and persistent offenders. At its best, however, it has made considerable contributions as an alternative to official data in the study of the distribution of juvenile delinquency and the testing of theories of it. Despite this, it has so far been less successful in illuminating serious and adult crime, and has continued the neglect of certain types of hidden crime that are often also neglected in official statistics, such as corporate and governmental crime, domestic violence, and sexual and physical abuse of children.

Further reading

There are very few up-to-date overviews of this area. Box (1981) presented a concise version of what he saw as the main findings of these studies and their implications for criminological theory. Although now dated in content, it is still worth a look for its approach. Hindelang *et al.* (1981) is still a key book for its summaries of their own and other research on methodological and other issues. O'Brien (1985) has a chapter giving an overview of the earlier studies conducted in the USA. More recently, the collection edited by Klein (1989) has a number of useful contributions, including a whole section on longitudinal self-report research. In particular, it contains a piece by Farrington which summarizes some key findings on self-reported and official offending from the Cambridge Study in Delinquent Development, and an article by Elliott and Huizinga on what experience has taught us about methodology in this whole area and how to improve it. Elliott *et al.* (1985) could be looked at as a well-known example of such research to test theory (of delinquency and drug use). Finally, Junger-Tas *et al.* (1994) contains the first results of an international self-report delinquency study, including a contribution from England and Wales (Bowling *et al.*, 1994). A much more detailed account of the research on which the previously mentioned article was based was published after our main text was written and is strongly recommended. It includes findings on participation in and frequency of offending, age and offending, and the initiation of and desistance from offending, based on the self-reports of a representative sample of 14–25 year olds (see Graham and Bowling, 1995).

chapter four

Victimization surveys:
total recall?

This chapter introduces the following key concepts or terms, which are also to be found in the glossary at the end of the book: Uniform Crime Reports; National Crime Survey; index crimes; victimology; national surveys; multiple victimization; local surveys; administrative criminology; victimless crimes; sampling frame; Postcode Address File; sampling error; non-respondents; 'booster' sample; measurement error; 'non-stranger' crimes; response bias; 'education factor'; target hardening; and evaluation study.

Victimization surveys involve the application of the sample survey to the measurement of crime; a representative sample of a chosen population is questioned on their experience of criminal victimization, that is, crimes committed against them. Those who use this technique are aiming to capture crimes which do not enter the official statistics because they are not reported to or recorded by the police. Thus, they hope to be able partially to quantify the dark figure of crime, while at the same time producing data on the public's experience of crime and the criminal justice system. An American development, victimization surveys soon spread to Europe – although a little later to Britain – and were quickly embraced by researchers and policy-makers alike as offering a real solution to the problem of 'counting' crimes. Victimization surveys, while creating an invaluable source of data, are not without their own problems and indeed their own dark figure; we must learn to treat them with the same degree of caution and scepticism as is afforded official crime statistics and self-report studies.

In this chapter we will trace the history and development of victimization surveys and the different objectives which the various types of survey satisfy. We will see that as this method of research has matured, so their original purpose has expanded and developed. While partially meeting their original objective, it was soon found that they could be put to other uses. We will examine the methodological issues associated with this type of research in

Although this study did produce some interesting results which were useful in later refinements of methodology, the victimization section of the survey was rather swamped by other questions (Durant *et al.*, 1972: 20–76). For example, 'do you think the magistrate wears a wig?' or 'are there proper flush lavatories in most prison cells? If no, how do they manage?' – something we all wonder about! Indeed, it is very easy for the victimization data to be overlooked when it is in competition with such fascinating topics.

The first major British survey was Sparks *et al.*'s (1977) study, *Surveying Victims*. The authors were concerned with testing the methodology of the victimization survey in order to ascertain the validity of such techniques. They carried out their research in three demographically different London boroughs, selecting three independent samples from each area – two of the samples were of known victims drawn from police records and the third was a random sample of residents. Their known-victim samples were designed to test how well people could recall and date victimizations; their random sample was used to explore wider methodological issues of definition and multiple/serial victimization. Sparks *et al.* were also interested in the wider use of such surveys and gathered information on people's perceptions, attitudes and experiences of crime and the criminal justice system. We will be looking at the methodological problems which they identified later; for now it is enough to note the importance of their study in the development of British victimization surveys. As an antidote to the enthusiasm shown elsewhere for this method of research, Sparks *et al.* (1977: 220) raised a cautionary hand and paused to ask: does it work? They posed the question: '[i]s it possible, by asking people directly about their own experiences as victims, to get a reasonably accurate picture of the amounts and kinds of law breaking which have occurred in a given area and period of time?' They concluded that, 'on balance our answer to this question is "Yes", but it is an answer with several important qualifications'.

The Home Office took the decision to fund a British national victimization survey in 1981 and the first report of the British Crime Survey (BCS) was published in 1983 (Hough and Mayhew, 1983). Using a representative sample of the population of England and Wales, over 10,000 respondents (aged 16 years or over) were interviewed on their experiences of victimization during the previous 12 months. A proportion of the sample, including all those who reported victimizations, were also questioned on more general issues surrounding lifestyle, fear of crime and attitude to the police. Also included in this section was a self-report element which explored the respondent's own law-breaking behaviour. The BCS has now completed five 'sweeps' (1982, 1984, 1988, 1992 and 1994) and is firmly established as an alternative source of crime data. During its lifetime it has undergone modification and a widening of its scope and focus – the fourth sweep, for example, included a section on self-reported drug misuse, and the 1994 BCS increased its sample size to 14,500.

This and other national victimization surveys serve the needs of administrative criminology by mapping the incidence of crime, facilitating both prevention and control policies. Those associated with the emerging school of left realism were critical of this method of large-scale research. Their criticisms centred around 'their lack of detail and their inability to deal with the fundamental fact that crime is both geographically and socially focussed' (Jones *et al.*, 1986: 4). They were interested in the risk of victimization which particular subgroups experience, such as women, minority ethnic groups and deprived inner-city communities. In order to be able to identify and emphasize the seriousness of the impact of crime upon these groups and the rationality of the fear of crime, the local crime survey was developed. We shall be returning to both the BCS and local surveys later in this chapter.

Victimization surveys, national or local, have been of little use to those people interested in making international comparisons. There have been too many differences in the method of collecting data and in the definition of criminal events for any direct comparisons to be confidently made between different countries. In order to gain a valid picture of the extent of unrecorded crime on an international scale, a standardized victimization survey was required which could collect comparable data in each country. In order to meet this need, the 1989 and 1992 International Crime Surveys were carried out (see van Dijk *et al.*, 1990; van Dijk and Mayhew, 1992). This ambitious undertaking involved a standardized victimization survey in 17 European and non-European countries, plus a version of the survey in three other countries. Although this project has presented us with some very valuable and interesting international comparisons, it has also raised a different set of methodological issues and problems. It is important to remember that data generated by such international surveys should only be used for the purpose for which they were intended – international comparisons – and they should not, for example, be used to make comparisons with official crime rates.

Victimization surveys, as we have seen, can be made to serve a variety of interests and to play many different roles in the formulation of both theory and policy. In tracing their development, we have so far glossed over the methodological issues which arise. These issues will be addressed next.

The trouble with surveys: methodological issues

Some of the methodological issues which surround victimization surveys are common to all types of survey research, while others are quite specific to victim research. Before addressing these issues we should first discuss the most basic limitation of the method: victimization surveys can only measure criminal incidents where there is an identifiable victim. They are therefore of no value in assessing 'victimless crimes' such as drug offences or consensual sexual acts. Sparks *et al.* (1977: 227) point out that victimization surveys can only be used to measure incidents which have been both perceived *and* defined as crimes; they cannot measure the total number of illegal acts which take place in society. Therefore, not only must a victim exist, but the person must also realise that s/he has been victimized. It is of little use asking respondents about corporate or environmental crime as they are likely grossly to under-estimate the occurrence of victimization. Victimization surveys are best suited to measuring what Steven Box (1981: 164) calls 'ordinary crimes', the very crimes which are most likely to enter the official statistics – theft, burglary and the like. They are less able to capture such crimes as rape and domestic violence, although some local surveys have been specifically designed for this purpose. Generally, then, victimization surveys are good at measuring certain types of crime, less suitable for others and exclude some altogether.

Who shall we ask? Sampling and sampling frames

Crime is still a relatively rare event (despite what you may hear to the contrary) and in order to capture sufficient incidents a large sample is required. Durant *et al.* (1972) found that of their sample of 1890 respondents, only 45 per cent recalled *ever* having been the victim of *any* crime. Even with a large sample, some crimes appear elusive; the 1982 BCS captured so few incidents defined as robbery that little could be 'said about the offence with any statistical precision except to emphasise its rarity' (Hough and Mayhew, 1983: 17). A sample not only has to be large enough to capture rare events but must also be representative of its population: the BCS aims to be representative of England and Wales as a whole, whereas local crime surveys have a much narrower population, such as a city or a housing estate. The results from such local surveys do not purport to be representative of anything other than their own population; despite this, wider generalizations are often made from their data.

Vital to the representativeness of any survey is the choice of sampling frame; before 1992 the BCS used the electoral register to generate its sample, as did many of the early local surveys. Use of the electoral register as a sampling frame is known to have certain limitations and produces a low response rate from certain subgroups of the population who could have a very different experience of victimization, such as minority ethnic and transient groups (see Sparks *et al.*, 1977). These problems were felt to be exacerbated in the 1980s by the introduction of the community charge and the subsequent greater number of omissions from the register – we can only speculate on the victimization profile of the 'poll tax dodger'. Some local surveys used enumeration districts to generate samples of households (Jones *et al.*, 1986), while others (such as Anderson *et al.*, 1990) began to use the Postcode Address File (PAF) in an attempt to avoid the possible distortions which the electoral register can create. The PAF has the advantage of being constantly updated (unlike the electoral register, which is updated annually) and suffers from few omissions. However, the use of the PAF has its own problems; it includes businesses as well as residential addresses and includes a higher proportion of void and empty dwellings than the electoral register. Nevertheless, the PAF has become the preferred sampling frame for victimization surveys, being considered to produce a more representative sample, and in 1992 the BCS began using this sampling frame in preference to the electoral register.

Another problem which is common to all survey research is sampling error: statistics which are generated from a sample can be used to produce estimates for the population but these estimates may be different from those which would be produced if the whole population were surveyed. We do not intend to discuss in detail the technicalities of sampling errors; there are plenty of good research methods texts available which do this. Local victimization surveys suffer from relatively high sampling errors due to their relatively small samples. The BCS, which uses a large sample, still has the problem of high sampling errors for 'rare' crimes such as robbery (Mayhew *et al.*, 1993).

Although response rates for victimization surveys are relatively high – the response rate for the 1994 BCS was a very respectable 77 per cent (Mayhew *et al.* 1994) and most local surveys achieve a similar figure – some thought must be given to those who make up the non-respondents. If the characteristics of the non-respondents are atypical of the sample, then their exclusion could radically affect the results of the survey. Mayhew *et al.* (1993) argue that non-respondents probably include a disproportionately high number of victims, but the opposite could equally well be true – incentive to participate in a victimization survey could be stronger for victims than for non-victims. Little is known about non-respondents (for obvious reasons) and we have to rely upon informed speculation gathered from studies of known victims using reverse record checks (see Glossary). The early American pilot studies incorporated into their main samples a subset of known victims and it was this group that yielded the lowest response rates (see Skogan, 1986: 109). Sparks *et al.* (1977) had similar experiences; their two samples drawn from police records had a combined response rate of only 35.1 per cent. The main reason for non-response was found to be that the respondents had either left the address or could not be contacted; the rate of refusal was not seen to be significantly higher than in the main sample. Because Sparks *et al.* had information on these non-respondents they were able to come to certain conclusions about their characteristics. While displaying no clear pattern, their analysis led them to conclude that

> it appears that female victims of violence tended to refuse to be interviewed more often than male victims of violence. It must be borne in mind, however, that overall . . . there was a greater tendency for women to refuse than for men. Overall, victims of theft refused less

frequently than victims of either burglary or violence, but conversely they were more often unable to be contacted by interviewers. Of those respondents who were known to have moved away from the address obtained from police records, no pattern emerges in relation to any of the categories of offence.

(Sparks *et al.*, 1977: 30)

Crawford *et al.* (1990) found that those who refused to complete their questionnaire for the *Second Islington Crime Survey* were more likely to have been recent victims of violent crime than those respondents who co-operated. It would seem clear from the evidence available that 'official' victims are a group who are difficult to survey and will be found in disproportionate numbers among non-respondents. However, we should not presume that victims who do not report incidents to the police exhibit similar behaviour patterns to this group. Response rates and the possible bias which they introduce remain a difficult problem for survey research which can only be partially solved by careful weighting of the sample to counter the biases.

Until recently, victimization surveys have dealt with samples of adults and have largely excluded the victimization experience of children. However, both the BCS and local surveys have begun to take an interest in this issue. The 1992 BCS introduced a 'booster sample' of teenagers, and a notable local study is Anderson *et al.* (1991) which was a combined self-report and victimization study of young people aged 11–15 in Edinburgh. They discovered a surprisingly high level of victimization; their work was followed up by Hartless *et al.* (1995) in Glasgow, who concluded that young people were 'more sinned against than sinning', that is, they were more often the victims of crime than the perpetrators.

Another group of people who are more often than not missing from victimization survey samples are those who are in institutions such as prisons, young offender institutions, hospitals and residential care homes. These groups are very likely to have different victimization experiences from the wider public.

Will they remember and will they tell? Measurement errors

Respondents are a tricky bunch, and they do not always behave in the way a researcher would wish or expect. In fact, surveys would be a whole lot more reliable without them! There are several areas of error which can be introduced by respondents giving inaccurate answers. Such factors have an important bearing on the design of the survey and the reliability and validity of the results (on these terms, see Chapter 3 or the Glossary).

Memory decay and telescoping

It was originally thought that respondents would easily recall incidents of victimization which they had suffered, since crime is a salient event in people's lives. Researchers soon discovered that respondents tended to forget victimizations which had occurred even in the relatively recent past and that memory decayed at a faster rate than they had anticipated. The very first pilot study (a survey of three police precincts in Washington, DC) asked respondents about victimizations occurring in the previous 15–18 months (the recall period) and also the 'very worst crime ever' they had suffered. The results showed that many more recent victimizations were recalled than those which were temporally distant. Furthermore, 60 per cent of the 'worst crimes ever' were reported as having occurred during the previous three years, a far greater number than we would expect (Hindelang, 1976). Durant *et al.* (1972) found the same phenomenon; of their respondents recalling ever having been a victim of crime, 22 per cent of them stated that it was less than 12 months ago. As the recall accuracy of respondents declines with the length of the recall period, some optimum period needed to be defined.

Recall periods present researchers with another problem: forward and backward telescoping. This occurs owing to respondents' inability to date events accurately; some events which occurred outside the recall period are brought forward in time (forward telescoping) and this results in an over-estimation of victimizations: similarly, events can be shifted back in time (backward telescoping) so that they are not captured in the recall period. This problem was identified at an early stage and different strategies have been adopted to minimize the effect. The panel design of the American NCS has provided the researchers with the opportunity to use the first interview to 'bound' the subsequent six interviews. Basically, respondents are asked to recall victimizations which have occurred since they were last interviewed, using a relatively short recall period of six months. This technique largely eliminates the problem of telescoping – forward telescoping can be checked and adjusted for and backward telescoping is partially resolved by the previous interview acting as a reference point and memory 'jogger' for the respondents. However, as with most good ideas, other problems are created by this method and it has not been adopted in other countries. We will not go into detail here, if only for the sake of international relations, but briefly the problems centre around the high cost involved in carrying out the survey and the difference in levels of victimization between 'stayers and movers', i.e. those who remain at the sample address and those who move on (for details, see Hindelang, 1976; Skogan, 1976; Block and Block, 1984).

Sparks *et al.* (1977: 66) investigated the phenomenon of telescoping in some detail; indeed, one of their three samples was specifically designed for this purpose. Using the reverse record check method they concluded that, by and large, temporal inaccuracies cancelled one another out – that is, forward telescoping was balanced by memory decay and backward telescoping. They decided in favour of a 12-month recall period which should be fixed in the respondent's mind in order for it to be a salient period. This they achieved by 'asking him [*sic*] to "bracket" the reference period in his own mind, and to recall "landmark" dates within it'. The 12-month recall period seems to have become the standard in Britain, being used by the BCS (strictly speaking, the BCS uses a recall period of 13–15 months – depending upon when the fieldwork is carried out – but only incidents falling within the 12-month period are used) and the majority of local crime surveys. The 1992 BCS found, again using reverse record checks, that memory decay or backward telescoping tended to occur with regard to less serious offences, while the more serious incidents of victimization were the ones which were most likely to be telescoped forward; this obviously has consequences for the validity of the survey results. Even if, '[o]verall, memory loss seems to exclude more incidents than "forward telescoping" includes' (Mayhew *et al.* 1993: 6), the results are likely to contain an over-estimation of serious incidents.

Concealment and fabrication
We need to consider whether respondents fail to report incidents to the survey interviewers for reasons other than memory decay or temporal displacement, and whether respondents report incidents which have in fact not happened to them. In other words, can the respondent be trusted to tell the truth?

It is known that measurement errors can occur in the form of under-reporting for particular types of crime, particularly sexual offences and domestic violence. The same crimes which are least likely to be reported to the police are also least likely to be captured by victimization surveys (Walklate, 1989). The 1982 and 1984 BCS had only one report each concerning rape (which were both defined as attempted rapes) and the *Merseyside Crime Survey* failed to find any reports of sexual offences against women (Kinsey, 1984). Some studies have found that domestic violence is more likely to be reported to the police than to survey interviewers; we can easily imagine how, at the time of the incident, a woman may have reason to report the crime to the police but later may not be inclined to reveal such a personal thing to survey researchers. Many local surveys, in response partly to the criticisms which have come from feminists, have tried to address the problem of under-reporting for these types of crimes in their survey design (see, for example, Jones *et al.*, 1986).

Feminist researchers remain dissatisfied with the findings of local surveys and have attempted to discover the true extent of what Stanko (1988: 40) calls the 'hidden violence against women'. Studies which have been specifically designed to investigate sexual and domestic violence have exhibited levels of victimization far beyond that found in general victimization surveys. For example, Painter (1991: 50) concluded her study by stating that '1 in 4 women have been raped at some time by some man'. Such studies should also be treated with caution; many of Painter's 'rapes', for example, would not have been defined as such under the law.

Little can be said with any certainty concerning the understandable reluctance of respondents to reveal certain incidents, and it is impossible to estimate the degree of under-counting which is involved. We do know the types of crime which are most likely to be affected by this kind of measurement error: sexual assaults and domestic violence, as we have discussed above, but also other crimes where the victim knows the offender, so called 'non-stranger' crimes. Apart from the general reluctance which respondents may have about revealing such incidents, they may also feel some degree of culpability or perhaps not recognize the incident as a crime (see Skogan, 1986).

Even less is known about the degree to which respondents fabricate victimizations and, although this was suggested as a methodological issue by Levine (1976), most researchers work on the premise that respondents are responsible and trustworthy, having nothing to gain by making things up. It is, however, quite plausible that some respondents, not wanting to disappoint the interviewer, may recall incidents which happened to friends or neighbours rather than to themselves personally. With the 'crime problem' so high on the media's agenda and therefore ingrained in the mind of the general public, respondents may also feel that 'something should be done' and fabricate incidents in the hope that it will somehow help.

The honesty of survey respondents is a difficult issue, and raising it serves to remind us what the results of any survey actually represent; they do not represent 'reality' but the responses certain people make to certain questions in particular circumstances, something which we shall return to later.

Do they matter? Response bias

If the measurement errors which we have been discussing were randomly distributed then they could be largely ignored; unfortunately, owing to response bias, this is not the case. As we have seen, measurement errors affect certain crimes in certain ways, producing under- or over-estimates of these events. There is another source of bias which is class-based and creates the 'education factor'. One surprising finding from many victimization surveys is that the education level of a respondent is positively correlated with reported victimization, particularly from violent crime. In other words, the better educated you are, the more likely you are to report being the victim of a crime. That more educated people are actually more likely to be victims is counter-intuitive and '[b]etween believing such a wild implausibility, and doubting the validity of the survey data, the choice should be clear' (Sparks, 1981: 34); such results are likely to be evidence of a response bias. Richard Sparks's explanation for this bias centres around the actual act of research and the reaction and response to it by socially different respondents:

> 'Being a survey respondent' is, in many ways, a middle class game; it requires a certain amount of verbal fluency and a capacity for abstract conceptualisation, both of which are to some extent concomitants (if

not consequences) of formal education. It would not be surprising to find that these classroom-like tasks would be better performed by those with more practice (in the classroom) at them.

(Sparks, 1981: 32)

The BCS found that its results displayed this apparent bias but only with regard to violent crime (Hough, 1986: 120). While agreeing with Sparks, Hough (1986: 121) highlights another issue concerning the definition of an event as a crime: 'those with more education may apply lower thresholds of seriousness when it comes to defining, in their own minds, attacks, assaults, threatening behaviour, etc.'. In other words, what the graduate may define as an assault, someone who left school at 16 may define as horseplay. We can only speculate on the reasons, while taking account of the under-estimation of violence and the inaccuracies in any calculations of risk which are produced by the operation of this apparent response bias.

A crime's a crime? Definitions

As we have seen, events can be defined in different ways by different people, and this issue of the definition of an event as a crime gives victimization surveys their own particular methodological problem. In some surveys the respondent's own definition of an incident as a crime is accepted; in others, the respondent is asked about particular incidents and the interviewer then defines these as criminal or not.

Because different surveys use different definitions and different ways of establishing whether an offence has taken place, comparisons between surveys are very difficult. Local survey data are often compared to BCS results, even though different definitions of crime are used. This problem of definition makes any meaningful international comparisons impossible without a standardized survey carried out on a collaborative basis (van Dijk and Mayhew, 1992).

Surveys do not necessarily use legalistic definitions of crime; this means that had the incident been reported to the police, it would not necessarily have been recorded (Walklate, 1989). This creates certain problems for those who wish to compare survey data with the official crime rates, but this is not always the primary aim of the survey. Where it is, then care should be taken to ensure that the survey definition matches the official definition of crime. The BCS applies legal criteria to the respondent's description before defining incidents as crimes. It uses 'a *nominal* definition of crime: a count of incidents which according to the letter of the law could be punished' (Mayhew *et al.*, 1993: 4; emphasis in original). Incidents defined in this way would still not necessarily be recorded if they were reported to the police: '[t]he police use an *operational* definition of crime'. That is to say, the police have their own organizational priorities and criteria for recording crimes (see Chapter 2), so there will always be some mismatch between the data sets.

A further problem connected with the definition and classification of criminal incidents comes from multiple or serial victimizations. Victimization surveys count crimes as discrete events, whereas for some individuals victimization may be a process, part of their everyday lives (Genn, 1988). Respondents for whom victimization is a part of life may not recognize their experiences as the types of discrete events asked for by the survey interviewer; they may therefore fail to recall any incidents. The crimes which are most likely to be affected are the very ones which already suffer from various forms of measurement error, such as sexual abuse and domestic violence.

The limitation of space has necessitated a certain amount of selectivity in discussing the methodological issues which relate to victimization surveys; you will find that other writers may highlight different issues (such as the method of administering the questionnaire) to which we have chosen to pay less attention. The main point is that victimization surveys have their own dark figure. Levels of reliability and validity vary according to the type of crime (and respondent) being explored; they 'present a clearer and more complete picture of *some* forms of criminality . . . but they do not give the *whole* picture' (Sparks *et al.*, 1977: 227; emphasis in original). Such issues require close attention when studying any survey data; results and conclusions drawn from such data should not be accepted at face value and thought must be given to the methods used in their production. As we have emphasized already, data are products and any data which have been generated by a survey should be treated as a subjective measure of a social process; questionnaires are tools constructed by researchers according to particular frames of reference, and their data are not 'facts' which reproduce real-life events (Hindess, 1973; Young and Matthews, 1992).

The uses of survey data

Now that we have an awareness of the methodological shortcomings and limitations of victimization surveys, we can proceed to an assessment of the usefulness of the data and a look at some substantive results which have come from these surveys. Sparks *et al.* (1977: 223), in their pre-BCS assessment of the future uses of victimization survey data, asked why we should bother to measure crime, particularly unrecorded crime. They listed several reasons why we should want to do this and how data from victimization surveys could be used.

- The crime rate is used as a 'social barometer' from which the general state or health of society is (rightly or wrongly) judged. Victimization survey data could provide us with a more accurate estimate of the 'true' crime rate.
- The official crime rate can change independently of a change in the total

volume of crime, and because of the size of the dark figure these data are likely to be very sensitive even to small changes in the public's reporting habits and the police's recording practices. Victimization surveys could be used to estimate the size of the gap between reported and unreported crime, and surveys repeated over time could be used to assess any 'real' changes in the crime rate.

- Victimization surveys could be used to examine the public's reporting habits in relation to their perception of crime and victimization in order to assess correlations between changes in reporting and recording and changes in the crime rate.
- Surveys could be used for crime prevention evaluations since official statistics, when used for this purpose, often gave a misleading impression. When an area is targeted for some crime prevention measure the result would often be an apparent increase in the crime rate owing to a change in reporting habits by the 'crime-sensitized' residents. It should be noted, however, that victimization surveys, when used for this purpose, can produce the same effect; residents may be more inclined both to define and to recall more criminal incidents to the survey interviewer.
- Victimization surveys could perform an important social function by focusing attention on the hitherto largely ignored plight of the victim.
- The data could be used as an alternative and more accurate measure for theories of crime which use the crime rate as their dependent variable. The greater validity of this alternative crime rate would be especially useful for explanations of crime which were interested in changes or trends over time, or those seeking a causal relationship between crime and unemployment (see Chapter 5).
- They could provide invaluable data for those concerned with victimology. Their data could be used to answer many questions concerning victims of crime. Who are they? Why some and not others? How and why do some people become chronic or serial victims? The data could also be used to explore the 'social *meaning* of criminal victimization' (Sparks *et al.*, 1977: 231; emphasis in original), that is, the way in which different groups define crime in relation to their own experiences of victimization.
- Survey data could be used in investigations of the societal reaction to crime: attitudes and responses to, and the consequences of, crime for individuals and society. Related to this are assessments of the fear of crime in relation to the risk of becoming a victim.

Sparks *et al.* correctly predicted many of the most important functions which such data now perform.

The British Crime Survey

The primary aim of the BCS was to provide an independent measure of crime which could be compared to the official figures found in *Criminal Statistics*.

In commissioning the surveys (a very costly undertaking) the Home Office hoped to be able to demonstrate that the rising crime rates were in part due to changes in both police practice and the public's reporting habits, and that the real risk of crime for most people was still very small. The first report presented us with the following thoroughly reassuring statistics for what the average person can expect:

- a robbery once every five centuries;
- an assault resulting in injury once every century;
- the family car to be stolen once every 60 years;
- a burglary in the home once every 40 years.

(Hough and Mayhew, 1983: 15)

The BCS is concerned with describing 'average' risks for 'average' people and the petty nature of most crime, reflecting a pattern which can be compared with that found in *Criminal Statistics*. Mayhew and Hough (1988) discuss the impact which the BCS has had on policy-makers, academics and the public. First, they state that the BCS has acted as a powerful vindicator of the inadequacies of the official statistics – that which has long been known to be true can now be more substantially demonstrated. The policy relevance of the BCS extends to crime prevention, victim support and sentencing. The BCS can be used by policy-makers to draw attention to problems and to define them, providing them with a policy data base. The BCS has made theoretical contributions to criminology – concerning the relationship between fear and the risk of crime and situational perspectives. It also provides researchers with a valuable data base for secondary analysis. Through the dissemination of its results by the informed media, the BCS has indirectly helped reshape the public's perception of crime.

The BCS is designed to be comparable to *Criminal Statistics*. Even so, only a subset comprising eight BCS crimes are used for such comparisons; these crimes account for approximately 60 per cent of all incidents being measured by the survey. Using this comparable subset, the 1994 sweep found that while recorded crime had increased by 111 per cent between 1981 and 1993, the BCS suggested an increase of 77 per cent over the same period (Mayhew *et al.*, 1994). This difference, however, is specific to the crimes of vandalism and violence; acquisitive crimes displayed a similar increase in both data sets. The divergence between recorded crime and the BCS could be due to an increase in reporting and recording for these two offences. If we look at the short-term picture for the period 1991–3 we can see a reversal of this trend; an increase in recorded crime of 7 per cent and an increase in the BCS subset of 18 per cent were evident across most crime categories. Both the reporting and recording of incidents decreased during this period. The authors suggest that the drop in reporting rates could be due to changes in insurance coverage, as one reason for reporting an incident to the police is to enable an insurance claim to be made. '[F]ewer incidents of property theft and damage mentioned were covered by insurance in 1993 (37%) than in 1991 (50%). There were also fewer claims made by insured victims in 1993 (37%) than in 1991 (43%)' (Mayhew *et al.*, 1994: 4).

So, the BCS can sometimes be used to explain increases in the rate of recorded crime and also any decline in the rate of increase. Explanations for changes in reporting and recording rates are also offered to us. The survey produces estimates of the total number of crimes occurring in the survey year; in 1993 it estimated a total of 18 million crimes occurring in England and Wales (separate figures are available for Scotland), but bear in mind that this only includes the types of crimes which the BCS is capable of measuring. An estimated 25 per cent of these 18 million crimes found their way into *Criminal Statistics* (Mayhew *et al.*, 1994). Thus we can place an approximate quantification on the dark figure of unrecorded crime, but one with certain limitations.

The BCS provides us with more than these 'counts' of crime; the data collected cover a host of crime-related topics, some of which are collected in every sweep to provide comparisons, and other areas are covered as they become topical. The research studies which have been published using BCS data are too numerous to list here, but they include investigations into household fires (May, 1990), racially motivated crime (Aye Maung and Mirrlees-Black, 1994), neighbourhood watch schemes (Dowds and Mayhew, 1994), drug abuse (Mott and Mirrlees-Black, 1993) and the perception of the seriousness of different crimes (Pease, 1988). Of particular interest are the studies concerning the fear of crime in relation to the risk of crime (see, for example, Mirrlees-Black and Aye Maung, 1994); it is women and the elderly who have the greatest fear of crime, the very groups who are, according to BCS figures, the least at risk of victimization. This mismatch between fear and risk is one of the issues taken up by local crime surveys, which we discuss shortly.

Although victimization surveys are offence-based, the BCS does offer us some valuable information on offenders. Data are available on the sex of offenders involved in crimes of violence and judgements concerning their ages. We are also provided with information on the types of crime which are most likely to be reported and therefore have the greatest prospect of being recorded. From this, we can begin to see how the profile of the known offender population has been constructed, and we can speculate how this may differ from the profile of all offenders. For example, if 'male crimes' (such as vehicle theft) have a higher rate of reporting than 'female crimes' this could account for some of the sex differences which are apparent in the official statistics of known offenders (for a detailed discussion, see Chapter 5).

The BCS provides an invaluable, high-quality data base for policy-makers and researchers, and it performs an important political role for the government when the 'crime problem' is so high on the public and political agenda. Although the survey's count of crime is always higher than, official figures, the data can be used to suggest that things are not as bad as they may seem – at least with regard to the rate at which crime is increasing. However, data have no loyalty, and they can bite the hand that funds them. This was demonstrated by the publication of a Labour Party report in 1995 which used BCS data to demonstrate that the risk of becoming a victim of burglary or violent crime had increased threefold while the Conservatives had been in power. The conclusion that 'everyone's a victim' was reached by presenting the data in a different form from that normally used (*The Independent*, 29 March 1995).

When rates of recorded crime were rising, the government was keen to emphasize the lower rates of increase which were evident in the BCS. While *Criminal Statistics* is showing a decrease in the crime rate, survey results which can interpret this decrease as being merely an illusion will be less welcome and will no longer fulfil one of their political functions for the party in power.

Local surveys

Local crime surveys are small-scale (relative to the national surveys) and geographically focused, often concentrating on particular vulnerable social groups. Numerous local surveys have been conducted in the last ten years. They have allowed particular problems to be located in terms of both area and victim group, have redirected traditional criminological concerns and emphasized alternative perspectives (for example, the feminist perspective).

In comparison to the government-funded BCS, local surveys have been thought to be politically independent; some perhaps are, but many are in fact funded by local authorities who have their own political objectives to meet, making the commissioned survey far from independent. Left realism developed partly out of the need for the Labour Party to have a practical (vote-winning) law and order platform, and this political genesis has sometimes made it and its theoretical stance a target for criticism. Some point to the political commitment of the local survey approach and highlight this as one of the strengths of the method; but where it does exist, it can be considered a weakness. What is required is an unbiased account of crime and victimization; political commitment could influence both the design of the survey and the reading of the data (Walklate, 1989: 49–50). However, the contribution to criminology through the development and refinement of the local victimization survey should not be overlooked.

> Left realist surveys are a practical attempt to provide an alternative and more total definition of the process of the construction of crime and its perception than offered by official criminal statistics and other survey technologies. Such a first step is vital to the development of constructs

and general laws which help to demystify social reality and lead to the identification of theoretical questions.

(MacLean, 1991: 246)

Local crime surveys can provide us with a wealth of information which is not available from national surveys; they allow us to move from the general and typical to the specific and atypical. The *Islington Crime Survey* focused upon a deprived inner-city area (at the time, Islington was the seventh most deprived area in England). Little wonder, then, that the researchers discovered levels of victimization which were higher than those found by the BCS. They were able not only to uncover a crime rate above the national average, but also to demonstrate how crime was geographically focused within Islington itself and the degree to which subgroups were subjected to multiple victimizations. Reporting and recording practices were investigated, and it was found that although the area had a reporting rate above the national average, the recording rate of the police was found to be below the average. This was obviously an area for local concern and could not have been discovered by large-scale national surveys (Jones *et al.*, 1986: 83–5).

In contrast to national findings, the *Islington Crime Survey* found that women were at greater risk of crime than were men and that 'people's attitude to crime is probably much in line with their experiences of crime, with the exception of older white people who are least likely of all groups to experience crime of any sort' (Jones *et al.*, 1986: 85). Crawford *et al.*, (1990) took up the issue of fear of crime in relation to the extent and risk of crime in the *Second Islington Crime Survey* and, more particularly, the gender difference which can be seen in any analysis of the fear of crime – women are much more likely to express 'fear of crime' than are men. They concluded that women's greater fear was far from irrational (as suggested by national surveys) but was directly related to women's experience of crime and victimization. Individual circumstances and past experiences can influence the impact of victimization, and therefore the fear of crime, independently of an individual's risk of crime (see Lea and Young, 1993; Young, 1988b).

This is only one example of a local survey. Other notable examples include *The Edinburgh Crime Survey* (Anderson *et al.*, 1990), and the *Merseyside Crime Survey* (Kinsey, 1984). Such studies share their own particular strengths and weaknesses, and all can provide us with information which would overwise remain unknown. They allow for the pinpointing of particular problems in particular areas which affect particular social groups, problems which may be lost in national data: '[t]his facilitates the rational allocation of resources and provides identifiable targets for local action' (Crawford *et al.*, 1990: 5).

In recent years, local victimization surveys have been used to investigate particular criminological phenomena – for example, high-crime areas. A well-known example of this is Farrington and Dowds's (1985) study of

Nottinghamshire's apparent high crime rate. Part of their study involved a victimization survey of Nottinghamshire and two other comparable counties to see whether the high crime rate could be attributed to different reporting habits by the residents. This was found not to be the case, and the researchers had to look elsewhere for an explanation. Unfortunately, Robin Hood was not discovered lurking in the forest; the county's 'odd' crime rate was found to be caused mainly by the more mundane factor of their police force's recording practices.

Localized surveys are also increasingly being used in evaluation studies to explore the impact of crime prevention measures. Does improved street lighting reduce crime or the fear of crime? Is the installation of closed-circuit television effective in deterring crime? Local surveys, either comparative or longitudinal, are used to provide answers to such questions. These evaluation studies often take the form of quasi-experimental research: 'measurements' are taken before and after implementation of the crime prevention measure (often referred to as 'target hardening'), and any observed difference is then attributed to the policy. An example of this can be found in Bennett's (1988: 252) evaluation of neighbourhood watch schemes. Using victimization surveys to measure changes in the crime rate and attitudes to crime, he found that, while crime rates were not seen to fall, there was an improvement in 'community cohesion' and a reduction in the fear of crime.

Most evaluation studies are carried out with care and precision, but there is the danger of such studies being misused and over-simplified. The use of highly localized surveys (sometimes involving just a few streets) to investigate a very specific variable holds some potential for abuse. What was a sophisticated research technique can easily become something rather different. Questionnaires can be cobbled together and students employed (at very little cost) to tramp the streets interviewing unsuspecting householders. Victimization surveys of any value are time-consuming, expensive and difficult. Surveys done at the drop of a hat (or research grant) should be treated with extreme caution.

Some conclusions

It was originally thought that victimization survey data, like self-report data, would allow criminologists partially to quantify their long-held obsession; these new forms of data would, it was hoped, eat into the dark figure of unrecorded crime, exposing both its size and nature. This process is sometimes pictured as a series of concentric circles (see Block and Block, 1984: 149–50); as new research methods are put into practice, so the dark figure is progressively revealed. However, the real picture is more complex than this.

Official crime statistics are concerned with recorded crime and known offenders; self-report studies, being offender-based, provide us with infor-mation on the wider population of both known and unknown offenders; victimization surveys are offence-based and provide information on those crimes which have been recorded by the police, those reported to the police but not recorded by them, and those which are not reported. Not only are the three data sets measuring different things, they are taking these measure-ments from three very different perspectives: those of the police, the offender and the victim, three perspectives which are unlikely to be congruent.

Many of the incidents which are captured by self-report studies and victimization surveys are the very types of crime which are most likely to enter the official statistics, while others tend to evade capture by any of these methods of data collection. Self-report studies and victimization surveys concentrate upon their own universe of crimes; self-report studies are good at counting offenders of a 'trivial' nature, while victimization surveys are suited to collecting data on 'ordinary' offences. Both are of limited use in collecting data on crimes of the powerful or white-collar crime; neither can tell us anything about homicide – successful murderers (or rather, those who remain undetected) are unlikely to confess their sins even for the benefit of research and their victims would be difficult to include in a survey sample.

Victimization survey data have a complex and overlapping set of relationships with both officially recorded crime data and that generated by self-report studies, relationships which need to be fully appreciated before such data are put to any use. However, the data produced by these surveys have outgrown their original purposes and can, in many instances, stand alone without the need for comparisons with other forms of crime data. Their silence with regard to certain crimes and largely on the nature of offenders can be excused – once it is understood – as they provide us with a vital piece of the criminological jigsaw.

Summary

The history of victimization surveys is outlined, from their birth in America to their continued development in Britain. The emphasis is upon the changing functions of these surveys as the full potential of this method of research was realized. Different types of survey were developed to meet different needs: the British Crime Survey (BCS) provided data at the national level, some of which could be compared to information found in *Criminal Statistics*, and local studies concentrated upon particular areas or subgroups of the population, providing detailed data of aspects which were obscured by the national surveys. Methodological issues are discussed in order that the data generated by such surveys can be fully appreciated and interpreted. Consideration must be given to the processes involved in the production of these data and the implications of these for the reliability and validity of survey results. The uses of the BCS are considered, from its 'counting' function to the provision of data concerning public attitudes to crime and the criminal justice system. Results from the 1994 sweep are outlined and comparisons made with official statistics of recorded crime. Local surveys and the different nature of their data are then considered. These surveys are often used by left realists to challenge the picture which emerges from both *Criminal Statistics* and the BCS, for example in regard to the relationship between the risk and fear of crime. The chapter concludes with a discussion of the relationship between data produced by victimization surveys and those produced by official statistics and self-report studies.

Further reading

Details of the early American victimization surveys can be found in Hindelang (1976) and Skogan (1976). Block and Block (1984) and O'Brien (1985) also provide valuable insights into the uses of survey data from an American perspective. The most concise overview of the methodological problems facing this method of research remains Sparks *et al.* (1977). Although their study is now nearly 20 years old, it remains relevant, as many of the methods suggested by them are in use today. There is also a useful discussion of methodological issues in a later article by Sparks (1981). Reference should be made to the actual studies themselves. The BCS produces a main report for each of its biennial sweeps, (for example, Hough and Mayhew, 1983; Mayhew *et al.*, 1993); these reports contain useful information concerning the methodology used, detailed results of the survey and comparisons with earlier sweeps and official statistics. Articles and reports are also available covering the many local surveys which have been conducted (for example, Jones *et al.*, 1986; Hartless *et al.*, 1995). The text edited by Maguire and Pointing (1988) contains several useful chapters, especially Chapter 16 (Mayhew and Hough, 1988) on the impact of the BCS, and Chapter 17 (Young, 1988b) which discusses the relationship between risk and fear of crime. Walklate (1989) and Zedner (1994) both provide a good overview of victimology and victimization surveys.

chapter five

Characteristics of offenders: the usual suspects?

This chapter introduces the following key concepts or terms, which are also to be found in the glossary at the end of the book: sex; race; class; peak age of offending; age–crime curve; male to female ratio; black; Asian; white; mugging; and underclass.

The aim of this chapter is to provide a 'taster', suggesting what crime data can and cannot tell us about the following key issues concerning the characteristics of offenders: age, sex, race and class. We have chosen to concentrate upon offenders rather than victims, but we recognize that the latter are equally deserving of our attention. However, the data concerning offenders, coming as they do from a wide variety of sources, have, in our opinion, the greater potential for misinterpretation.

Official offenders are found in disproportionate numbers among certain subgroups of the population (the young, males, black people and the lower social classes) with the popular image of the offender sharing these characteristics. But what might the dark figure of the offender look like? If pulled from the shadows, might we find a member of the Women's Institute – a middle-aged, middle-class, white woman – making jam with stolen fruit? We shall examine each of our chosen variables – age, sex, race and class – in turn, asking whether alternative sources of crime data confirm the official picture of the offender.

Age: young guns?

It has been stated that '[o]ne of the few facts agreed on in criminology is the age distribution of crime' (Hirschi and Gottfredson, 1983: 552). Folk devils are traditionally pictured as youthful, and indeed each generation of adolescents seems to produce a new moral panic (see, for example, Cohen, 1973; Pearson,

1983). A single glance at criminological research and theory is enough to convince anyone of the importance of the age–crime connection, and we could be forgiven for thinking that the whole criminological enterprise has been built mainly upon the activities of young people. Could this concentration upon youth be misplaced, having been produced by a distorted official picture of the offender? Could the dark figure of the offender be a pensioner?

Official offenders

Criminal Statistics relating to 1993 (Home Office, 1994a) indicates a prevalence rate of 1150 known offenders per 100,000 of the population for indictable offences. The peak age of known offenders using this information is 18 years for males (8702 per 100,000) and 15 years for females (1995 per 100,000); after these ages the rate drops steadily, although less steeply for females. This produces the distinctive age–crime curve (strictly speaking, of course, we mean age–offender curve) – a sharp rise to the peak age then a gradual decline. This suggests that crime is overwhelmingly a young person's game, something which is entered into during adolescence only to be abandoned by many as maturity takes over. This picture is reflected in the Offenders Index, which shows, for example, that

> [t]he proportion of the male population born in 1953 known to be 'criminally active' [defined as someone who has been convicted of an offence at the age in question] increases rapidly with age to a peak of 11 per cent at age nineteen. The known 'criminally active' proportion of the population tails off gradually after that age to reach 4 per cent at age thirty four.
>
> (HOSB 14/95: 7)

The slightly older peak age produced by the Offenders Index is explained by the fact that this measure only counts convictions for standard list offences and does not include cautions (see Chapter 2). The correlation between youth and crime might be thought to be due in part to differences in the frequency of offending by individuals at each age, with the younger offenders each clocking up a greater number of appearances in the offender data in any year. This seems plausible given the energy and enthusiasm of youth. However, more detailed research by Farrington (1994: 516), using self-report data, concludes that 'individual offenders commit offences at a tolerably constant frequency during their criminal career'.

Young offenders

We can construct a case which suggests that Official Statistics are biased in such a way as to over-represent young offenders and under-represent the older offender. The control and surveillance of youth by various agencies (for example, the family and school) increases the risk of detection for young people. Young offenders tend to carry out their crimes in groups, unlike older offenders who more often work alone. Research has shown that group offenders are more readily apprehended than the lone offender (Hirschi and Gottfredson, 1983). Youths have less access to and control over private places, so that their crimes are more likely to take place in public, again increasing the chances of detection (Pearson, 1994). There is some evidence of differential reporting practices by victims of shop theft which work in favour of the elderly (see Farrington and Burrows, 1993). This particular offence is rarely reported without the offender being identified. These are all issues which make it reasonable to assume some degree of bias within the official statistics which has the effect of over-emphasizing the crimes of the young.

Adult offenders and offences

A factor which is probably even more relevant is the 'unintended de-emphasis of "crimes" committed by adults' (Pearson, 1994: 1193). The hidden crimes of domestic violence and sexual abuse are not offences which we would associate with youth. Young people are in no position to indulge in tax evasion or Social Security benefit fraud; both are 'crimes' which in any case, shy away from *Criminal Statistics*. The extent of white-collar crime cannot even be estimated by available data, but we can hazard a guess that the peak age of offending for this does not come in the late teens. Steffensmeier and Allan (1995: 109) state that, 'white-collar offenders apparently reach their peak level of criminality at about the time they reach the peak of their conventional careers'. Many of the darkest of dark figures of offences then, can be seen to involve older offenders.

We can see that the age–crime curve varies between offence categories (see Wilson and Herrnstein, 1985; Farrington, 1986, 1989; Tarling, 1993) and that it is most pronounced for those 'ordinary' crimes which are most readily captured by official statistics. This could have the effect of producing a misleading picture of disproportionately young known offenders. Gottfredson and Hirschi, however, reject any differences in the age–crime curve, not only between offences but also over time, demographic groups and place. Using a variety of official and self-report data, they seductively try to convince us that the age effect does not vary (Hirschi and Gottfredson, 1983; Gottfredson and Hirschi, 1990). Even in prison, 'when "practically everything" is held relatively constant, the age effect is much like the age effect in the free world' on the pattern of offending by prisoners (Hirschi and Gottfredson, 1983: 562). According to these writers, age is the 'master variable'.

Self-reported offenders

Self-report studies have traditionally concentrated upon the activities of youth and have discovered prevalence levels which are higher than those suggested by official statistics (see Chapter 3). Knowing that the majority of young people are up to no good does not help us very much as we need to be able to compare their behaviour to that of the adult population. The Cambridge Study in Delinquent Development enables us to examine and compare patterns of offending at different ages. Farrington (1989) presents data which show the proportion of the cohort admitting specific offences at certain ages. It reveals a not unexpected picture. Certain offences decline dramatically with age; for example, 'theft of vehicle' is admitted by 15.2 per cent of respondents when aged 15–18 years but by only 5.5 per cent when aged 26–32 years. In contrast, other offences do not decline, and some increase with age, such as 'theft from work'. The self-report element of the British Crime Survey provides us with valuable data concerning older respondents (Mayhew and Elliott, 1990). Its results are broadly in line with the Cambridge study. BCS analysis has also revealed a declining age–crime effect with respect to drink-driving (Riley, 1985) and drug taking (Mott and Mirrlees-Black, 1993). Overall, self-report data suggest that while the peak age of offending is relatively young, the shape of the age–crime curve is offence-dependent and the curve for offenders measured in this way is probably considerably flatter than that produced by official offenders.

Growing up

The majority of teenage offenders have a relatively short criminal career ahead of them, in contrast to the average 30-year-old offender who has a longer career remaining (Farrington, 1994). In other words, most young offenders do not carry on to become adult offenders. This gives criminology a new puzzle to solve; as Gottfredson and Hirschi (1990: 131) put it, 'at the point where the criminal group has been created, it begins to decline in size'. Theory not only has to confront the onset of criminal behaviour among a large proportion of young people but also desistance from it. Desistance has become a favourite topic for the rational choice perspective and it would seem to involve a range of factors such as the offender receiving some awful fright while committing an offence (see Clarke and Cornish, 1985; Cusson and Pinsonneault, 1986).

Pearson (1994: 1195) comes to the conclusion that '[w]e simply do not have the evidence . . . to state with any confidence the actually existing relationships between "youth" and "crime"'. So much for age being the only undisputed issue in criminology. In our view, age as a predictive variable can be applied with some confidence to certain 'ordinary' offences – those offences which are most readily measured by official statistics, self-report studies and victimization surveys. While the emphasis of criminological theory and policy is on these 'ordinary' crimes, the concentration upon youth is not misplaced. However, if we were to turn our energies to those offences with the largest dark figures, then age becomes less relevant as a variable.

Sex: men behaving badly?

The relative rarity of female crime and the resulting 'gap' between the sexes is quite clear from *Criminal Statistics* and can be traced back in history, providing us with an enduring predictor of official criminality (Maguire, 1994: 275). The official statistics suggest that women tend to commit a relatively narrow band of offences in comparison to men, and the wide variations between offence categories can distort the overall picture. The preponderance of male offenders and the general pattern of male and female crime is not peculiar to England and Wales but can be observed world-wide (Harvey *et al.*, 1992). We have already come across Pollak's (1961) suggestion that the dark figure is a woman (see Chapter 1). In exploring this proposition, we do not need to consider the connection between women's ability to fake orgasm and their lack of official criminality. We have the more reliable, if rather more mundane, measuring instruments of self-report studies and victimization surveys.

Official offenders and their offences

Criminal Statistics provides information on known offenders from which we can calculate the male to female ratio: in 1993 the ratio for indictable offences was approximately 4.5:1, that is, for every 4.5 males found guilty or cautioned for an indictable offence there was one female (figures taken from Home Office, 1994a). The ratio for summary offences was, at 2.4:1, considerably smaller, but still represents a difference worthy of attention. If we examine the total number of offenders, we can see that females account for only 24 per cent of persons found guilty or cautioned for all offence types. Although the overall ratio of male to female crime is both significant and interesting in itself, it is useful to break this down into offence categories so that the variation in offending rates can be seen (Tables 5.1 and 5.2).

Table 5.1 Ratio of male to female offenders found guilty or cautioned for indictable offences: England and Wales, 1993.

Violence against the person	5.7:1
Sexual offences	75.0:1
Burglary	23.1:1
Robbery	13.5:1
Theft and handling stolen goods	2.8:1
Fraud and forgery	2.8:1
Criminal damage	9.4:1
Drug offences	9.4:1
Motoring offences	20.6:1

Source: Adapted from Home Office (1994a: Table 5.11)

Table 5.2 Ratio of male to female offenders found guilty of non-motoring summary offences: England and Wales, 1993.

Criminal damage >£2000	16.5 : 1
Offences under the Public Order Act 1986	17.0 : 1
Offence by prostitute	0.01 : 1
Drunkenness	16.5 : 1
Common assault	7.0 : 1
Assault on constable	5.5 : 1
TV licence evasion	0.5 : 1
Taking and driving away	33.0 : 1
Other	9.5 : 1

Source: Adapted from Home Office (1994a: *Supplementary Tables*, vol. 1, Table S1.1)

Indictable offences

We can see that some crimes are overwhelmingly a male preserve. The most notable difference in offence patterns occurs for *sexual offences*, explained largely by the fact that these offences are mainly defined as male crimes. Other offences committed mainly by males include the categories of *burglary* and *motoring offences*. The offence categories of *theft and handling stolen goods* and *fraud and forgery* have the lowest ratio and, if the proportions of male and female offenders committing certain crimes is examined, these categories are confirmed as the types of offences for which women are most likely to be found guilty or cautioned: 75 per cent of all female offenders fall into this category compared to 46 per cent of all male offenders.

Summary offences

An examination of summary offences explains the lower overall ratio for these crimes: the ratio has been reduced by the two crime categories in which females outnumber males – *offence by prostitute* (an offence mainly defined as one committed by women) and *TV licence evasion* (the person who 'opens the door' is the one who is prosecuted, and the woman of the house is both more likely to be at home and more likely to answer the door (Hedderman, 1995)). If these two rather special offence categories, comprising 80 per cent of all female summary offenders, are discounted, the male to female ratio increases to 15 : 1.

Self-reported offenders

As we know (see Chapter 3) early self-report studies suggested that the relative contribution of female offending had been underestimated. However, further work has led some researchers to conclude that the discrepancies between self-report data and official measures are an illusion. The issue which affects these studies when looking at sex differences is the trivial nature of the majority of the items being measured; even those items defined as 'serious' do not, it is claimed, 'represent especially dastardly behaviour in the eyes of the general public' (Hindelang *et al.*, 1981: 145). Once this and issues concerning the frequency of offending were taken into account, the studies produced sex-differentiated offence patterns which broadly matched the official statistics. What have more recent self-report studies got to say about sex and crime?

Bowling *et al.* (1994) found a male to female ratio of 1.25 : 1 – for young people aged 14 and 15 who admitted offending during the previous 12 months. The ratio is much smaller than that found in official data but it is not directly comparable because of the narrow population (in relation to age) which the self-report study surveyed. The ratio was found to increase in line with offence seriousness; for 'wounding someone with a weapon' – the most serious item – the ratio was 4 : 1 (Bowling *et al.*, 1994). Thus, the broad trends found in official data were reflected in this study – females were involved in fewer offences overall than males, and this was particularly evident for more serious offences. Another example comes from Hartless *et al.* (1995), who found a disproportionate number of males admitting to certain items: fighting in the street, vandalizing a car, assaulting someone, and stealing from a car. Results from the self-report element in the BCS show a familiar pattern: males are more likely to admit to committing any of the items and the male to female ratio increased with the seriousness of the crime (Mayhew and Elliot, 1990). The BCS provides some limited offender-based data for violent offences. The 1992 sweep of the BCS concluded that

> [m]ost violence is perpetrated by men, whether directed against men or women. However, one in five incidents of violence against women were committed by other women, and a further 6% by men and women acting together . . . But women offenders caused less injury.
>
> (Mayhew *et al.*, 1993: xii)

This is broadly in line with our other findings.

Reporting offences

The data from victimization surveys which tell us about the public's reporting behaviour are useful to this discussion. We know that one of the most important factors relating to a victim's decision to report an incident is the perceived seriousness of the offence (see Chapter 4). If it is accepted that women tend to commit less serious offences, then there is the possibility of some under-reporting occurring for the types of crime in which women are most involved. The victim–offender relationship also has a bearing upon reporting behaviour: offences where the victim knows the offender are less likely to be reported than so-called 'stranger' crimes. This has the effect of producing an official under-count of the arguably mainly 'male crime' of domestic violence – the extent of which is believed to be under-estimated in both official and victimization data (see, for example, Walklate, 1989). When these types of offences (where the victim knows the offender) are reported and recorded, the offender is, of course, identified, although not necessarily cautioned or found guilty. However, other mainly 'male crimes', such as car theft, have high rates of reporting (because of the demands of insurance companies), but not necessarily high rates of detection, and so some 'balancing out' probably occurs.

Chivalry

Farrington and Burrows's (1993) survey of retailers' experiences as victims of shoplifting provides some interesting results: they discovered a discrepancy between the retailers' account of apprehended shoplifters and the police recording of offenders which suggested that '[a]t some stage from apprehension to recording, there seems to be some discrimination in favour of females' (Farrington and Burrows, 1993: 63). Shoplifting comes under the offence category of 'theft and handling stolen goods', a category which has one of the smallest official male to female ratios. Farrington and Burrows's results suggest that this ratio is in truth even narrower. It is also interesting to note that the retailers studied had a policy of not reporting shoplifters who were elderly or heavily pregnant. As we know, old women outnumber old men and men do not get pregnant. This gives some credence to Pollak's assertion that women are treated less harshly in this instance by their victims and the police. However, no overall agreement has been reached; Morris (1987: 81) concluded that, '[e]vidence for the preferential treatment of women by the police *because they are women* is weak' (emphasis in original). It is true that women are more likely to receive a caution than men, but this should not be taken as evidence of chivalrous treatment. Their high rate of cautioning can be accounted for by the fact that women tend to commit less serious offences and to have fewer, if any, previous convictions.

Overall, alternative sources of crime data seem to confirm the official picture of male and female patterns of offending. There is no evidence to suggest that females are responsible for a disproportionate amount of the dark figure of crime; on the contrary, many mainly 'male crimes' (domestic violence, sexual offences, etc.) would seem to be under-reported. Crimes of the powerful are also under-represented in official statistics and most likely to be perpetrated by males (Box, 1983). The suggestion from official statistics that women tend to be involved in less serious crimes than males is confirmed by self-report studies. Victimization surveys point to an under-reporting of these crimes and therefore an under-count of female offenders, but these factors do not undermine the broad trends exhibited by official statistics. The various biases in the data may cancel one another out – some work in favour of women, others in favour of men. We can conclude that official statistics provide a broadly valid indication of the relative contributions made by males and females to offending.

Race: criminal discrimination?

Black people seem to be disproportionately represented among the known offender population, at least for certain sorts of offences (Fitzgerald, 1993a). There are two basic ways in which we can interpret this: black people have a higher involvement in crime than other groups, or black people are more likely to be drawn into, and less likely to be filtered out of, the criminal justice system. Others dismiss these either/or explanations. Rather, they say, both propositions are true; there is higher black involvement in crime *and* the criminal justice system is discriminatory. These two factors interact and 'aggravate each other in a vicious circle of mutual amplification' (Reiner, 1993: 3). We shall highlight some of the problems involved in the interpretation of crime data which relate to race in order to demonstrate why it is so difficult to come to any firm conclusions.

Offenders in prison

Statistics about the prison population provide us with a useful starting point to any debate concerning race and crime, presenting us with an interesting, yet atypical, sample of offenders. The Home Office publishes data which detail the ethnic origins of prisoners. These data reveal that black prisoners account for a disproportionate number of the prison population. In 1993, 9.7 per cent of the prison population were classified as black, while the proportion of black people in the national population was estimated to be only 1.3 per cent (figures exclude foreign nationals; HOSB 21/94). Prisoners from other ethnic origins (for example, Asian and Chinese) are found in proportions equal to or less than what would be expected from their numbers in the population.

Prison represents the 'end of the line' as far as the criminal justice system is concerned, and very few offenders get this far. Only a minority of offenders are identified and charged. Of those who are sentenced, about one-sixth receive a custodial sentence (HOSB 19/1994). Prison statistics then, can only inform us about an atypical group who are in prison; we cannot necessarily extrapolate from their characteristics to make generalizations about the population of offenders.

Those arrested

We do not know the ethnic characteristics of those people who become official offenders (those who are cautioned or found guilty and thus make their way into *Criminal Statistics*) but we have some data on arrests provided by the Metropolitan Police Department (MPD). These data, which categorize arrest rates according to skin colour, show that those classified as black make up a disproportionate number of all arrests and the majority for *street robbery of personal property* (HOSB 17/89). This may tell us more about the construction of the suspect population in London than it does about black involvement in crime; for example, policies and practices in surveillance, stop and search and arrest may make black people more likely to be processed (see McConville *et al.*, 1991). We cannot conclude from these data that black people are more likely to be *criminal* as they may simply suggest that black people are more likely to *be criminalized*.

Samples of known offenders

Much research has been carried out tracing the passage of offenders from minority ethnic groups through the criminal justice system using data generated from research on samples derived from official sources. It has been found that black people are more likely than other groups to be:

- stopped by the police (Willis, 1983; Norris *et al.*, 1992);
- arrested (Smith and Gray, 1985; Walker *et al.*, 1990);
- sent for trial rather than cautioned (Landau and Nathan, 1983; Commission for Racial Equality, 1992);
- remanded in custody (Shallice and Gordon, 1990; Hood, 1992);
- tried at the Crown Court (Jefferson and Walker, 1990; Brown and Hullin, 1992);
- given a harsher sentence (Hudson, 1989; Hood, 1992).

(For a review covering the majority of relevant research studies, see Fitzgerald, 1993a.)

Such results could be taken as an indication of racial discrimination within the criminal justice system. However, the interpretation of data from these types of study is very complex. In order to isolate the effect which race may have upon an individual's treatment, all other relevant variables must be held constant, such as propensity to offend, seriousness of the offence, employment status and social class. Most studies attempt to do this but it is a difficult task; see, for example, Roger Hood's (1992) study of race and sentencing. In her review of available research, Fitzgerald (1993a: 5) concludes that, after taking all relevant factors into account, 'some residual, unexplained ethnic differences remain' which can only be accounted for by racial discrimination. Reiner (1993: 4), however, is of the view that we cannot 'conclusively pin down' discrimination because of the difficulties involved in identifying and controlling all other relevant variables.

Young, poor and working-class

The demographic profile of the black population differs from that of whites (for a summary using Census data, see Home Office, 1994b). If black people are disproportionately represented among the lower socio-economic groups and have a young age profile (both factors which are associated with involvement in crime) we should not be surprised that they have a higher crime rate. Some studies have shown that once such 'extra' variables have been taken into account, ethnic origin no longer appears as a significant factor contributing to official offending (see Ouston, 1984), that is to say, young disadvantaged blacks are no more likely to be offenders than their white counterparts. Other studies, however, have found that discrepancies in rates of offending remain evident after controlling for age and class (Walker, 1989), suggesting that young, disadvantaged blacks are more likely to be offenders than young disadvantaged whites. Lea and Young (1993) have argued that black people have an extra disadvantage – being a member of a minority ethnic group – which makes their experience of economic and social inequality different from their white counterparts, causing them to have a higher involvement in crime.

The Asian crime rate

Pakistanis and Bangladeshis have a similar demographic profile to blacks, and have arguably suffered from as much discrimination, yet research and the official data have consistently shown them to have a lower crime rate (see, for example, Mawby *et al.*, 1979). This lack of Asian criminality has been less controversial than the issue of black crime and generally accepted as 'real'. No one has suggested that the dark figure is an Asian. The Asian stereotype is very different from that applied to blacks and it 'militates (for the moment) against invoking the discourse of criminality' (Jefferson, 1993: 37). Jefferson, writing in the early 1990s, hinted that things were about to change. Two years after his paper appeared, there was a prediction of an 'Asian crime time bomb' (*The Independent*, 22 July 1995) and of a new moral panic involving young Bangladeshis and Pakistanis. This prediction is partially based upon the knowledge that both groups have a young age profile and large numbers are reaching the peak age of offending (see HOSB 21/94; Home Office, 1994b). Such a meteoric rise from criminal obscurity to folk devil can only be successfully investigated by disaggregating the Asian category which is used in much research. Until this is done the extent of any new crime wave will be masked by the more affluent Indian members of this category (Fitzgerald, 1995).

Self-reported offenders

As we saw in Chapter 3, some early American self-report studies suggested that blacks offended at the same rate as whites but that blacks were more likely to be official offenders. Later studies highlighted a difference in the validity of responses between minority ethnic groups suggesting that self-report data were less valid for black offenders, producing an under-estimation of their offending. This issue is yet to be settled and there is no agreement on the extent or cause of the problem (see Junger, 1989; Bowling, 1990). Seriousness and frequency of offending were also seen to have been neglected in many early self-report studies; once taken into account, a different picture of race and crime emerged which was more in line with the official data (Elliott and Ageton, 1980). Most British studies have chosen to ignore race as a variable or else were conducted before race and crime was an issue (for example, the cohort used for the Cambridge Study in Delinquent Development has no members from minority ethnic groups). A recent exception can be found in the section of the International Self-report Delinquency Study which relates to England and Wales (Bowling *et al.*, 1994: 56). They found that black respondents, were no more likely to report offending than other groups, and less likely for certain offences. There was, however, a lower response rate from non-white respondents, making it possible that 'the sample may be skewed towards a low-offending group of ethnic minorities'. The discrepancy between their results and official data may be further explained by the issues of frequency and seriousness of offending, both of which were neglected in their study. The authors do not consider differences in the validity of the responses to be an issue, claiming that 'there is no evidence in the UK at present which suggests that ethnic minority respondents have less valid responses than whites'. Their results are rather inconclusive, partly because the study was concerned with making international comparisons rather than with the specific issue of race. Overall, the available data from British self-report studies tells us little about the actual offending behaviour of minority ethnic groups.

Victims and reporting

From victimization surveys emerges a picture of race-differentiated victimization stemming from racially motivated incidents and the intra-racial nature of much crime (see Jones *et al.*, 1986; Bowling, 1993; Mayhew *et al.*, 1993; Aye Maung and Mirrlees-Black, 1994). There is also evidence to suggest that reporting of incidents is affected to some extent by the perceived skin colour of the offender. Shah and Pease (1992: 198), using BCS data, describe a complex relationship between ethnicity, offence seriousness and reporting behaviour, concluding that 'the first stage in making offenders potentially available to the penal system is discriminatory', that is to say, victims are more likely to report an incident when the offender is black. The BCS details the characteristics of certain offenders but it does not explicitly state the proportion of incidents which are reported to involve a black offender.

Is a little knowledge a dangerous thing?

Crime data which relate to race suffer from all the usual deficiencies plus their own particular problem. This concerns the sensitivity of the whole question of black crime. Some of those who interpret the official data as a reflection of discrimination argue that by drawing attention to the differential crime rates of blacks, and indeed by collecting race-related data, the fire of racial discrimination is fuelled and the image of the black criminal is reinforced (Gilroy, 1982; Gutzmore, 1983; Carr-Hill and Drew, 1988). However, racial discrimination within the criminal justice system (and within society) is impossible to identify and address without 'proper evidence' of its operation. The official data are difficult to interpret, but this is partly because there is so little available.

Unfortunately, it is often the least meaningful data (such as MPD arrest figures) which come to the public's attention via the mass media and are the cause of much misunderstanding and controversy. A good example of this is the connection between mugging and race which can be traced back to the mid-1970s when the MPD first released data suggesting that this was a *black* crime (see Hall *et al.*, 1978; Lea and Young, 1993). Twenty years later, the debate is still very much alive, as the Police Commissioner found when he brought up the subject in July 1995. Reaction in the press ranged from the condemnation of Sir Paul Condon as a racist to the conclusion that all muggers are black men. The possibilities for misinterpretation of such data are limitless, especially when they are repackaged for mass consumption.

There would appear to be a move towards collecting more race-related data within the criminal justice system. For example, police forces are now obliged to record the skin colour/ethnic appearance of all persons who are subject to stop and search procedures. Such information, on its own, will tell us very little about police discrimination or patterns of offending. Data collected at different points and by different agencies in different ways are more of a hindrance than a help in the task of interpretation. The criminal justice system, by keeping only one cautious eye open, is providing us with a very limited picture of race and crime. While we would be reluctant to suggest that *Criminal Statistics* should classify offenders by race, such a move would provide us with a firmer base from which comparisons could be made and other forms of data developed. If we must look, then better to look with both eyes open.

In the meantime, we can only come to certain conclusions. The official picture suggests that black people do have a higher involvement in some offences than do whites, while other minority ethnic groups appear to have lower rates. There is some evidence of racial discrimination within the criminal justice system and in the reporting habits of the public. Although this evidence is inconclusive, the existence of discrimination should not surprise us, as it would merely be a reflection of the wider discrimination which exists in society. We cannot say with certainty that black people are more likely to have a higher involvement in crime than other groups, but their disadvantaged socio-economic position and young age profile provide us with reasons, other than race, to think that they might.

Class: on the caboose of the train?

The link between social class and crime seems to be well established and 'constitutes the basis for most of the leading sociological theories of crime' (Rutter and Giller, 1983: 132). This being so, we might expect to find firm empirical evidence which demonstrates this relationship. Although there are no routinely collected official data concerning the class of offenders and we must rely upon information generated from research on samples derived from official sources, the data from such studies are unequivocal in displaying the connection between social class and known offending. However, when we examine other forms of crime data the issue becomes less clear-cut. Indeed, some evidence suggests that we should move further up the train and look for offenders in the first-class carriages.

Offenders in prison

A survey of the adult prison population, commissioned by the Home Office, classified prisoners by social class based upon their most recent employment prior to imprisonment. It was found that 18 per cent of prisoners were from the Registrar-General's social classes I, II and III non-manual (compared to 45 per cent of these classes in the general population), 41 per cent from social class III manual (37 per cent of the general population), and 41 per cent from classes IV and V (19 per cent of the general population) (Walmsley *et al.*, 1992). It is clear from these data that the lower social classes are disproportionately represented in the prison population. An earlier survey of adult male prisoners revealed a similar picture; Mott (1985) found that 75 per cent of the prisoners in her study were last employed in a manual occupation.

Samples of known offenders

Miller *et al.* (1974), Wadsworth (1979) and Ouston (1984) all found a strong negative correlation between social class and known offending behaviour: those from lower social classes were more likely to be known offenders than those from higher social classes. Harris and Webb (1987) found that less than 8 per cent of their sample of boys on supervision orders had white-collar parents, and in Hagell and Newburn's (1994) study of persistent young offenders only 8 per cent of the male heads of household were in non-manual employment. In a study of court defendants, it was found that only 5 per cent of defendants (excluding those charged with motoring offences) were from classes I and II (Bottoms and McClean, 1976).

Ecological studies

Clelland and Carter (1980) highlight ecological or areal studies (usually using official data) which support the link between class and crime. Such studies have consistently shown offenders to be geographically concentrated in particular areas, usually the most economically and socially deprived: the inner city and, in Britain, outer council estates (see Foster and Hope, 1993). However, offenders living in deprived areas are not necessarily themselves low-status, which is to suggest that perhaps such data are tempting us into an ecological fallacy. Hence, we cannot automatically come to conclusions concerning the class of offenders from aggregate area data. On this occasion, however, Clelland and Carter suggest that common sense allows us to reject the notion of an ecological fallacy occurring:

> If class–crime relationships based on ecological data are spurious, it can only be due to especially high crime rates of 'middle-class' people living in 'lower-class' areas or to especially low crime rates of the 'lower-classes' who reside in 'middle-class' neighbourhoods. There is no research which supports these implausible interpretations.
>
> (Clelland and Carter, 1980: 330)

Offender bias

Various studies have been carried out to identify the presence of class bias in the construction of the known offender population. Research has found that the unemployed (we will discuss ways of defining class later; for now we can take employment status to be one rough indication of class position) are more likely to be stopped by the police (Smith, 1983), stopped and searched (Kinsey, 1984) and to receive a custodial sentence (Crow and Simon, 1987; Crow et al., 1989). Some of these differences, however, can be attributed to behaviour, offence seriousness and frequency of offending. The police's treatment of juvenile offenders has been shown to be affected by the perceived class of the offender; Bennett (1979) found that middle-class juvenile offenders were more likely to receive a caution than working-class offenders when arrested for the same kind of offence. Landau and Nathan (1983) found the police more readily prosecuting so-called 'latchkey' children. Such studies suggest that there exists class discrimination within the criminal justice system which has the effect of drawing greater numbers of the lower social classes into the system. We have already discussed the problems of identifying and isolating discrimination; however, we can conclude that

> it remains probable that social status is sometimes influential at the stage of deciding whether or not to prosecute, or even whether or not to report, certain crimes. 'Young people' in one part of a city might receive an oral warning for 'rowdiness', whereas 'youths' in another area might be prosecuted or formally cautioned for similar behaviour interpreted as 'disorder'.
>
> (Ashworth, 1992: 183)

Offence bias and opportunity

Certain offences are both more likely to come to the attention of the criminal justice system and more likely to involve offenders from the lower social classes. For example, those who defraud the Department of Social Security are more likely to be prosecuted than those who defraud the Inland Revenue (see Cook, 1989). White-collar crime is far less likely to enter the official statistics than 'ordinary' crime (see Croall, 1992). There is also a very clear class distinction in the opportunity to commit these two sorts of offences. Other offences do not have this class distinction; for example, illegal drug use 'has historically crossed class boundaries' (South, 1994: 400). However, the lower social classes are more likely to purchase their drugs in high-risk situations and, perhaps, to resort to crime in order to finance their drug taking. The drug trade, on the other hand, is controlled at the top by offenders whose collars are not only white, but 'pristine, and hand-stitched in silk' (Hobbs, 1994: 459).

Self-reported offenders

Self-report studies caused quite a stir when they apparently failed to find a relationship between social class and self-reported offending (see Chapter 3). Box and Ford (1971) concluded that the available evidence did not support a class–crime link. Tittle and Villemez (1977: 495), in a self-report study of adults, claimed that their findings 'suggest that social class is almost irrelevant for criminality'. Tittle *et al.* (1978) went on to analyse 35 self-report studies which explored the relationship between class and crime; they concluded that the relationship was a myth: '[T]he implications undermine the purported class/criminality relationship which fuelled so much theoretical activity in sociology. Thus, numerous theories developed on the assumption of class differences appear to be based on false premises' (Tittle *et al.*, 1978: 654).

Whoops! This was quite a blow to those who had laboured for so long over class-based theories of crime, but help was at hand. Hindelang *et al.* (1979: 995) declared that the discrepancy between self-report and official data was an illusion created by the misinterpretation of self-report studies and incorrect comparisons made between different data sources. Self-report and official data, they claimed, did not 'tap the same domain of behaviour' and therefore direct comparisons should not be made. Clelland and Carter (1980) mounted a comprehensive critique of Tittle and others who were debunking the class–crime connection. Their main criticisms surrounded the definitions and measurement of both class and crime which were used in self-report studies. Class, they pointed out, had two aspects to it, culture and economic resources. Many studies failed to recognize this and contented themselves with defining the lower classes as the lowest economic stratum – the *poor* – a section of the population who are notoriously difficult to find and survey. Many studies, which used occupation as a basis for class, eliminated the unemployed from their analysis, while others combined categories of social class or occupation in an arbitrary manner. They considered many of the items dealt with in self-report studies to be too trivial to be classified as criminal offences, citing the example 'walking on grass . . . where it is prohibited to do so'. They rather caustically stated that

> criminologists have spent an unconscionable amount of energy investigating peccadilloes . . . we have no theory of the relationship of class to the commission of trivial offences. Nor do we see that it would matter much should such a relationship be found.
>
> (Clelland and Carter, 1980: 332)

A self-report study by Thornberry and Farnworth (1982) defined offences to match those in the official statistics, and using the social class of their adult respondents (rather than class of family, as was used in many studies which looked at juveniles) found no major discrepancies between their results and official data. Indeed, they concluded that the 'association between status and criminality is seen to be quite robust' (Thornberry and Farnworth, 1982: 516).

Farnworth *et al.* (1994) blamed the inadequate measurement of both class and delinquency for the absence of a class–crime relationship in self-report data. Rather than measure class according to occupational status, they used the concept of underclass, defined in this case as persistent unemployment and/or dependence on welfare benefits, and concentrated upon 'street crimes' of a non-trivial nature. They concluded that it was between these categories – underclass status and street crime – that the 'strongest and most consistent class–crime associations are found' (Farnworth *et al.*, 1994: 32).

It would seem that the strength of the relationship between class and crime found in self-report data depends upon the particular definitions used by the researchers. After the initial skirmish, it is now generally accepted that there is a correlation between class and offending behaviour – 'known' and 'actual', and that the latter relationship can be demonstrated by self-report studies. Many research studies begin by first controlling for, or matching their subjects by, social class. Others, purposefully, sample only the lower social classes, or else take their sample from predominantly lower-class areas. 'This reflects a widespread belief in the importance of SES [socio-economic status], but of course it often prevents the correctness of this belief from being tested' (Farrington, 1994: 546). The Cambridge Study in Delinquent Development took its sample from a 'typical working-class, residential area . . . The area was not prosperous, but not especially impoverished . . . Judged on their fathers' occupation, 93.7 per cent [of the sample] were working class' (West, 1982: 7–8). Such studies can only tell us about working-class offenders and offences, and are of limited value in our present quest.

Intra-class offences

Victimization surveys can be used to make inferences as to the likely class of certain types of offender from knowledge of who is at greatest risk of victimization. The BCS and various local surveys have demonstrated that the risk of burglary is particularly high for individuals living in the poorest housing estates and those with low incomes (Jones, 1986; Mayhew *et al.*, 1993). From this we can infer that lower-class offenders are preying on lower-class victims, unless we wish to believe that middle-class burglars are travelling to poor areas hoping to find something worth stealing. This is unlikely, as there is little disagreement about the social class of 'ordinary' burglars.

Intra-family offences

There are some data available from the victims of certain offences from which the class of the offender can be inferred – offences which we could call 'intra-family', where the class of the victim will correspond (in most instances) to the class of the offender. Levi (1994) cites Australian and American studies of the victims of homicide which indicate that a disproportionate number are lower-class and a majority are killed by close family members, and data showing that the incidence of child abuse is 62 per cent higher among the very poor. Levi (1994: 307) argues that 'it is implausible that these differences are the result of definitional bias by doctors and coroners'. However, it seems quite plausible that doctors and coroners could be influenced by the perceived attitudes and demeanour of the parents and by the stereotypical image of the 'good parent'. Smith (1989b) concluded that there was no class distinction in the incidence of domestic violence, but analysis of the 1988 and 1992 sweeps of the BCS showed that this offence was much more likely to occur in 'socio-ecomonically deprived' households (Mirrlees-Black, 1995: 4). Similarly, Painter (1991) found working-class women twice as likely to be victims of domestic violence as women from higher classes. We know that domestic violence is likely to have a substantial dark figure which makes it difficult to reach any final conclusions, but there is evidence from both national and local surveys which indicates that the lower social classes are more likely to be perpetrators and victims of this offence.

Whose class?

So far we have been cavalier in our use of the term 'class', gaily skipping from one definition to another. Such behaviour cannot be allowed to continue and the question must be posed: what exactly do we mean by 'class'? The most commonly used classification in research in Britain remains the Registrar-General's, which classifies class according to occupational status. This, however, causes problems in classifying the unemployed, including those who have never worked, and in embracing changing family structures. Such a classification does not always correspond to an individual's or family's socio-economic status. Various other variables which relate to class position have been used in studies. Farrington (1994: 547) lists the following indicators of class position which have been commonly used in criminological research:

- income;
- housing;
- overcrowding;
- possessions;
- dependence on welfare;
- family size.

Different results could be obtained depending upon the researcher's conceptualization of social class, making comparisons between studies less meaningful. The point to be made is that before talking of a class–crime correlation, we should be clear just exactly what and who we are talking about.

How well does the class distribution of known offenders reflect the characteristics of the offending population? Self-report research, having largely abandoned the proposition that 'a class–crime link is a myth', demonstrates a relationship which is broadly similar to that found in official data. Victimization survey data further confirm the official picture, providing us with an insight into the intra-class nature of much crime and the class-differentiated risks of victimization. However, the whole question of class and offending is tied up with issues concerning different types of offences and different opportunities to commit these offences. It would, perhaps, be useful to follow Braithwaite's (1981: 49) suggestion of a more offence-specific approach, asking why certain types of crime are committed by the 'powerless' and other crimes by the 'powerful'? Such an approach, coupled with an appreciation of the differential rate at which these two types of offences and offenders come to the attention of the criminal justice system, may prove fruitful in unravelling the relationship between class and crime.

Ordinary offences and ordinary offenders

We can state, with varying degrees of confidence, that known offenders are likely to be disproportionately young, male and lower-class. Race is a rather more difficult variable to deal with. Only a small minority of known offenders are black, but the proportion who are is greater than we would expect from their numbers in the general population. This small, but disproportionate number of black known offenders is also likely to be young, male and from the lower classes.

It would seem that the characteristics of known offenders are shared by their victims. Studies show that victimization tends to be both intra-racial and intra-class (see, for example, Jones *et al.*, 1986; Mayhew *et al.*, 1993). Recent research has for the first time highlighted the extent to which young people are victimized (Hartless *et al.*, 1995). There is some dispute concerning the differential victimization rates of males and females; many surveys (including the BCS) reveal males to be at greatest risk (Mirrlees-Black and Aye Maung, 1994). Others argue (see, for example, Crawford *et al.*, 1990) that such findings do not fully take into account the hidden crimes of domestic violence and rape which women suffer but which are not easily captured by any method of data collection (see Chapter 4). Generally, however, offenders are seen to prey upon their own kind or intimates.

Perhaps the official statistics are not so bad after all. Their validity, as far as the characteristics of offenders are concerned, can be broadly corroborated by alternative data sources. Many self-report studies sample the very groups most likely to be known offenders (young lower-class boys) and local victimization surveys often focus upon areas with a high official crime rate (the inner city and council estates – areas which are also likely to have a disproportionate number of individuals with known offender character-istics). Little wonder, then, that such studies reflect the official picture. The available data have said all they can, but that is not to suggest that these issues are settled. The loose consensus which exists has partially developed from the view that '[a]ny findings which seem counter-intuitive or even a little surprising should be disregarded on the ground that they are probably artifactual' (Sparks, 1981: 44). Sparks was talking about the early develop-ment of victimization surveys, but we have come a long way since then. Now, 'surprising findings' should be used to alert us to the need for further research. Much of the empirical evidence which is used to demonstrate the relation-ships which we have discussed is too fragile for anything to be taken for granted. We should not blame the data for this. These data sources measure and evaluate the *crime problem* in the way in which it has been socially, academically and politically defined – overwhelmingly a problem of petty property and less serious personal offences committed by disaffected youths. 'Ordinary' offences committed by 'ordinary' offenders.

However, as Steven Box (1983) pointed out, this is only *one* crime problem. Another, that of corporate and white-collar crime, would produce a very different offender profile:

> Few people become aware of crimes of the powerful or how serious these are, because their attention is glued to the highly publicized social characteristics of the convicted and imprisoned population. It is not directed to the records, files, and occasional publications of those quasi-judicial organisations (such as the Factory Inspectorate in the UK or the Federal Drug Administration in the US) monitoring and regulating corporate and governmental crimes.
>
> (Box, 1983: 13)

The 1970s witnessed some radical criminologists turning their attention towards crimes of the powerful (see, for example, Carson and Martin, 1974) while others busied themselves deconstructing the picture which the official data portrayed. This reprieve for working-class boys was not to last – Steven Box, sadly, is no longer with us and many of the radicals, perhaps having had their Bob Dylan records stolen, have become grey and realistic. Left realist and mainstream administrative criminology focus their gaze firmly upon conventional definitions of crime and, therefore, offenders. It is, they argue, these crimes – burglary, robbery and the like – which are of most concern to us all, especially the working classes, given the intra-class nature of much victimization. But *this* crime problem is the one which we hear most about, while the other criminals 'in their coats and their ties are free to drink Martinis and watch the sun rise' (Dylan, 1988: 532). If we knew how many people were killed (murdered?) as a result of their employer's negligence or how much the Exchequer lost through creative accounting practices (theft?), would we worry less about pub brawls or having our car taken for a 'joyride'? Left realists argue that we would not. Perhaps they are right, but it would enable us to redefine the nature and extent of the 'crime problem' and the offender population.

If we want to find the 'real' dark figure of the offender then we need to look further than the deprived inner city and beyond a sample of working-class boys. The Women's Institute may not be such a bad place to start, if only to gain access to the members' rich husbands. Also, as Box (1983) suggests, we need to look at other sources of information which are not conventionally thought of as 'crime data'. As far as ordinary crime goes, the characteristics of the dark figure are probably fairly well represented by known offenders. We can speculate with some confidence that the dark figure of the burglar, for example, shares the same characteristics as official burglars and that 'he' is probably lurking on some run-down housing estate.

Summary

This chapter examines the characteristics of offenders in relation to age, sex, race and class, using official and alternative sources of crime data. *Criminal Statistics* includes information on the age and sex of offenders, and this provides a clear picture of the known offender which can be compared to data from studies which seek to identify 'actual' offenders. Race and class are more difficult variables to deal with. Data are available relating to the race and class of the prison population and from research carried out using samples of known offenders. Such data can only reveal a partial picture of the racial and class make-up of the known offender population. The overall image of the known offender as young, male and lower-class is broadly reflected in the data from self-report studies and victimization surveys. This can partially be explained by the way in which the 'crime problem' is currently defined, emphasizing as it does the offences most likely to be perpetrated by these subgroups of the population. The issue of race is more difficult to disentangle, and there is no simple explanation for the presence of a disproportionate number of black people in the known offender population.

Further reading

Tarling (1993) provides data concerning the characteristics of offenders and summaries of major research findings. The text edited by Walker (1995) contains several useful chapters, especially Chapter 9 (Hedderman, 1995) which is concerned with male and female patterns of offending, and Chapter 10 (Fitzgerald, 1995) which discusses the difficulties involved in interpreting race-related crime data. The *Oxford Handbook of Criminology* (Maguire *et al.*, 1994) is similarly useful: Chapter 12 (Farrington, 1994) on criminal careers; and Chapter 24 (Pearson, 1994) on youth and crime. Fitzgerald (1993a) and Reiner (1993) provide a concise and critical overview of research relating to race and crime. The original literature concerning the ability of self-report studies to demonstrate a class–crime link are still well worth reading, for example Box and Ford (1971); Tittle *et al.* (1978); and Clelland and Carter (1980). Reference should be made to primary sources of data, for example *Criminal Statistics* and other official data (Home Office, 1994a; 1994b), reports from the BCS (Aye Maung and Mirrlees-Black, 1994), local surveys (Farrington and Burrows, 1993), and self-report studies (Bowling *et al.*, 1994).

chapter six

Interpreting trends:
quantum leaps?

This chapter introduces the following key concepts or terms, which are also found in the glossary at the end of the book: 'offences against morale'; black market; professional crime; unemployment rate; claimant count definition; personal consumption; experimental research.

In this chapter we shall look at what crime data can and cannot tell us about trends in crime. First, we shall examine what everybody 'knows': that there has been a dramatic increase in crime since the Second World War. We shall travel back to the 1930s, when '[c]rime, other than public disorder, was not a noticeable feature of ... society' (Morris, 1989: 16), and follow the accelerating crime rate through the years and into the 1990s. Our primary focus in this section will be upon offence-based data. Before setting off on this journey, we shall attempt to remove our rosy spectacles, remembering that things often seem as if they used to be better when viewed from the present. As Geoffrey Pearson (1983: ix) reminds us, 'for generations Britain has been plagued by the same fears and problems as today'. Forewarned is forearmed, as they say. Having gained an appreciation of the difficulties involved in interpreting both long- and short-term trends in crime, we shall look at one example of how such trends are interpreted. We shall look at the assumption often made that a rise in the rate of unemployment is linked to an increase in the crime rate.

Sixty-one years of crime

In 1934 there were 233,259 recorded indictable offences in England and Wales (Smithies, 1982). In 1995 this figure had reached over 5 million. Twenty-two times the number of recorded crimes is an alarming increase – imagine this book being 22 times as long as it is. Dwarfing the *Oxford*

Handbook of Criminology, it would be impossible to read in bed. To what extent does this massive increase in recorded crime represent an increase in actual criminal behaviour? Is Britain 22 times as criminal as it was 61 years ago?

We know that crime figures can go up and down independently of a change in the number of crimes being committed, affected as they are by reporting and recording behaviour and changes in legislation. Increases in the crime rate have been explained by a variety of factors, including the increased number of police, improved recording systems (brought about, for example, by computerization), the widespread availability of telephones (making it easier for the public to report incidents), increased insurance cover (also making it more likely that incidents will be reported), reduced public tolerance of violence and the break-up of traditional communities (both contributing to higher reporting rates) (Maguire, 1994). Factors such as these suggest that a greater proportion of criminal incidents are entering the official statistics, rather than that more are being committed. The growth of criminology itself may have contributed to uncovering crimes which were once hidden from the police and public's view; 'systematic data collection often *follows*, rather than generates, new insights and perspectives' (Maguire, 1994: 237; emphasis in original). Suggestions have been made that the crime rate expands in line with the organizational capacity of the criminal justice system (see, for example, Cohen, 1985). A general point which could be made is that '[t]he extent of [officially recorded] criminal behaviour is likely to vary over time in approximate relation to the public and official concern about criminality' (Gurr, 1976: 21).

An alternative perspective accepts the general trends which the crime rate displays and explains them in terms of changes in opportunity; that is, crime rates rise and fall in line with the number of opportunities to commit criminal offences which exist in society. Trends in the crime rate have also been accounted for using measures of population change, and some evidence has shown that the size of the birth cohort is related to the crime rate (Field, 1990; Tarling, 1993). In the past this argument was often used to link rising crime rates to the proportion of young people in the population, but more recently an ageing population has been used to explain a fall in crime rates (see Steffensmeier and Harer, 1991).

Since the advent of victimization surveys we no longer have to rely solely upon official data when attempting to interpret long-term trends (Box, 1987). As we saw in Chapters 2 and 4, the British Crime Survey (BCS) has since its inception shown an increase in the number of criminal incidents occurring, but the increase has been less than that suggested by the official statistics. We must remember that crime rates generated by victimization surveys do not represent the 'true' crime rate – they have their own set of weaknesses and are simply products of a different nature. However, it is now generally accepted that an increase in the total volume of crime has occurred, even if the actual extent of this increase is uncertain (Maguire, 1994).

Crime rates and the War

The 1930s witnessed a steady rise in recorded crime figures (an upward trend which began in the mid-1920s) but the year-to-year increases were not sufficiently sharp to cause political or public alarm. Between 1934 and 1938 the total number increased by 21.3 per cent (Smithies, 1982: 2). Although as a percentage increase this figure appears substantial, the actual numerical counts of crime were low (certainly compared to today's standards); burglaries, for example, numbered fewer than 40,000 a year. New forms of criminal activity were emerging during this period, most notably the organized theft of motor vehicles – the motor car was still a relatively rare and therefore valuable commodity. Even so, the actual number of car thefts was too small to be counted separately in the figures. The motor car not only attracted the professional thief, but also created a new type of offender: traffic offences accounted for 67 per cent of non-indictable crime in 1934 (Smithies, 1982: 42).

The crime wave which was predicted to occur as a result of the blitz and blackout regulations with the onset of war (bombed properties and pitch blackness providing great opportunities for theft and other offences) seemed not immediately to materialize. Between 1941 and 1943, indictable crime rose by only 3.9 per cent. However, this overall rate conceals the wide variations which existed in different parts of England and Wales; for example, Manchester suffered a rise in indictable crimes of 20.4 per cent over this period, while the rate in Leicester fell by 24.4 per cent (Smithies, 1982: 171). Statistics which relate to single towns or cities which do not reflect the general trend within a country are difficult to interpret. The War caused a great deal of upheaval in organizational practices and personnel throughout England and Wales, which may account for some of the local and regional variations in the crime figures.

As the War progressed, so the rate of increase accelerated. Overall the years 1939–45 witnessed a 69 per cent increase in the rate of indictable crime (Morris, 1989). This increase should be viewed in conjunction with the loss in population which also occurred; for example, the civilian population of London fell by over 2 million. Much of this 'population loss' consisted of young men, the very group considered to be most at risk of committing offences. The prevalence rate (offenders per 1000 population) displayed a steady increase throughout the war: from 10 in 1938 to over 15 by 1944 (Smithies, 1982: 2). While losing a proportion of the civilian population, Britain 'suffered' an influx of military personnel which may well have contributed to the rising crime rate. Wilson and Herrnstein (1985: 436), reflecting upon the fall in American crime rates which occurred during this period, remind their readers of the exportation of 'millions of men during their crime-prone years to foreign lands'. It was on British shores that some of these 'crime-prone' Americans landed. However, it is difficult to calculate the direct effect which the presence of the military had on the crime rate. American offenders tended to be dealt with by their own military police and courts, whereas Canadians were more often dealt with by their host's legal system (Smithies, 1982). Also related to the wartime crime rate was the presence of substantial numbers of 'deserters' in the population: it has been estimated that in London alone there were some 20,000 deserters living off their wits (and crime?) by the end of the War (Morris, 1989).

The War produced a wave of new offences and offenders as the British government sought to control first the country's morale, and then the market and supply of goods. During the first 18 months of the War there were many prosecutions for 'offences against morale', for which some quite draconian prison sentences were meted out (Smithies, 1982). Rationing brought with it an upsurge in the black market and influenced other forms of crime, especially theft. The tight controls which were placed on the market resulted in the growth of prosecutions for white-collar crimes. The black market involved

> not only the kinds of people who would, under normal circumstances, be involved in shady dealings on the margins of the law, but large numbers of middle class people who would never have considered themselves criminals in the commonly understood sense of the term.
>
> (Morris 1989: 18)

The pattern of crime throughout the War was dominated by property offences; the offences of larceny (theft) and breaking and entering (burglary), for example, accounted for just over 90 per cent of indictable crime by 1945. Although our focus here is not on offender data, it is interesting to note that the age profile of known offenders found guilty of property offences progressively shifted during the war years. Those aged over 29 years accounted for the largest increases in the numbers found guilty of such offences. According to Smithies (1982: 195) this is a reflection of the increase in white-collar and professional crime.

One category of property crime which did decrease during the War was 'fraud and false pretences', displaying a fall of 18 per cent. This fall has sometimes been explained by the fact that the population were obliged to carry identity cards, something which may have been an obstacle in perpetrating such offences. The rate for this crime category resumed its upward trend when identity cards were abolished in 1952 (Morris, 1989: 36) – a useful 'fact' for those who advocate the reintroduction of the identity card to Britain. However, fraud and forgery are likely to have a very large dark figure. Thus any 'facts' concerning this offence can be interpreted in many different ways.

Violent and sexual offences increased, but there was no significant rise in the number of homicides. The rate of increase for violent offences accelerated towards the end of the War, with one of the most serious offences, felonious wounding (acts endangering life), displaying the sharpest rise. The increase in violence is not thought to be linked to the rise in professional crime, but to the general social upheaval and conflicts of the War (Smithies, 1982: 152) and to the 'fact that in wartime the normal standards of behaviour and restraint are not infrequently suspended in the context of the belief that life itself is uncertain' (Morris, 1989: 20).

The Second World War was a period of 'exceptional circumstances' and it is difficult to come to any firm conclusions about the nature and extent of crime during this time, not least because publication of *Criminal Statistics* was suspended for the duration of the War, casting some doubt upon the accuracy of the retrospectively published data. The fact that the police service was heavily depleted in numbers and under pressure from the special problems and duties which the War brought, suggests that rates of recording probably fell during this period. Reporting by members of the public could also have decreased, as their minds were concentrated upon other, more pressing issues. Despite these possibilities, we can speculate that the rise in recorded crime which is evident for this period is a reflection (if an under-estimation) of a 'true' increase in certain forms of criminal behaviour, some of which were caused by 'the insatiable demands of the black market' (Smithies, 1982: 189).

Crime rates and prosperity

The rate of recorded crime continued to rise in the years immediately following the end of the war. The period 1945–50 displayed hitherto unprecedented increases in the crime rate. However, some sense of proportion should be maintained: the actual number of recorded crimes (as opposed to percentage increase) was, at its highest, less than half a million, a figure which has subsequently come to be viewed as a 'low' crime rate. The increase peaked in 1950, and there followed a brief lull during which the trend was reversed and recorded crime began to fall slightly.

It was from 1955 onwards that recorded crime displayed the 'true beginnings of the modern crime problem' (Morris, 1989: 90). A sharp and sustained increase in the crime rate occurred. By 1960 the figure had reached three-quarters of a million (a 70 per cent increase since 1955) exceeding 1 million by 1964 (Maguire, 1994: 257). This increase was evident across all offence categories; notable increases occurred in relation to offences involving motor vehicles (theft of and from vehicles) and other property offences (theft and burglary). As motor cars returned to the roads after the War and became ever more abundant, they became more vulnerable as fewer car owners had secure parking facilities. Unlike in the 1930s when they were the province of the professional criminal, motor vehicles became increasingly targeted by younger offenders. Property offences were seemingly rising in direct proportion to the number of 'attractive, portable consumer goods entering the market' (Wilson and Herrnstein, 1985: 413). Not only were there many new 'stealable' goods but also these items were, it has been argued, less well guarded than they once might have been. Houses were more likely to be left empty during the day: women entered the labour market in increasing numbers; families took holidays away from home; domestic technology cut down the time spent on housework. The new supermarkets and self-service petrol stations increased the opportunity for shoplifting and other forms of theft (Wilson and Herrnstein, 1985: 410–16; Felson, 1994). McClintock and Avison (1968: 273) attributed some of the increase in property crime to a 'growing attitude of carelessness toward property resulting from a greater material prosperity in the general population'. They were of the opinion that many of these crimes were preventable and that research studies were required to establish methods of crime prevention. This, of course, turned out to be prophetic.

Violent crime also increased dramatically during this period, doubling between 1955 and 1960 (Morris, 1989: 91). Racial conflict and violence became an issue with the increase in immigration, and violence generally was thought to be increasing because of the emergence of youth subcultures (see Cohen, 1973; Pearson, 1983). Throughout the 1950s and 1960s, however, violent crime remained a small proportion of the total (about 5 per cent). Within the category there were wide variations; for example, the number of homicides remained fairly constant, while malicious woundings increased over threefold between 1955 and 1965 (McClintock and Avison, 1968: 273).

It was during the late 1950s and 1960s that the post-war baby boom came of age, so increasing the number of potential offenders in the population. This change in the age structure can be used to account for some, but not all, of the trends in recorded crime. An examination of prevalence data leads us to conclude (if these figures are taken at face value) that during this period an increased population of offenders was committing crimes at an increased rate (Morris, 1989: 90–91). Some have accounted for this apparent increased criminality as being the result of the formation of a 'critical mass of young people outnumber[ing] or overpower[ing] their would-be controllers' (Wilson and Herrnstein, 1985: 425). Others had previously concluded that the War years had produced a more delinquent generation of young people (Wilkins, 1960; cited in Morris, 1989); this theory collapsed when subsequent cohorts of children became even more delinquent.

The most interesting aspect of this 'crime wave' was that it occurred during a time of prosperity and full employment, creating for criminology, according to some commentators, an aetiological crisis which allowed (forced) the discipline 'to expand and burst out of its positivist straitjacket' (Maguire, 1994: 241). As the accepted causes of much crime – poverty and deprivation

– were 'pushed into an increasingly remote past' by the combination of economic growth and the welfare state, crime continued to rise (Morris, 1989: 93). Some looked for a sociological root to the causes of crime, while others abandoned the quest altogether. According to Young (1988a), the emerging school of left radicals neatly side-stepped the issue by denying that there was any real increase in crime; the apparent rise in crime rates was, they argued, merely a reflection of the social construction of official data. Other social commentators busied themselves with the question of the disappearance of poverty and, rather than rediscovering it, concluded that it had never gone away (see, for example, Townsend, 1979). The intimate link which trends in crime and other socio-economic conditions have with criminological theory underlines the importance of distinguishing the illusory from the real.

Crime rates and decline

Recorded crime continued to rise throughout the 1970s and into the 1980s, with an average annual rate of increase of approximately 5 per cent. There were, however, significant fluctuations in this annual rate; for example, an 18 per cent rise in 1974 and a 3 per cent fall in 1979 (Maguire, 1994: 257). There is a danger of attaching too much importance to short- or medium-term trends as such changes can often be the result of legislative or definitional changes. For example, the 1968 Theft Act redefined and reclassified many offences and thus distorted the figures for burglary and theft of motor vehicles; the 1971 Criminal Damage Act changed the rules for recording this offence, resulting in a massive increase in the numbers appearing in *Criminal Statistics* between 1971 and 1981 (Walker, 1981; 1995). Despite this, year-to-year changes in the official crime rate tend to be 'wielded as matters of momentous importance ... almost always rising and therefore always weapons with which to attack the government of the day' (Wiles, 1971: 205).

During the 1980s the offence categories which involved rape and drug trafficking were seen to increase most sharply; both displayed an average annual rise of 10 per cent (Maguire, 1994: 259). In the case of rape, there was evidence of an increase in police recording of reported offences (Smith, 1989a). The official response to drug trafficking changed during the 1980s; 'of all areas of crime control, drug trafficking has been at the forefront of stimulating developments in terms of legislation and the organisation of law enforcement' (Dorn *et al.*, 1992: ix). There is little doubt that drug trafficking has actually increased over the years, but the increase in recorded offences has also been accentuated by the official response.

Burglary figures almost doubled during this decade: from 0.6 million in 1980 to just over 1 million by 1990 (Home Office, 1989; 1993). We have victimization data concerning this offence dating back to 1972 provided by the General Household Survey (1972–81) and the BCS (1981–91). While police figures show a 189 per cent increase in the recorded incidence of burglary between 1972 and 1991, the General Household Survey and the BCS data reveal a smaller increase of 61 per cent (Hough and Mayhew, 1983: 8; Mayhew *et al.*, 1993: 42). The discrepancy has been attributed to a steady increase in reporting rates. So, while burglary probably did increase substantially during the 1980s, the increase was less than that suggested by *Criminal Statistics*.

The 1990s dawned with a recorded crime rate of over 4½ million which began rising at an average rate of 16 per cent a year. The new decade saw the categories of theft, burglary and fraud increase substantially, but it was vehicle crime which soared. Theft of and from vehicles increased by approximately 57 per cent between 1988 and 1992 and accounted for 28 per cent of notifiable offences in 1992 (Home Office, 1993: 23). This increase was greater than the increase in the number of vehicles licensed, suggesting that 'proportionately more cars [were] stolen or stolen from' (Walker, 1995: 17).

The 1992 sweep of the BCS indicated a somewhat less dramatic rate of change. Over all categories of offence where comparisons were possible (the 'comparable subset') the BCS showed a 14 per cent increase between 1987 and 1991; figures for these same offences as counted by *Criminal Statistics* increased by 39 per cent. The mismatch between the data sets can be accounted for by an increase in reporting. In 1991, 50 per cent of the comparable subset of BCS offences were reported to the police, compared with only 36 per cent in 1981. Recording by the police remained stable overall, with some variation between offences. The result of this increase in reporting was a contraction of the dark figure.

> In 1981, the BCS estimated that for the comparable sub-set, there were 4.5 BCS incidents for every one incident recorded by the police – due to non-reporting and non-recording. This had dropped to 4.4 in 1983, to 4.1 in 1988 and to 3.4 in 1992.
>
> (Mayhew *et al.*, 1993: 16)

Figures of recorded crime relating to 1992 and 1993 indicated that the upward trend was beginning to slow down: a 6 per cent increase in 1992 was actually followed by a 1 per cent fall in 1993 (Home Office, 1994a). The BCS suggested that a drop in both reporting and recording had occurred between 1991 and 1993, along with a smaller biennial increase in the rate of BCS offences (Mayhew *et al.*, 1994). These two things, taken together, help us to understand and interpret the trend displayed in *Criminal Statistics*. It would appear that, at least among these particular offences, a slowing down in the rate of increase did occur, but this was less pronounced than indicated by recorded crime statistics, owing to a change in reporting and recording habits. Information such as this is, in itself, interesting and worthy of study. It also demonstrates how one of the dark figures (that measured and exposed by the BCS) can contract and expand over a relatively short time period.

Most recently, the Home Office has released figures which show that recorded crime fell by 5 per cent in 1994 and 2 per cent in 1995 (HOSB 19/95;
3/96). This is the first time in forty years that there have been three consecu-
tive falls in recorded crime. Before we cheer at this news, we should note that
some of the more serious offence types actually showed increases. Figures for
1995, for example, display increases in homicide and robbery of 3 per cent
and 14 per cent, respectively (HOSB 3/96). An overall fall in the crime rate is
significant for the government; indeed, it is very good news. Currently the
decline is being largely attributed (by the government) to new and improved
policing methods. It is too early for us to proclaim a reversal in crime trends;
for example, the 5 per cent fall in recorded crime which occurred at the end of
the 1980s was followed by a 31 per cent increase in the first two years of the
1990s (HOSB 19/95). Short-term trends often turn out to be the lull before
the storm. Data from the next sweep of the BCS may offer us some clues to aid
our interpretation by providing us with information concerning any changes
in reporting and recording behaviour. If the current downward trend displayed in *Criminal Statistics* continues, some may conclude that the mid-
1990s have produced a more law-abiding society where fewer crimes are
committed. Alternatively, and more plausibly perhaps, it could be concluded
that as the police have to deal with increasing reports of incidents, so they
record fewer of them as crimes; as the public grow used to a high crime rate,
so they change their reporting habits; as fewer people can afford high insurance premiums, so they have less reason to report crime.

On the up and up

The rate of recorded crime over the last 60 years has shown remarkable
resistance to wildly differing economic and social conditions. Through a
world war, full employment, the swinging sixties, hyperinflation and
economic decline, the crime rate has doggedly continued its skyward
projection, apparently unstoppable. Carr-Hill and Stern (1979: 271) concluded their analysis of trends in crime by stating that, 'since, on an empirical
basis, the process generating criminal statistics differs substantially from year
to year, it is difficult to say whether actual offences have decreased or
increased. The verdict must be "not proven"'. Pearson (1983) in a rather
pessimistic mood, stated that there is

> no way of making sure-footed judgments about whether movements in
> recorded crime reflect actual alterations in criminal activity; or shifts in
> public tolerance; or changes in policing; or some messy permutation of
> any of these factors. Statements about rising crime (or about falling
> crime) can neither be regarded as true nor false in this strict sense.
> Instead, we must regard them as logically *undecidable*.
>
> (Pearson, 1983: 218; emphasis in original)

These conclusions were reached before the availability of alternative data; now the verdict would have to be rather different. National victimization surveys allow us to track one particular set of offences and enable us to see the 'messy permutations' which result in changes in the recorded figures for these offences. Trends in other forms of crime remain more difficult to interpret, but as new research and improved data collection methods begin to 'discover and count' more of these crimes, so the long-term trends may be even better understood.

The population of England and Wales is (probably) not 22 times as criminal as it was 61 years ago: we have a larger, more efficient police service which records more incidents as crimes, and a more vigilant and less tolerant public who report more crimes. Such suggestions, and the evidence from the BCS, lead us to believe that the rise in crime is less than that indicated by the official statistics. There is also evidence of a substantial increase in 'actual' crime (that is crimes committed) which can be explained, in part, by the existence of many more criminal opportunities. Different offences have displayed varying rates of growth, which it is useful to study and interpret, but this does not 'distract from a striking picture of consistent long-run growth in crimes whose origins are diverse' (Field, 1990: 4). We can also see that the overall picture of crime in the 1990s is very similar to that of the past. McClintock and Avison (1968: 273) noted that,

> [t]hroughout the present century, the vast majority of indictable crimes annually recorded by the police has consisted of larcenies [theft] and breaking offences [burglary]. Offences against the person have remained a very small proportion of all crime, accounting in recent years for less than five per cent of the total.

In 1995, violent crime accounted for 6 per cent of recorded crime (HOSB 3/96). The picture of crime was, and remains, one dominated by property offences. Of course, the total is much bigger and the types of property crime have changed over the years (as have the types of violent crime). Overall, official statistics tell us something about the broad trends in some crimes, but we only know this because of the availability of alternative data.

Unemployment and crime: the devil finds work for idle hands?

In the never-ending quest for causality, the criminologist has sought out correlations between crime and other variables. After largely failing to find individual differences between criminals and non-criminals, the search party packed away their tape measures and refocused their sights. During the 1950s and 1960s (periods of economic growth, low unemployment and rising crime) many theorists sought causal explanations for crime in the social situations of offenders. The economic crisis of the mid-1970s saw a renewal of interest in a link between economic conditions and the crime rate. As crime rates continued to rise in periods of recession, so unemployment became and remains a key variable proposed in the explanation of crime.

We shall look at two different types of research which are used to demonstrate the link between unemployment and crime: aggregate-level studies which compare fluctuations in the crime rate with fluctuations in the unemployment rate, and individual-level studies which examine the offending behaviour of actual individuals. The former type is concerned with correlations between a change in the crime rate and a change in the unemployment rate, while the latter is concerned with whether employment status has an effect upon a person's propensity to offend.

Aggregate-level studies

Much research has been carried out using aggregate data, some looking specifically at property crime (the type of offence most readily associated with unemployment) and others at all crime. While unemployment displays an upward trend, correlations between it and the crime rate are easily found. However, as Roger Tarling (1982: 29) points out,

> [b]ecause crime has generally been increasing, any other series [aggregate data from some variable] that exhibits the same overall trend will be highly correlated with it. It would not be difficult to find a range of other measures, some obviously irrelevant, which mirror the crime figures equally well and more consistently.

He offers us the example of ice cream consumption. Of course, no one would be tempted down the path of causation with this particular variable (except those of us with sensitive teeth!), but unemployment is another matter. Most contemporary criminological theories sit happily with a causal relationship between crime and unemployment (for summaries, see Box, 1987: 36–52; Pyle and Deadman, 1994: 339–40; Farrington *et al.*, 1986a: 335–6). The empirical evidence, however, is contradictory, and a consensus is yet to be reached as to the nature of the relationship between unemployment and crime. Let us examine the reasons why this task is so difficult and why we share Bottomley and Pease's (1986: 138) sentiments of being 'basically pessimistic about the use of routine statistics to do more than locate possibilities'.

Other dark figures?
As we know, the recorded crime rate does not represent a 'true' measure of the total volume of crime, and changes over time can mean many things other

than a change in offending behaviour. The unemployment rate presents us with similar problems. It is an administrative construction measuring the number of individuals who are officially defined as unemployed, on the basis of the 'claimant count definition' – that is to say, individuals who, for benefit claiming and other purposes, are able to register as available for work. This narrow definition excludes many individuals who do not have full-time paid employment – the dark figure of the unemployed? Those excluded from the official count include many lone parents, those working at least 16 hours per week, the sick and disabled and, of greatest significance to our discussion, the majority of those aged under 18. Changing work patterns and family structure affect the size and shape of this dark figure. Like recorded crime, the official unemployment rate is also affected by changes in legislation. For example, the 1986 Social Security Act effectively removed those aged 16 and 17 from the register (see Hill, 1990). Dickinson (1993: 19) states that while there are 'strong indicators that the claimant count underestimates unemployment by a wide margin', by adjusting the data for legislative changes in the definition, consistency over time can be achieved. We can be in no doubt that an under-estimation occurs and are rather more pessimistic about the possibility of adjusting the data to make accurate comparisons over time. We must bear in mind, then, that aggregate studies are actually examining correlations between two data sets which share a common problem, in that they measure only the number of *recorded* crimes and the number of individuals *recorded* as unemployed. This does little to inspire confidence in any conclusions drawn from such data.

A useful stand-in?

Unemployment is often used by researchers as a proxy for economic disadvantage. For example, John Wells (1995) amasses evidence to show that the unemployment–crime link is stronger than currently supposed. However, he concludes his paper by stating that

> [m]ass unemployment and the growth of single parenthood have resulted in poverty on a scale without precedent since [World War II] with 1 in every 4 children currently from families in receipt of Income Support [the state-defined minimum benefit] . . . [A] society with such large numbers of children in poverty runs the risk of massive criminal delinquency.
>
> (Wells, 1995: 5)

This sounds as if his *real* interest lies in a link between poverty and crime. Why not, then, compare numbers defined as poor with the crime rate? The full answer to this question is beyond the scope of this book. Put simply, there is no agreement as to the definition of poverty. Unlike the USA and many European countries, Britain does not have an official poverty line. It appears that counting offenders, official or otherwise, is child's play compared to defining what is a poor person (for a discussion of definitions of poverty, see Ringen, 1989; George and Howards, 1991). The poor, whoever they are, are as likely to be found among lone parents, low-paid and part-time workers (and students?) as they are among the unemployed. We should also note that being officially labelled as unemployed has no simple link with an individual's command over economic resources. Unemployment rates can only provide the roughest of guides to the extent of poverty. The lesson from this is that those primarily interested in poverty as a criminogenic variable should avoid aggregate studies of unemployment rates and concentrate their research efforts at the individual level.

It is also true that unemployment itself can act as an indicator of other aspects of social deprivation. Employment status is associated with many other criminogenic variables, such as social class, educational achievement and age. Aggregate studies are unable to disentangle the direct effect of unemployment from these other variables. We shall return to this issue later when we look at individual-level studies.

An ecological fallacy?

The finding that the crime rate is positively correlated with the unemployment rate should not be taken as an indication that it is the unemployed who are responsible for the increased crime rates (see Bottomley and Pease, 1986: 138). In order for causation effects at the individual level to be attributed to unemployment, it must be shown that the unemployed are more likely to commit crimes than those in employment. This is not possible from aggregate data. 'In order to draw conclusions about individuals, it is necessary to carry out research based on individuals' (Farrington et al., 1986a: 336).

Which way round?

Causal order is difficult to determine from aggregate studies. 'While unemployment may cause some people to commit crime it is also possible that for others involvement in crime and a criminal record causes unemployment or at least exacerbates their difficulties in securing jobs' (Tarling, 1982: 28). Dickinson (1993: 25), while recognizing that for some individuals this may be true, finds it 'implausible to suggest that it could account for the large and rapid movement of unemployment'. Of course, no one has ever suggested this. However, much crime is perpetrated by young people before they officially enter the labour market – while they are still in compulsory education or else under 18 years of age and therefore not classified as unemployed – who may later find that their criminal record adversely affects their job prospects. Despite this, it is usual to think in terms of unemployment causing crime. Bottomley and Pease (1986: 135) argue that this is due to an illogical bias in our way of thinking: '[t]hat is to say, it seems to come more easily to people to think of events as causes of future events than consequences of prior events'.

The consensus of doubt? (Chiricos, 1987: 188)
Cautionary points to one side, how closely does the unemployment rate mirror the crime rate? What do the numerous aggregate studies tell us? It rather depends on which side of the fence we choose to stand. The existence of a relationship between unemployment and crime has increasingly become a political issue,

> as unemployment and crime are perhaps the two major social problems to be faced by governments in the 1990s. In the United Kingdom, the Conservative government wishes to deny any direct causal relationship between the two because this would imply that making a priority of reducing inflation at the expense of high unemployment would negate its attempts to control burgeoning crime levels. The political import-ance of the relationship and the research effort devoted to testing it has however failed to produce any clear consensus.
>
> (Hale and Sabbagh, 1991: 400)

The cynical among us might think that the lack of a consensus is due to the political importance of the issue. Conclusions often *seem* to follow the researcher's (or funding body's) own basic political instinct.

The many reviews of existing empirical research reflect this lack of consensus and generally fail to arrive at any firm conclusion. Roger Tarling's (1982) review found that, overall, more studies demonstrated a lack of an unemployment–crime relation than could show its existence. He concluded his review of 30 studies by stating that

> it is clear that unemployment is not the sole determinant or even the major determinant of crime ... [However] some evidence of a relationship persists suggesting that unemployment is a factor in the causation of crime, although it may not be a major factor.
>
> (Tarling, 1982: 32)

Box's (1987: 96) 'labour of love' could only conclude that the relationship was inconsistent, even when alternative sources of crime data were used.

Particular studies can be picked out which claim to demonstrate less equivocal results. Jackie Orme's (1994: 1) Home Office study analysed the relationship between the rates of increase in unemployment and crime at police force level. Her examination of the data failed to demonstrate a 'consistent significant correlation between unemployment and recorded crime'. In contrast, Dickinson (1993) reported a clear correlation between the unemployment rates of young males and domestic burglary committed by young males. Critical analysis of both these studies (something which we shall resist here) could find enough methodological weaknesses to question each study's findings. It remains true that 'politicians and others can find apparently respectable support for their diametrically opposing views' (Pyle and Deadman, 1994: 339).

Cantor and Land (1985) attempt to explain why aggregate studies produce such differing results. In times of high unemployment there exist two forces which pull against one another, opportunity and motivation. The latter increases owing to financial hardship and causes property crimes to increase. The former decreases as homes are better guarded and there are fewer goods available to steal, thus producing a fall in property crime. The combined effect of these forces is said to be responsible for the 'weak and inconsistent' results which aggregate studies often produce (Cantor and Land, 1985: 321). This sounds like a compelling argument. However, Hale and Sabbagh (1991: 401) have since suggested that the methodology used by Cantor and Land is 'fundamentally flawed'. And so the 'adversarial positivism' continues (Brake and Hale, 1992: 114).

A wider focus?
Some studies have examined links between crime and wider indicators of the state of the economy. The most extensive and notable is Simon Field's (1990) Home Office study, *Trends in Crime and their Interpretation* (but see also, for example, Pyle and Deadman, 1994). Field (1990: 5) concluded that 'economic factors have a major influence on trends in both property and personal crime' [e.g., offences of violence]. Increases in property crime were found to be correlated with a downturn in personal consumption (the average amount spent by each person in a year), while increases in personal crime were correlated with increases in personal consumption. He explained these findings mainly in terms of changed opportunity and motivation, a similar argument to that of Cantor and Land (1985). Motivation to commit property crime is greatest during a fall in consumption (although opportunity is less). Similarly, the opportunity to commit personal crimes is greatest during periods of rapid consumption growth, at least for those offences more likely to be recorded, when people spend more time out of the home (see Felson, 1994).

This, he argued, causes the year-to-year fluctuations but the effects are short-lived and the crime rate soon returns to its long-term trajectory. He notes that crime and the economy display similar short-term fluctuations, but the underlying trend of rates of both is one of consistent growth. The similarity in both rates is quite startling and could lead us to believe that economic growth has been the major determinant of the long-term rise in the crime rate.

The unemployment rate, Field (1990: 7) concluded, was not an important variable in the explanation of fluctuations in the crime rate: '[o]nce the effect of personal consumption on crime is taken into account, no evidence emerged, despite extensive statistical testing, that unemployment adds anything to the explanation of any crime'. An increase in the rate of unemployment lags a year or so behind a fall in consumption and yet fluctuations in the crime rate were seen to follow consumption trends. Others have argued that because unemployment rates and consumption growth are so closely related to one another, there is no value in including both measures in any analysis (Reilly and Witt, 1992).

Individual-level studies

There have been very few British studies which look at the connection between unemployment and crime at an individual level. The Northumbria Police (1980) found that greater numbers of the unemployed than employed were arrested. A self-report study of young people in Northern Ireland discovered that the unemployed admitted more offences than the employed (Gormally et al., 1981). The trouble with such studies is that there are many variables which can make an individual prone to both crime and unemployment. In order for unemployment to be causally linked to an individual's criminality, these other variables would have to be matched in the comparison group. The growth of youth unemployment during the last two decades has made this issue all the more relevant. The group who are most at risk of committing offences are also those most likely to be unemployed.

The most convincing study of individuals to date is Farrington et al. (1986a), an analysis of data from the Cambridge Study in Delinquent Development. These researchers cunningly avoided the problems of controlling for other relevant variables by looking at differences in each individual's offending behaviour during periods of employment and unemployment. Having previously found that unemployment was correlated with both official and self-reported offending (West and Farrington, 1977; Farrington, 1979; West, 1982), they went on to discover that members of their cohort were more likely to offend while unemployed than when in employment, although this difference was only evident for property crimes:

> [t]his was true even when the analysis was restricted to youths who had all been unemployed and who had all committed officially recorded crimes, suggesting that unemployment was related to crime independently of the many individual differences between convicted and unconvicted persons.
>
> (Farrington et al., 1986a: 351)

They found that this effect was strongest for those individuals who were already predisposed towards offending (measured by a variety of socio-economic factors). Farrington et al. highlight the weaknesses in their analysis: the small numbers involved, the relatively short periods of unemployment and the generally low rates of youth unemployment at the time of the study.

A complete unknown?

Our initial pessimism has quickly turned into deep depression. Tarling (1982: 32) suggested that '[i]t seems unlikely that additional aggregate studies would clarify the issues'. Few seem to have heeded his words. While the rates of unemployment and crime remain high, the temptation to demonstrate aggregate correlations between them is too great for many to resist. Causal relationships found in the social world are never simple. Some processes can be reproduced in the sterile conditions of the laboratory, but 'real' life is a complex web of interacting variables which we could never fully hope to identify, let alone hold constant for research.

> Yet our brains and our newspapers lead us into temptation to think of simple causes. Although textbooks warn that correlation does not imply cause, nonetheless it is *only* through seeing correlations that we start thinking about causes. To ask us to eschew thinking causally about these relationships is probably fruitless.
> (Bottomley and Pease, 1986: 137; emphasis in original)

The strength of aggregate studies is that they allow us to see correlations which may be indicative of causal relationships. Their weaknesses appear when their data are asked questions which they cannot hope to answer. If researchers are interested in causation, they must leave the warmth of their offices and stop tinkering with secondary data.

The work of Farrington *et al.* (1986a) demonstrates what could be the most fruitful way forward for research in this area: longitudinal self-report studies carried out over several years using large samples, examining individuals' offending and employment careers. However, these types of complex, long-term studies are often prohibitively expensive. Furthermore, Farrington *et al.* (1986a: 352) suggest that the only way to prove 'unambiguously that unemployment causes crime . . . [is] in a randomised experiment in which employment levels were systematically varied'. They are not suggesting that people are randomly sacked from their employment to see whether or not they commit crimes (this would be considered a trifle unethical) but rather that an experimental group is assisted in gaining employment and their offending behaviour compared to a control group who are not. This introduces a whole new form of data – that produced by experimental research, which have not been discussed in this book (see Farrington *et al.*, 1986b, for a review of experimental data). We will only say that we do not share their enthusiasm for such research methods, except when we fantasize about building a simulated prison in the basement of the university in which we can incarcerate and observe both staff and students (see Haney *et al.*, 1981).

We are in little doubt that economic factors have an important role in the causation of crime. Unemployment represents but one possible indicator of economic deprivation and, on its own, is of limited use as a causal variable. The impact of unemployment is much influenced by individual circumstances and the different ways in which being unemployed is subjectively experienced (see Lea and Young, 1993). The 'meaning' of unemployment can also change at the aggregate level, for example, unemployment in the 1990s may be a different experience generally, compared to that of, say, 20 years ago. Using unemployment to explain crime raises many more questions than it answers. While the nature of unemployment has changed dramatically over the years, the nature of crime displays consistencies which are more startling than any changes. For example, the young have always been 'crime-prone', but they have not always suffered from high rates of unemployment. The infamous Mods and Rockers may have disrupted many a bank holiday, but the majority of them were back at work by the Tuesday.

The trouble is that we expect unemployment to cause crime; indeed we can easily imagine how it might. Not only can we see how the devil might find work for idle hands, but also how such work provides illegitimate means for satisfying material need, and, at the same time, some measure of excitement lacking in the often dull life of the unemployed (see Gottfredson and Hirschi, 1990: 163). The reality is that, for many people, work is an unfulfilling experience both mentally and financially. It has even been suggested that the widely held belief that unemployment causes crime actually results in higher rates of recorded crime. During periods of high unemployment the public and police will expect a rise in crime and this could result in an increase in the fear of crime, leading to higher reporting rates and increased surveillance and control of 'problem populations' by the police. The end result of these factors would be an increase in the rate of recorded crime, thus fuelling the belief and the fear (Box, 1987: 157).

Well-meaning criminologists should think twice before implying in a simplistic way that it is the unemployed who are to blame. Those concerned with economic causes of crime should investigate a range of variables instead of concentrating upon employment status: for example, material deprivation, conditions of work, the level of state benefits and the conditions attached to receiving them, and future employment prospects. It will then perhaps become clearer how unemployment affects the crime rate and individuals' offending behaviour. Box (1987) presented evidence which showed that the extent of income inequality was consistently correlated with crime rates. In light of the widening inequality in Britain's income distribution (Joseph Rowntree Foundation, 1995) this economic measure may be worthy of scrutiny. Of course, suggesting that a more equal distribution of income would result in less crime is rather unpalatable to some political positions.

To conclude, asking the official data whether unemployment causes crime is akin to asking hospital porters to perform brain surgery on the grounds that they know how to get to the operating theatre. The data appear to hint at the existence of some kind of correlation between unemployment and crime.

This, together with what we already know about the possible causes of crime, suggests that explorations of these variables at the individual level may prove fruitful. As we have seen, few have chosen this path and there is a tendency to repeat the same exercises without moving further forward. The value of matching crime and unemployment rates has been exhausted and it is time to move on to new pastures.

Summary

Recorded crime in Britain is traced over a 61 year period, with due attention to the many problems of interpreting such official statistics as measures of trends in crime. Increases in recorded crime can occur for many reasons other than a change in the 'actual' number of criminal acts being perpetrated. The arrival of national victimization surveys has allowed 'actual' increases in some crimes to be separated from increases caused by changes in reporting and recording behaviour. The difficulties which are involved in demonstrating a relationship between crime and unemployment are highlighted by consideration of two methods of research: aggregate-level and individual-level studies. Data from aggregate studies fail convincingly to reveal a strong correlation between the rates of crime and unemployment, and insufficient research has been carried out using individual-level studies. The chapter concludes by suggesting that future research on this topic should concentrate on individual-level studies and take a broader focus on economic conditions.

Further reading

Historical accounts of trends in crime and offenders are found in Smithies (1982), which covers the Second World War, Morris (1989), detailing the period from 1945 to the 1980s, and McClintock and Avison (1968), who discuss trends in recorded crime from the beginning of the century to the mid-1960s. Pearson (1983) provides a fascinating historical account of youth crime. Details of more recent trends in crime can be found in Maguire (1994) and Walker (1995). As always, primary sources should be consulted: *Criminal Statistics* and BCS reports such as Home Office (1994a); HOSB 19/95; and Mayhew *et al.* (1994). The theoretical debate about crime and unemployment is summarized by Box (1987), who also provides an excellent overview of both aggregate- and individual-level studies. Useful summaries can also be found in Tarling (1982) and Pyle and Deadman (1994).

chapter seven

Conclusion: carry on counting?

This chapter introduces the following key terms and concepts, which are also to be found in the glossary at the end of the book: ethnographic research; qualitative methods and data; individual pathology; appreciative stance; correctionalist viewpoint; displacement; left idealism; right realism; relative deprivation; corporate crime.

In this final chapter, we do not intend to repeat the conclusions and summaries which have already been provided in each of the earlier chapters. Instead, we outline some of our own personal views about the whole field of crime data that we have covered, and make a few comments about the direction in which it might go in the future. As part of this, we also point out some of the aspects of the field that we have neglected in this book. We begin this part of the task in the next section.

Numbers are not the only data

This book has mainly been concerned with a particular kind of crime data, that provided by official statistics, self-report studies and victimization surveys. In some respects, all three provide a similar type of product – quantitative data, whether produced by official bureaucracies or by survey methods. This focus may have left the impression that we consider these data to be the preferred, or even the only data to consider in relation to crime. This is not our view at all. Although we concentrate on these particular forms in this book, we believe that other kinds of data are essential for the criminological enterprise. In fact, a combination of different strategies, methods and data (what we have previously referred to as 'triangulation') is generally to be preferred.

As we have made clear throughout this book, the three types of data considered have certain limitations on their own terms, as quantitative data.

It is often necessary or desirable to conduct special research studies in order to unravel some of the puzzles which are thrown up by them. We should, however, like to add two points which are broader than this. First, there are some important areas that are very difficult to investigate with official data and survey methods. To paraphrase the familiar lager commercial, we need other ways of reaching the parts that these methods cannot reach. As Hobbs (1994: 442) puts it, in connection with one of them, that of professional crime: 'Until gangsters, armed robbers, fraudsters and their ilk indicate their enthusiasm for questionnaires or large-scale social surveys, ethnographic research, life histories, oral histories, biographies, autobiographies and journalistic accounts will be at a premium'. These alternative data also need critical assessment, especially in the light of the circumstances under which they were produced. However, what are often called 'qualitative methods' and 'qualitative data' are too valuable to ignore.

Our second point is that such qualitative data should not necessarily be regarded as second best, a kind of fall-back to be employed where the large-scale quantitative sort is unavailable. Not only can qualitative methods access regions other methods cannot reach, but they can also provide a different kind of data that makes a distinctive contribution of its own. The information produced by official statistics and survey methods is abstracted from rich and complex settings populated by human agents who attribute a variety of meanings to their experiences. Much of this is lost in the translation of fragments of these experiences into large-scale, summarizing quantitative data. Small-scale qualitative studies can contribute much to our understanding of the contexts in which offending, victimization and the processes of criminal justice occur. They can provide us with a sense of the unitary character of particular settings and groups which is often lost in the production of large-scale data – see, for example, Foster (1990) on local and family traditions of petty crime, and Hobbs (1988) on entrepreneurship in the criminal subculture and the Criminal Investigation Department in the East End of London. In addition, they can give us valuable accounts of the overall experiences of individuals and the social meanings given to them in real situations. They can, therefore, provide us with in-depth material which fleshes out the bare skeleton provided by quantitative data.

Crime statistics and the honest politician

Another area that we have been unable to cover in this book is the politics of crime statistics. Some years ago, Morris and Hawkins (1970) published a book with the intriguing title *The Honest Politician's Guide to Crime Control*. Cynics might suggest that this was a serious mistake, for it was clearly a book with a very small or even non-existent market. The use made of crime data by politicians is a fascinating area of study in itself. As we have seen in our survey of trends in recorded crime, there has been little good news for governments of the day. Increases in recorded crime were handy for those aspiring to power (as in the election campaign of 1979, in which law and order was a major platform for the Conservatives), but more than a little inconvenient once in office. Little wonder, then, that Home Secretaries over recent years have sometimes been glad to refer to British Crime Survey (BCS) figures in order to suggest that the increases in crime were actually not as bad as the official statistics seemed to suggest – a healthy (albeit not disinterested) scepticism at last about these figures.

Such scepticism has a habit of evaporating as times change. As we were writing this final chapter, statistics of recorded notifiable offences were released by the Home Office which showed that the number had fallen by over half a million since June 1993, giving the largest percentage fall since records began over a hundred years ago (*The Times*, 28 September 1995). The Home Secretary (Michael Howard) is quoted as saying: 'I believe these figures mark a real turning of the tide against crime'. Like King Canute before him, Michael Howard appears to have discovered the secret of controlling the waves. Gone is any scepticism about these figures. Gone is any reference to BCS data (which, as we saw earlier in the book, seemed to suggest that fewer of those crimes committed against people were being reported to the police in the most recent period covered). Instead, we hear a number of reasons for the fall, which is taken at face value: the growth of closed-circuit television; new initiatives by the police, including the targeting of known offenders; and the courts responding to his repeated pleas for a tougher sentencing policy, with the result that the prison population had risen by a quarter in the preceding two and a half years.

We would not wish to deny the efforts of many of those working in the field, and that a number of initiatives appear to have produced promising localized results with certain sorts of offences. It is, however, misleading to imply that the crime rate is so clearly within the power of the Home Secretary and criminal justice system to control. If it were so, we should also rightly hold them responsible for the enormous increases in crime in England and Wales over recent years. As Morris and Heal (1981: 49) concluded some years ago at the end of their review of research evidence about the effectiveness of the police in crime control: 'At the risk of some oversimplification the message most obviously to be drawn from this review is that it is beyond the ability of the police to have a direct effect on a good deal of crime'. Similarly, the idea that more and longer prison sentences act as a deterrent against crime seems to ignore the fact that many offences are never detected, and that the threat of prison may not loom large in many potential offenders' minds. Finally, a further element in what the Home Secretary apparently has in mind – a tougher sentencing policy which has an appreciable effect on the crime rate by taking offenders out of circulation – was declared as impractical and 'unthinkable' by a Home Office study some years ago for a variety of reasons, 'not the least of which is the intolerable burden it would place on the prison system' (Brody and Tarling, 1980: 36).

How Kenneth Baker must envy Michael Howard's apparent ability to control the (crime) waves. As Home Secretary back in 1991, on the eve of the publication of crime figures showing a very substantial increase, he was also having to contend with the continuing decline in clear-up rates that we outlined in Chapter 2. He was reported as saying that too much attention was given to police performance in clearing up crime (*Guardian*, 26 June 1991). The emphasis on the clear-up rate created 'a grossly distorted picture' of what the police did and what the public wanted. The criminal statistics, he said, ignored the time spent on such aspects as incidents of nuisance, domestic disputes, traffic work, rescuing stray animals, street patrolling, giving directions to people and assisting lost children. He went on to announce that Her Majesty's Inspectorate of Constabulary would in future be publishing information on this previously unmeasured workload. Whatever their motives, politicians under pressure often say more interesting things than those who are not. In this instance, some fundamental issues are raised about the role of the police and how to measure their performance of it.

Useful for what?

One of our favourite seaside postcards features a man stooped over a pile of horse droppings in the street, about to shovel them into a bucket (a rare sight in contemporary Britain). A small boy looks on, with a puzzled expression on his face. 'Hey Mister', he shouts, 'what yer goin' to do with that?' 'Put it on my rhubarb when I get home', the man replies. 'Ugh', says the boy, 'we have custard on ours'. Products of any kind should be judged according to the purpose to which they might be put. Horse manure works wonders in the garden but not on the dinner table. So it is with crime data. Any data set will be more useful for some purposes than for others. Maguire (1994: 247) made this point well in relation to *Criminal Statistics*:

> Despite the caution with which they are now treated by criminologists and Home Office statisticians alike, and despite the increasingly high profile given in *Criminal Statistics* to comparative data from the British Crime Survey, these statistics remain the primary 'barometer of crime' used by politicians and highlighted by the media. They are also – a use to which they are much better suited – influential in the resource and strategic planning of the Home Office and police forces.

As Bottomley and Pease (1986: 169) say, virtually all official statistics are *records of decisions* (of which they are a very careful and detailed account) made in a variety of contexts, rather than *an attempt to represent* aspects of crimes and offenders. In order to understand or interpret such data, we need to appreciate that they are products of interactions in particular social and legal contexts: 'This is one of the reasons why comparative statistical studies, between jurisdictions or over extended periods of time, are bound to be such difficult exercises' (Bottomley and Pease, 1986: 169). Especially important is the way in which such data are regarded by those who have a role in producing them. Any measures that are seen as reflecting on the capacities and qualities of those involved present particular difficulties: 'those that are seen as "productivity measures", "success rates" and the like, require much more subtlety in their interpretation' (Bottomley and Pease, 1986: 169). The figures used to measure police performance, for example, are often not created independently but produced by the organization. They are not only social constructions but are also open to manipulation and disputes about interpretation. If we take the institutionalist perspective, official statistics become useful in a different way – as the object of enquiry in their own right, as a window through which we can come to appreciate a whole range of processes of discretion, law enforcement and criminal justice. It may be a window in which the glass is frosted, or the curtains at least partly drawn, but this is precisely why further investigation and research are necessary.

The power of numbers

This book has illustrated the various problems involved in trying to count crime and offenders by three major methods. Despite these problems, there is little doubt about 'the predominance of numbers as a descriptive medium' (Maguire, 1994: 236). This is true in politics, in the mass media, in policy-making circles and in the academic discipline of criminology. Although the early radical criminology of the 1970s (see, for example, Taylor et al., 1973) had little inclination to delve into the realms of quantitative data, the more recent 'left realists' are major exponents of the local crime survey. As Maguire (1994: 237) points out, even researchers who favour qualitative methods 'routinely produce quantitative data to reinforce and "legitimate" their findings'. Although we can 'ask whether "crime" (or any particular category of crime) is a phenomenon which can sensibly be described merely by adding up totals of diverse actions and incidents' (Maguire, 1994: 237), it is unlikely that things will change very much where concise and seemingly authoritative statements of the scale of a problem and our response to it are required. Having said this, there can be too many crime surveys, where these take precious time and funding away from more fundamental research. We have already noted the limitations of aggregate statistics which are produced without much regard for explanation and understanding. There is a need for careful detailed research studies, as well as a need to 'carry on counting'.

It is certainly true that considerable progress has been made in counting crime and offenders since the first half of the twentieth century (when only official statistics were available), or even since 20 years ago. Furthermore, this progress has not been restricted within local or national boundaries; despite the difficulties involved, international comparative work has been conducted. From a 'realist' perspective, many years spent desperately seeking the dark figure have brought results. In the USA and in Europe, for example, we now have regular victimization surveys, such as the BCS in Britain. Despite their limitations as measures of crime and offenders, considerable progress has been made in providing more and better information of various kinds in official statistics, and other developments along these lines seem to be round the corner. There also seems to be some prospect of systematic recurrent self-report surveys of high quality to enhance our knowledge of the prevalence and frequency of offending measured in this way. We would welcome this. We are already in a position to identify certain key patterns and trends in a way that was not possible in the past. Also needed, however, are those special research studies and theoretical work to provide us with more satisfying explanations for those patterns and trends. Other kinds of research and data are particularly important with those dark figures which appear largely to elude official statistics, victimization surveys and self-report studies, such as white-collar crime and domestic physical and sexual abuse.

A drift from aetiology?

Aetiology (the science of causation) is a term borrowed from medicine, as are a number of other terms which have been used in criminology and the sociology of deviance, such as epidemiology, prevalence and so forth. These terms seem to indicate the legacy of a clinical model, in which deviance and crime were seen as manifestations of something that was wrong with the individual and that offenders were suffering from something akin to a disease (the notion of individual pathology). Such notions are less common in the contemporary discipline of criminology, at least for the majority of offenders; this is surely due in part to the revelations of the studies that we have considered in this book. No longer is it possible to see most crime as the province of a group of clearly identifiable, 'defective' individuals. Offending is not only widespread but also seen to be committed, at least in small quantities, by individuals with a broad range of characteristics and backgrounds. Little wonder, then, that one response to the results of the early self-report studies was to suggest that, if most people had been involved in offending in some way, there was actually little to explain. Such a view was, of course, superficial, ignoring as it did the enormous variations in frequency and seriousness of offending which were sometimes obscured by the early studies.

Nevertheless, it is certainly true to say that the search for the 'causes of crime' had fallen from favour as the main focus of academic enquiry in the 1970s, in the British context. One reason for this was certainly that the critiques of official statistics and the self-report studies of the 1960s undermined the confidence of criminologists in their data. If official data were not to be trusted, self-report studies had their own problems and appeared to be throwing up findings which some found hard to believe. What, in the end, were the 'facts' to be explained? Without those, it was difficult to see the way forward. Secondly, the advent of the new theoretical perspectives in the 1960s brought with it the view that the old emphasis on aetiology and the measurement of crime was in any case misplaced. The labelling perspective, for instance, saw criminality as a status conferred upon individuals and groups by various audiences rather than a property inherent in individuals or their behaviour. It was the process of their criminalization that should be studied, rather than the rule breakers and the reasons for their behaviour. Both labelling and radical perspectives also forcefully made the point that the definition of crime itself was a political process, which reflected the structures of power and wealth of the wider society. To accept the definition of one's subject matter uncritically seemed to be a major error. Early radical criminology found it entirely unsurprising that poor people tended to hit out at a society in which the odds were stacked against them. To ask why was a bit like asking why Robin Hood gave the Sheriff of Nottingham such a hard time, or why people did not pay their poll tax; the answers were obvious. What was more worthy of investigation was the way in which societies which were founded on gross inequalities and exploitation defined crime and criminals in a way that reflected and reinforced those features, and in effect succeeded in blaming the downtrodden for the problems whose real origins lay elsewhere. Conventional forms of crime data and the focus upon aetiology, especially at the individual level, seemed to be part and parcel of a process of mystification which identified certain individuals as the problem, rather than the society and its political economy.

Further resistance to the emphasis on aetiology was to be found in those who argued for an *appreciative stance* towards deviance and crime. David Matza (1969), in an influential volume, argued that traditional perspectives had concentrated on aetiology to the exclusion of almost all else because of the *correctionalist viewpoint* that they adopted. The correctionalist stance involved an overriding concern with preventing, reducing or getting rid of the phenomenon under study. The discovery of causes of the behaviour in question was seen as a key to such a corrective enterprise. In Matza's view, this stance systematically interfered with the capacity to understand the phenomenon. This was a major defect in any attempt at a comprehensive sociology of deviance. Instead of viewing deviance as a form of *pathology* in need of *correction*, he argued, we should regard it as *diversity* that we should *appreciate*. Appreciation, a form of understanding without pre-judgement of what was studied, clearly did not not have much time for quantitative data; first-hand familiarity with the social worlds of those under study, qualitative methods (such as participant observation) and qualitative data were clearly the way forward.

Matza's position was only one example of a strongly anti-quantitative current which was present in the sociology of deviance at this time, which also had little time for the traditional aetiological quest. Such a quest had also, to some extent, discredited itself by the wilder excesses of the Lombrosian project and its failure to produce convincing returns after many years of effort. We therefore find a turning away from the aetiological quest in Britain, by sociologists towards such topics as reactions to deviance, and among criminologists, such as those at the Home Office, towards pragmatic concerns such as situational crime prevention. In the USA, however, the search for the causes of crime continued unabated. Here, a great deal of time, money and effort was expended in testing theories of delinquency and crime, often using self-report measures. Here we find the evidence tending to support such approaches as control theory, often in combination with elements from other perspectives (see, for example, Elliott *et al.*, 1985).

Back to aetiology?

We are not suggesting that aetiological research disappeared completely in Britain during the 1970s. Clearly, for a number of researchers, it was business as usual – see, for example, Farrington (1994) on human development and criminal careers. We are merely suggesting a trend or current away from that enterprise at that time, especially among sociologists. There is, however, evidence to suggest that interest in this topic has been returning over recent years. Two examples may serve to illustrate.

First, there is the work from the Home Office Research Unit on rational choice theories of crime. The earlier work on situational crime prevention had ultimately proved to be limited because it could not, on its own, deal with the problem of displacement (the possibility that situational measures would merely displace much of the crime from the area in which measures had been instituted to other places, other times, or other forms of crime). Because it was not concerned with offenders, but only with offences and the situations in which they occur, a situational perspective alone could not say how offenders would behave when confronted with preventive measures. Rational choice theories try to fill this gap by looking at the way in which offenders make decisions about offending in particular situations, and in relation to particular types of crime. They therefore mark a return to collecting data about and from *offenders*, as well as about offences. Such perspectives are valuable in that they take seriously the need to understand some aspects of the point of view of the actor. They do not, however, generally look beyond those decision-making processes to the wider contexts in which they and the actors are located, perhaps because they are primarily interested in that knowledge which might lead to immediate situational policy measures for *controlling* crime.

Second, there is the highly influential work of the left realist school. Jock Young and his colleagues have urged a return to aetiology (see, for example, Young, 1986). Young (1994: 74) also argues that in many countries since the Second World War (and in their criminologies), there has been an '[a]etiological crisis' – owing to 'the existence of rising affluence and welfarism concomitant with increased crime and delinquency'. For Young, the coexistence of these two developments constituted the major puzzle and challenge for those countries which experienced them and for their criminologists. 'Social democratic positivism' (Young, 1994: 72), the 'consensus' of opinion 'that one of the major causes of crime was impoverished social conditions', was apparently completely foxed by this coexistence, and '[t]he subsequent development of criminology is an attempt to come to terms with the crisis' (Young, 1994: 78). We are told how four major schools of contemporary criminology dealt with this crisis. One variety of radical criminology ('left idealism') and the new administrative criminology of the Home Office denied its existence; only right realism (Wilson and Herrnstein, 1985), and his own left realism were perceptive enough to recognize it and provide explanations.

Not everyone subscribed to the consensus in the earlier period referred to by Young. J. B. Mays (1963; 1967), one of the authors quoted by Young to illustrate the sense of puzzlement about what was going on, had no problems in understanding the way in which improving social and economic conditions could be accompanied by rising crime; in fact, he spends a whole chapter on this very issue. In this, he draws heavily on a perspective that was explicitly designed to deal with this sort of question, and was part of the conventional sociological wisdom of its day – Merton's (1957) theory of anomie. Similarly, despite the many merits of Young's account in helping us to understand broad developments in thinking about crime, it is a little too sweeping to suggest that whole swathes of criminologists were engaged in the 'great denial' in the later 1960s and the 1970s: a denial which 'had many facets, all of which had in common the denial that crime or criminality had "really" risen' (Young, 1994: 78). In our view, the picture is more complex. Many of those who had been influenced by the intellectual ferment of that period, including the critiques of official statistics, had certainly been left unsure about what those statistics could tell us about trends in crime, and had turned to other sorts of research questions that they believed would be more rewarding. One result of this was indeed the 'loss of aetiology' (Young, 1986: 19) that we have discussed. With hindsight, a different theoretical and political agenda, and informed by alternative sources of data unavailable at the time (such as a number of sweeps of the BCS), it is easy to represent those in the past as missing the 'obvious'.

The return to aetiology urged by the left realists is very welcome, for we need more research to provide explanations for trends and patterns in crime data. Their emphasis is on 'relative deprivation in certain conditions as being the major source of crime: that is, when people experience a level of unfairness in their allocation of resources and turn to individualistic means to attempt to right this condition' (Young, 1994: 108). It will be interesting to see how this idea (which is by no means a new one in sociology and criminology) fares in the light of research. The left realists appear to have been preoccupied with other aspects of their agenda and have done no empirical work on this as yet. In addition, despite the stimulating and important work so far, it is certainly true to say that left realism has in practice largely failed to engage in the analysis of such areas as corporate crime, and that some modification of its approach and field of interest is required in order for it to do so (Pearce and Tombs, 1992). Such observations seem to lend some weight to the view that the approach has tended in practice to concentrate on 'conventional' or 'ordinary' crime. We can talk. This book has been mainly concerned with forms of crime data which shed light on a particular 'crime problem'. As we have suggested, other sorts of data, such as those involving offences often dealt with by other regulatory bodies (for instance, in the areas of pollution and environmental health, trading standards, advertising, health and safety at work, taxation) will yield a rather different picture (Box, 1983). Not all of these offences are necessarily defined or treated as crimes by the criminal law, but this does not mean that the very definition of crime cannot be contested.

In the quest to understand crime data, a range of perspectives should be employed. Explanations of patterns and trends, once established by careful and critical use of the different kinds of available data, can take place at a number of different levels. No doubt something can be learned from the insights produced by the work in such perspectives as rational choice, situational and control theory. But a wider perspective is also required which will relate people's experiences to the structural contexts in which they are located, as the left realists and others have argued. Ultimately, in order to provide that broader picture, we need a political economy of crime (see, for example, Taylor, 1994). For example, we in Britain need to understand the impact on crime of a number of years of policies which have stressed the need for free markets, self-help and rolling back the state, in order to generate enterprise; we need to understand the impact of very high unemployment and an increasingly unequal distribution of income and wealth. We feel that these conditions have created the ideal environment for the growth of certain enterprises not quoted on the Stock Exchange. Such developments as the growth of trafficking in controlled drugs also need a global perspective in order to be fully understood. Ultimately we come back to aspects of whole societies or significant groups within them. For example, some criminologists have found Merton's (1957) theory of anomie worth developing if used for one of its original (and often neglected) purposes – to understand some of the more robust and dramatic differences between societies in their rates of serious crime (Rosenfeld and Messner, 1995). Such structural frameworks are also needed to understand the growth of crime in Britain and many other countries over recent decades. Although it may be helpful to regard many offenders as making 'rational choices', they do so in broad circumstances that are not of their own choosing.

A final word

In the first chapter of this book we outlined three perspectives on crime statistics: realist (not to be confused with 'left realism'), institutionalist and radical. We indicated at the end of that chapter that our own position was rather closer to the last two than to the first. However, much of this book has been framed in terms of the basic realist questions, about the extent to which crime data can tell us about the nature, extent and distribution of crime. Such a perspective has always been dominant in the world of politics, the mass media and citizens. It has also been the dominant perspective among criminologists. A failure to give a systematic appreciation of it would be a major defect in a book of this kind. The literal meaning of the term 'data' is 'things that are given'. We hope we have said enough in this book to indicate that the data we have discussed should never be accepted as given, but are products, socially constructed, often reflecting the dimension of power. The three positions are in any case not necessarily irreconcilable: realist analyses, if open-minded enough, can learn much from the questions asked by the other two perspectives.

Summary

Data from official statistics, self-report studies and victimization surveys need to be complemented by special research studies, including those which offer the distinctive contribution of more qualitative approaches and data on those sorts of offences and offenders which are not well served by any of these three sources. A knowledge of crime data teaches us not to take the claims of politicians about law and order at face value. Assessments of the 'usefulness' of such data need to take into account the circumstances under which they were produced and the purposes for which they might be used. Aggregate statistics remain the favoured medium for talking about 'the crime problem', and some progress has been made in identifying broad patterns and trends. The explanation of such patterns and trends was somewhat neglected in Britain for a number of years, but now seems to be firmly on the agenda. A broadly based approach to this task is advocated, which may include societal and global analysis. Finally, it is concluded that realist, institutionalist and radical perspectives all have contributions to make to our understanding of crime data.

Further reading

Attention should be given to those research studies and other types of crime data which have not been systematically surveyed in this text. *The Oxford Handbook of Criminology* (Maguire *et al.*, 1994) is perhaps the place to start. The chapter by Nelken (1994) on white-collar crime could be read as an example of an area that has been neglected in the forms of data which have been the focus of this book. The chapter by Young (1994) on 'current paradigms in criminology' is recommended as one view of recent theoretical developments and emphases in the discipline. The chapter by Taylor (1994) illustrates what is meant by the 'political economy of crime'. All the chapters in *The Oxford Handbook* have extensive bibliographies and suggestions for further reading.

Glossary

(Terms that are cross-referenced within the glossary appear in italics.)

Administrative criminology   A term often used to describe that criminology in which the main concern is with policy-relevant research aimed at controlling and reducing crime and improving the effectiveness of the criminal justice system.

Aetiology   A term from medicine which refers to the causes (or our knowledge about them) of a disease in an organism. It has been imported from there and used to refer to the causes of crime and deviance.

Age–crime curve   Produced by the different prevalence rates of offending at particular ages. In the case of official data, for example, it is a graph with a distinctive shape: a sharp rise to the *peak age of offending* followed by a gradual decline. It allows us to see which age groups are most involved in offending.

Annual prevalence rate   See *prevalence*.

Anomie   A key concept in Durkheim's (1952) analysis of suicide rates, subsequently adapted and developed in *Merton's anomie theory*.

Appreciative stance   A viewpoint advocated by Matza (1969) which stresses the importance of in-depth understanding of social phenomena without prejudgement of what is being studied, in contrast to the *correctionalist viewpoint*.

Asian   A term used to distinguish those people who appear to originate or descend from the Asian continent. Where people are self-classified by ethnic origin, as in *Prison Statistics* (since October 1992), Asian is used in the British context as a broad category to describe those who consider themselves to be of Indian, Pakistani or Bangladeshi descent, whether or not their birthplace was the UK (HOSB 21/94).

Black   A term used to describe or classify people in terms of a particular skin colour or ethnic origin. It can be used as a generic term to distinguish between those with *white* skin and those with non-white skin (black), or to classify skin colour into subgroups of *white*, black, *Asian* and 'other'. The latter classification was used, until October 1992, by the Home Office to describe the ethnic composition of the prison population. *Prison Statistics* has since adopted the classification used by the Census and many other research studies in which people are self-classified by ethnic origin. Here, black is used as a broad category to describe those who consider themselves to be of black African or Caribbean descent, whether or not their birthplace was the UK (HOSB 21/94).

Black market The illegal trade in goods or currencies, especially in violation of official controls or rationing.

'Booster' samples These consist of subgroups of the population being surveyed, such as minority ethnic groups and teenagers, who are of particular interest to the research. Their numbers are increased in the sample to allow for the separate analysis of data relating to them.

Bounding techniques Attempts to reduce *telescoping error* by providing boundaries to the period under investigation which will have more relevance to subjects than mere dates; for example, 'since last Christmas', 'since leaving school'.

Claimant count definition A narrow definition of the unemployed which is used to calculate the *unemployment rate*. It includes only those people who declare themselves to be available for work and actively seeking work in order to be eligible to claim certain social security benefits. It excludes, for example, those who are sick and many lone parents.

Class A concept used in the study of social stratification to refer to categories of people who share a common relationship to the system of production, distribution and exchange. In many research studies, measurement of it is based upon an individual's or family's socio-economic status or position. In Britain, class is often measured by using the Registrar-General's classification which groups individuals into classes according to their occupation.

Classification of offences The allocation of recorded offences to particular offence types by the police.

'Cleared-up' offences An offence is said to be cleared up if someone has been charged, summoned or cautioned for it, if the offence is admitted and 'taken into consideration' by the court, or if there is enough evidence to charge a person but the case is not proceeded with (for example, because the offender is below the age of criminal responsibility or is already serving a long custodial sentence, or the victim is unable to give evidence).

Clear-up rate A percentage figure expressing the proportion of crimes recorded by the police which can be described as *cleared-up offences*. Often referred to as the 'detection rate'.

Conflict theory A term used to describe certain perspectives which see society as being characterised by conflict rather than consensus, and such matters as the formulation and application of criminal law being much influenced by interests and the power structure of society (see, for example, Quinney, 1970).

Control theory A theory which sees people as becoming free to commit crime or delinquency as a result of the weakening of their social bonds to the conventional social order.

Corporate crime Offences committed by, or on behalf of, business corporations in the furtherance of their interests. Usually regarded as a type of *white-collar crime*. The term 'organizational crime' is sometimes used, in order to include offences relating to public as well as private organizations.

Correctionalist viewpoint A stance in the study of deviance and crime which has an overriding concern with preventing, managing, reducing, or getting rid of the phenomenon. The focus is normally upon such matters as *aetiology* or the effectiveness of different strategies and measures in achieving those objectives.

Cross-sectional design A research design in which all the data are collected at one particular point in time. Data can, of course, be collected on what happened in the past, but the validity of this is dependent on, for example, the memories of respondents.

'Cuffing'   The practice of deliberately not recording a crime as such by a police officer.

Cultural deviance theory   A theory which sees crime or deviance as resulting from a process of learning deviant norms and values.

Dark figure   The figure for unrecorded crime or undetected offenders, that is to say, those not included in official statistics. In this book the term is also used in a qualitative sense, to refer to our picture of the characteristics of those hidden crimes or offenders.

Delinquency   This normally refers to law violations (usually of juveniles), but sometimes used more loosely to refer to any kind of youthful misconduct. In the USA, 'status offences' are those acts which are offences only if committed by persons within a certain age category.

Deviancy amplification   A concept used in the attempt to show that many of the ways in which societies respond to deviance may have the effect of increasing rather than decreasing the amount of such behaviour.

Deviant behaviour   Behaviour which breaks the rules which are accepted or enforceable within any social grouping. Its coverage is therefore wider than that of crime.

Discovery of crime   Awareness or recognition that a crime has taken place, or is taking place, by the police or members of the public. For various reasons, such recognition is not always a straightforward matter.

Displacement   One possible outcome of *situational crime prevention* measures in which some crime is merely displaced to other places, times or other forms of crime, rather than being prevented.

Ecological fallacy   The erroneous assumption that statistical correlations emerging from aggregate data (for example, for areas) necessarily identify correlations at an individual level (for example, the characteristics of the individuals who commit crime).

'Education factor'   The observation that the education level of respondents is positively correlated with reported victimization, particularly from violent crime. A *response bias* which has important implications for victimization surveys.

Epidemiology   A term from medicine, referring to the study or knowledge of the extent, distribution and spread of diseases in a population. It has since been used in criminology and sociology to refer to the study of the extent and distribution of phenomena such as crime.

Epistemology   The philosophy of knowledge – its nature, how it is derived, tested and validated, and the limits to understanding. There are a number of different positions on such issues, which lead to differing conceptions of criminological knowledge.

Ethnographic research   Research which attempts to gain in-depth and detailed understanding of social settings and the lives of subjects, by methods such as *participant observation*.

Ethnomethodology   A sociological perspective which focuses upon the way in which people use practical reasoning, stocks of knowledge (often tacit), language and so forth to accomplish a whole range of activities, including the production of reports and official statistics.

Evaluation study   Research which aims to assess the effectiveness or impact of some policy or change, such as *target hardening*.

Ever variety measures   Measures sometimes used in self-report delinquency studies to ascertain the range of different types of offence ever engaged in by respondents. 'Last year variety measures' measure the range over the last year.

Experimental research   This research method seeks to mirror the approach adopted by some of the natural sciences. The aim is to infer causation by isolating the effect of the variable under investigation by holding other confounding variables constant. There are, however, practical and ethical problems concerning the use of human subjects in an experimental setting (see Kelman, 1978).

Feminist criminology   A term loosely used to describe those studies conducted from a broadly feminist viewpoint which have sought to correct the neglect of the topic of women and crime, criticize those who have studied it in unsatisfactory ways, and do research on women as offenders and victims which does not distort or marginalize their experiences.

Folk devil   A category or group of persons, or a particular individual, who come(s) to represent evil or the embodiment of a particular problem. The portrayal of such a person or group is seen as involving elements of stereotyping and scapegoating.

Frequency   The number of offences or convictions within a period of time. A frequency rate (often referred to as the general offending rate) is obtained by dividing the number of offences by the number of persons in the group in question, or by expressing the rate in terms of offences per 100,000 persons, for example.

'Gate arrests'   A term used by police officers to refer to arrests which may be made of persons on release from prison for offences for which they have not already been processed.

General offending rate   See *frequency*.

Governmental project   The long tradition of investigations, by the state and others, which has attempted to improve the workings of criminal justice and the overall governance of the population by monitoring crime patterns, policing, courts and prisons.

Incidence   In medicine, this term refers to the number or rate of appearance of new cases of a disease in a population within a specified period of time. Although sometimes used in a similar way in criminology, it is usually used more loosely to refer to aspects of the *frequency* of offending (or victimizations) over time.

Index crimes   Part of the *Uniform Crime Reports* comprising the eight 'most serious' crimes which are defined and recorded in a consistent manner throughout the USA in order to provide a basis for comparisons over time and between areas.

Indictable offences   Offences that are tried at the Crown Court, although initial proceedings usually take place at magistrates courts.

Individual pathology   A concept suggesting that deviance and crime can be understood in terms of there being something wrong with the individual, such as a defective biological or psychological make-up.

Institutionalist perspective   A viewpoint stressing that official crime statistics are socially constructed, the products of a range of social and organizational processes and interactions, and should be studied as such, rather than used as measures of crime and offenders.

'Known' offenders   A term used to describe offenders who have been found guilty or cautioned for offences.

Labelling perspective   A sociological approach to the study of deviance which focuses upon the definition of deviance, social reactions to it, and their consequences.

It is therefore concerned with the origins of labels, their application, and their effects.

Last year variety measures   See *ever variety measures*.

Left idealism   A term used by *left realists* to refer to those criminologies of the left, heavily influenced by the *labelling perspective*, which are seen to focus to an excessive extent on the role of the state and its agencies in the study of crime. The result is seen as a romanticized, unrealistic view of much crime and of many offenders, together with a lack of attention to those causes of crime and its growth which are located in the structural positions of individuals.

Left realists   A group of criminologists emerging in Britain in the 1980s with a social democratic political orientation (see, for example, Young, 1986; 1992; 1994).They claim to be 'realistic' about crime (to take it, and people's fears of it, seriously), and have been involved in a number of local crime surveys in collaboration with local authorities. Compare *left idealism*.

Life histories   Research studies in which detailed information is collected from and about individuals (often only one) with the major focus on their lives and experiences, and how those persons interpret these.

Local surveys   Small-scale victimization surveys which focus upon a particular area or subgroup of the population, such as inner cities or minority ethnic groups. They are concerned less with trends over time or comparisons to official statistics, being more interested in specific problems and experiences.

Lombrosian project   The attempt to develop a scientific theory of crime and criminals, based on the assumption that criminals can be distinguished from non-criminals, for example in terms of their physical or psychological characteristics.

Longitudinal design or study   A research design in which, for example, the same group of individuals is followed through their development over time, enabling the collection of data at a number of stages. Also referred to as a 'cohort study'.

Male to female ratio   The number of male offenders to every one female offender. It is used to demonstrate the relative contributions made by males and females to offending.

Measurement error   Non-sampling errors which are introduced into survey data by factors such as memory decay and *telescoping*. Often, owing to *response bias*, measurement errors are not randomly distributed and under these circumstances they have an important bearing on the validity of survey data.

Merton's anomie theory   A very influential theoretical framework designed to account for variations in rates of *deviant behaviour*. For Merton (1957), a society which stresses money success for all, but without a corresponding stress on legitimate avenues for achieving it, can expect chronic anomie (an erosion or breakdown in accepted norms for conduct). This will manifest itself in high rates of deviant behaviour, especially among those in the lower social strata, who have limited access to legitimate opportunity structures. The theory is often classified as one of the main *strain theories* of crime.

Moral panic   A concept which suggests that the social response to some social problem, condition or episode is in some way over-hasty, ill judged or out of proportion to the threat or scale of the problem. Some of the problems involved in the use of the concept are examined in Waddington (1986).

Moral statisticians   A group of statisticians of the nineteenth century who attempted to apply methods and quantitative techniques which had mostly been developed in the natural sciences to 'moral' (or social) phenomena.

Mugging   The term in popular use to describe the offence of 'street robbery of personal property' (robbery is defined by *Criminal Statistics* as the use or threat of force to a person immediately before or at the time of a theft). Mugging has been a contentious topic since the 1970s, when there was a suggestion that there was a *moral panic* about it and a connection made with *black* youth (see Hall *et al.*, 1978; Lea and Young, 1993).

Multiple victimization   Also referred to as 'repeat victimization'. This occurs when many incidents of victimization are experienced by the same individual or household over a relatively short period of time, as when a household is repeatedly burgled. Surveys may produce an under-estimation of this type of victimization as there is often an upper limit placed on the number of incidents which each respondent may recall. The term 'multiple victimization' is often used to include those types of victimizations which can be viewed as a process, being a recurrent part of life for some victims, such as domestic violence and sexual abuse, rather than the type of discrete events counted by victimization surveys. These are also likely to be under-estimated in survey data as respondents may fail to recall any such incidents, not recognizing them as the type of event being asked for by the survey interviewer. The term 'serial victimization' is sometimes used to distinguish this second type of multiple victimization.

National Crime Survey (NCS)   The US equivalent of the British Crime Survey. The NCS was the first national victimization survey to be established.

National surveys   Large-scale victimization surveys which aim to produce data that are representative of an entire country, such as BCS and *National Crime Survey*. Such surveys are designed to facilitate comparisons with the official statistics of recorded crime. They are generally repeated at regular intervals in order to reveal trends in crime and in reporting and recording behaviour.

'No crimes'   Incidents initially recorded as crimes but which, upon further investigation and according to rules laid down by the Home Office, are 'written off' in the statistical returns made by police forces.

Non-respondents   Those individuals who are selected for a sample but not interviewed for the survey owing to refusal to take part or being uncontactable. As a group, non-respondents are important because they may have different characteristics and experiences from the actual respondents.

'Non-stranger' crimes   Those offences where there is an existing relationship between the offender and the victim. These types of offences (such as domestic violence and some sexual offences) are likely to be under-estimated in both official and survey data owing to the reluctance of the victim to report or reveal the incident.

Notifiable offences   Those offences for which police forces are required to produce statistical returns for the Home Office, which then form the raw material for publication in *Criminal Statistics*. They are mostly *indictable* and *'triable either way' offences*.

Offence mix   The mixture of different offence types, the composition of which may vary between areas and create different problems for policing within them.

'Offences against morale'   These were introduced during the Second World War to guard against the public becoming demoralized; for example, publishing statements relating to the war which were 'likely to cause alarm and despondency' (Smithies, 1982: 7).

Offenders Index   A large data base kept by the Home Office which details the criminal records of all those convicted of a *standard list offence* in England and Wales between 1963 and the present. It excludes cautions.

Official statistics   Statistical data which are compiled by official agencies, such as the police and courts, often for publication on the authority of the state.

Panel effect   Effects on data which are due to the repeated collection of such data from the same respondents over a period of time, for instance, a decline in the quantity of information forthcoming owing to decreasing enthusiasm of respondents.

Participant observation   A research method in which the researcher overtly or covertly collects observational data while participating in the setting or lives of those being studied.

Peak age of offending   The age in any population with the highest *prevalence rate* of offenders. For example, the peak age of known offending for males is currently 18 years, which means that there are more offenders aged 18 per 100,000 of the population than there are of any other age.

Personal consumption   The average amount spent per person in a year. Used as an indicator of a country's economic prosperity.

Positivism, positivist   Terms which are generally taken to refer to the position that the assumptions and methods of the natural sciences are an appropriate model for the social sciences. They raise issues about what those assumptions and methods are (for these are often more varied in the natural sciences than users of the term seem to allow), but also about the implications of the differences in subject matter between the two areas of enquiry. They have come to be used as terms of criticism and in so many ways in practice that they are often a source of confusion.

Postcode Address File (PAF)   The preferred *sampling frame* for British victimization surveys. It is used in preference to the electoral register as it has the advantage of being constantly updated and suffers from fewer omissions.

Predictive validity   The ability of a measure (such as self-reported delinquency) to predict a seemingly related event (such as official convictions) at a later date.

Prevalence   Measure of the number, or percentage (prevalence rate) of a population who have ever committed a certain act or been convicted of an offence ('ever', or cumulative prevalence), or who have done so within a specified time period (for example, if the period is one year, the measure is called 'year prevalence' or annual prevalence rate). The term is also used to refer to the estimated number or proportion of a population who have been a victim, once or more, of an offence (the prevalence of victimization).

Primary and secondary clear-ups   In the past, primary clear-ups referred to those achieved by charge, summons or caution, and secondary clear-ups those achieved by other methods. More recently, the Audit Commission has adopted a slightly different distinction, in which secondary clear-ups include only those offences 'taken into consideration' which have not previously been recorded by the police and 'those which involve attributing an offence to someone already charged or convicted of another offence' (HOSB 5/95: 24).

Principal offence rule   In the statistics about offenders in *Criminal Statistics*, only one offence is shown, generally that for which the most serious penalty has been or could be given.

'Prison write-offs'   Offences cleared up by an admission by someone already serving a custodial sentence for another offence.

Professional crime   There is some disagreement as to the exact nature of professional crime, but it can be loosely characterized by a degree of specialization and skill, economic motives, the organized nature of the activities and the relatively long duration and intensity of the professional criminal's career.

Qualitative methods and data   Methods and data in which the outcome is not primarily statistical in form, but which gives priority to qualitative description and understanding, using such methods as *participant observation* and *life histories.*

Race   A group or category of persons connected by common descent. It is a term commonly used when making comparisons of such matters as the behaviour and treatment of three broad groups: *black, Asian* and *white.* There is some controversy over the use of this term as it 'reflects the particular historical, political and economic circumstances which effectively "racialise" particular groups by attaching racial labels to them' (Fitzgerald 1993b: 54).

Radical criminology   Criminology which is committed to fundamental change in the discipline, the way we treat crime, and the wider society. That which emerged in the 1970s was much influenced by the *labelling perspective* and Marxism. See also *left idealism* and *left realism.*

Radical perspective on crime statistics   This stresses that the organizational processes and everyday interactions which lead to such statistics (see *institutionalist perspective*) are affected by wider social structural arrangements. Definitions of crime and their application may therefore be structured by such elements as class and power. Patterns of offending may also be regarded as in some way a response to such arrangements.

Rational choice perspectives   Perspectives on offending which focus upon the choices people make in different situations of opportunity and in relation to particular types of crime.

Realist perspective on crime statistics   A term coined by Biderman and Reiss (1967: 2) to refer to that approach which is concerned with the extent to which such data represent 'the real crime that takes place'. It therefore focuses upon such matters as their accuracy, reliability and completeness as a measure of crime. From this viewpoint, *self-report* and *victimization studies* can be seen as ways of making our knowledge of the extent and nature of crime more complete.

Recording of crime   The act of making a record of an incident as a crime by the police in the records kept by them, after an initial examination to see whether prima-facie evidence exists that a crime has been committed.

Reference period   In asking research respondents to recall past events, this is the period of time specified for which they are asked to do so, for instance a one-year period in a victimization survey.

Registrar-General's Classification   See *class.*

Relative deprivation   A term used by *left realists* to refer to the situation in which 'people experience a level of unfairness in their allocation of resources' (Young, 1994: 108). More extensive discussions of the concept and the various ways it has been used can be found in some of the literature on social inequality and poverty, for example, Runciman (1972) and Townsend (1979).

Reliability   Extent to which a research measuring instrument (such as a self-report questionnaire) produces identical scores when used to make a number of measurements of the same object.

Reporting of crime   The act of informing the police that a crime has taken or is taking place.

Response bias Non-random *measurement errors* caused by the tendency for certain types of respondent to answer certain survey questions in a particular way. This can produce a systematic under- or over-estimation of certain items in the data.

Reverse record check Check for the *validity* of a measure (such as self-reported delinquency) by comparing its results against past records (for example, official data) of the same or related events.

Right realism A term used by *left realists* to describe the work of American writers, Wilson and Herrnstein (1985), who take seriously the increase in crime over recent decades and the need to explain it. Their perspective is seen to come from the right of the political spectrum, stressing such matters as individual differences, the socialization process, and the rewards and punishments associated with crime, in its explanation.

Sampling error The term used to describe differences between the estimates produced by a sample and the statistics which would result from a survey of the whole population. Sampling error presents particular problems for *local surveys* using relatively small samples, and for all *victimization surveys* attempting to capture rare incidents, such as robbery.

Sampling frame A 'list' of all members of the population being surveyed from which a sample can be drawn; for example, the electoral register and the *Postcode Address File*.

Secondary clear-ups See under *primary and secondary clear-ups*.

Self-report study A method used to investigate crime or other rule-breaking behaviour by asking people directly about their involvement as the perpetrators of such behaviour.

Sex In Chapter 5 this term is used in preference to gender because we are discussing differences between male and female offenders in line with the practice in *Criminal Statistics*.

Situational crime prevention Policies attempting to reduce crime by changes in features of the situations in which it is likely to occur, for instance improved locks and bolts, and changes in environmental design.

Social disorganization A term used by the Chicago School of urban sociology to refer to an absence of stable or common standards in behaviour and culture in an area and a breakdown in community institutions, leading to ineffective socialization of children and poor social control.

Standard list offences Offences for which records are kept in the *Offenders Index*. They include all *indictable* and *'triable either way' offences*, together with a number of the more serious *summary offences*.

Strain theory A theory which views deviance or crime as being rooted in frustrations, contradictions and other problems confronting individuals or groups. *Merton's anomie theory* is often cited as a sociological strain theory.

Summary offences Offences which, if they get to the stage of court proceedings, are tried at a magistrates court. Many are, however, motoring offences, for which fixed-penalty proceedings may often be employed instead (as in the case of parking fines).

Target hardening A type of *situational crime prevention* measure, for instance the fitting of improved locks and bolts.

Telescoping error Inaccurate placing of incidents inside or outside the period specified in research studies of past events, such as crimes.

Test–retest procedure Test for *reliability* in which a research instrument or measure is administered to a group of subjects and then administered at a later time to the same group. The two sets of results are then compared to see how closely they correspond. The closer the correspondence, the more reliable the measure is usually thought to be.

TICs Additional offences which are admitted by a defendant and 'taken into consideration' by the court when sentencing.

'Triable either way' offences Offences which may be tried either at a magistrates court or at the Crown Court.

Triangulation The use of more than one method or sort of data in investigating a research problem, thereby attempting to counter the weaknesses of any one with the strengths of another.

Underclass A term first coined by Myrdal (1962) in the USA to describe those members of society who have been economically marginalized. The term is used in Britain in two different ways: those at the bottom of the social structure who suffer from a type of poverty which is usually long-term and characterized by dependence on welfare benefits and exclusion from full participation in society, or a subgroup of the poor who are seen as 'undeserving' and alienated from society. According to Gardiner (1995: 372), the use of the term has 'become widespread and diverse without foundation in rigorous empirical evidence, [and] the use of such a term beyond a popular metaphor is limited'.

Unemployment rate A measure of the level of unemployment in any population, which can be calculated in a number of different ways. In the UK the 'official' unemployment rate is calculated using the *claimant count definition* which produces an under-estimation of the number of people of working age who are without work.

Uniform Crime Reports (UCR) The US equivalent of *Criminal Statistics*, compiled by the Federal Bureau of Investigation (FBI). They contain reports of all major crimes recorded by the police.

Validity A term with a range of uses, but in this book used to refer to the extent to which research instruments and data are actually measuring what they were intended to measure or are thought to measure.

Victimization survey or study A method used to investigate crime by asking samples of the general public to recall crimes committed against them during a recent period.

Victimless crimes Those offences where there is no obvious or actual victim in the usual sense of the word, as in the case of drug offences, prostitution and consensual sexual acts (see Schur, 1965).

Victimology The study of crime from the perspective of the victim rather than the offender.

White A term used to describe or classify people in terms of their skin colour or broad ethnic origin. It can be used as a generic term to distinguish between those with white skin and those with non-white skin or as one of a number of subgroups; for example, the police record the skin colour/ethnic appearance of all persons subject to stop and search procedures using a number of categories, one of which is 'white'. Where people are self-classified by ethnic origin, as in *Prison Statistics* (since October 1992), white is used as a category to describe those who consider themselves to be of European descent, whatever their birthplace or nationality (HOSB 21/94).

White-collar crime 'Crimes committed by persons of respectability and high social status in the course of their occupations' (Sutherland and Cressey, 1960: 40). For details of the problems with the concept and more recent studies, see Nelken (1994). See also *corporate crime*.

References

Adler, F. and Laufer, W. S. (eds) (1995) *The Legacy of Anomie Theory*. New Brunswick, NJ: Transaction Publishers.

Akers, R. L. (1964) 'Socio-economic status and delinquent behaviour', *Journal of Research in Crime and Delinquency*, 1: 38–46.

Anderson, S., Grove Smith, C., Kinsey, R. and Wood J. (1990) *The Edinburgh Crime Survey*. Edinburgh: Scottish Office.

Anderson, S., Kinsey, R., Loader, I. and Smith, C. (1991) *Cautionary Tales: A Study of Young People and Crime in Edinburgh*. Edinburgh: Centre for Criminology, University of Edinburgh.

Ashworth, A. (1992) *Sentencing and Criminal Justice*. London: Weidenfeld and Nicolson.

Atkinson, M. (1978) *Discovering Suicide*. London: Macmillan.

Aubert, W. (1952) 'White collar crime and social structure', *American Journal of Sociology*, 58: 263–71.

Aye Maung, N. and Mirrlees-Black, C. (1994) *Racially Motivated Crime: A British Crime Survey Analysis*, Research and Planning Unit Paper No. 82. London: HMSO.

Barclay, G. (ed.) (1995a) *Digest 3: Information on the Criminal Justice System in England and Wales*. London: Home Office Research and Statistics Department.

Barclay, G. (1995b) *The Criminal Justice System in England and Wales*, 3rd edn. London: Home Office.

Beirne, P. (1993) *Inventing Criminology: The Rise of 'Homo Criminalis'*. Albany, NY: State University of New York Press.

Belson, W.A. (1975) *Juvenile Theft: The Causal Factors*. London: Harper and Row.

Bennett, T. (1979) 'The social distribution of criminal labels', *British Journal of Criminology*, 19: 134–45.

Bennett, T. (1988) 'An assessment of the design, implementation and effectiveness of neighbourhood watch in London', *The Howard Journal*, 27: 241–55.

Berger, A. S. and Simon, W. (1974) 'Black families and the Moynihan report: a research evaluation', *Social Problems*, 22: 145–61.

Biderman, A. D. and Reiss, A. J. (1967) 'On exploring the "dark figure" of crime', *Annals of the American Academy of Political and Social Science*, 374: 1–15.

Black, D. (1970) 'The production of crime rates', *American Sociological Review*, 35: 733–48.

Block, C. R. and Block, R. (1984) 'Crime definition, crime measurement and victim surveys', *Journal of Social Issues*, 40: 137–60.

Block, R. and Block, C. R. (1980) 'Decisions and data: the transformation of robbery incidents into official robbery statistics', *Journal of Criminal Law and Criminology*, 71: 622–36.

Bottomley, A. K. (1979) *Criminology in Focus*. Oxford: Martin Robertson.

Bottomley, A. K. and Coleman, C. A. (1976) 'Criminal statistics: the police role in the discovery and detection of crime', *International Journal of Criminology and Penology*, 4: 33–58.

Bottomley, K. and Coleman, C. (1981) *Understanding Crime Rates*. Farnborough: Gower.

Bottomley, K. and Coleman, C. (1995) 'The police', in M. A. Walker (ed.) *Interpreting Crime Statistics*. Oxford: Clarendon Press.

Bottomley, K. and Pease, K. (1986) *Crime and Punishment: Interpreting the Data*. Milton Keynes: Open University Press.

Bottoms, A. E. (1994) 'Environmental criminology', in M. Maguire, R. Morgan and R. Reiner (eds) *The Oxford Handbook of Criminology*. Oxford: Clarendon.

Bottoms, A. E. and McClean, J. D. (1976) *Defendants in the Criminal Process*. London: Routledge & Kegan Paul.

Bowling, B. (1990) 'Conceptual and methodological problems in measuring "race" differences in delinquency', *British Journal of Criminology*, 30: 483–92.

Bowling, B. (1993) 'Racial harassment and the process of victimization', *British Journal of Criminology*, 33: 231–50.

Bowling, B., Graham, J. and Ross, A. (1994) 'Self-reported offending among young people in England and Wales', in J. Junger-Tas, G. J. Terlouw and M. Klein (eds) *Delinquent Behaviour among Young People in the Western World*. Amsterdam: Kugler.

Box, S. (1971) *Deviance, Reality and Society*. London: Holt, Rinehart and Winston.

Box, S. (1981) *Deviance, Reality and Society*, 2nd edn. London: Holt, Rinehart and Winston.

Box, S. (1983) *Power, Crime and Mystification*. London: Tavistock.

Box, S. (1987) *Recession, Crime and Punishment*. London: Macmillan.

Box, S. and Ford, J. (1971) 'The facts don't fit: on the relationship between social class and criminal behaviour', *Sociological Review*, 19: 31–52.

Braithwaite, J. (1981) 'The myth of social class and criminality reconsidered', *American Sociological Review*, 46: 36–57.

Brake, M. and Hale, C. (1992) *Public Order and Private Lives: The Politics of Law and Order*. London: Routledge.

Brody, S. and Tarling, R. (1980) *Taking Offenders out of Circulation*, Home Office Research Study No. 64. London: HMSO.

Brown, I. and Hullin, R. (1992) 'A study of sentencing in the Leeds magistrates courts: the treatment of ethnic minority and white offenders', *British Journal of Criminology*, 32: 41–53.

Burrows, J. and Tarling, R. (1982) *Clearing Up Crime*, Home Office Research Study No. 73. London: HMSO.

Campbell, A. (1986) 'Self-report of fighting by females', *British Journal of Criminology*, 26: 28–46.

Cantor, D. and Land, K. C. (1985) 'Unemployment and crime-rates in the post-World War II United States: a theoretical and empirical analysis', *American Sociological Review*, 50: 317–32.

Carr-Hill, R. and Drew, D. (1988) 'Blacks, police and crime', in A. Bhat, R. Carr-Hill and S. Ohri (eds) *Britain's Black Population*. Aldershot: Gower.

Carr-Hill, R. and Stern, N. (1979) *Crime, the Police and Criminal Statistics*. London: Academic Press.

Carson, W. G. and Martin, B. (1974) *The Factory Acts*. London: Martin Robertson.

Carson, W. G. and Wiles, P. (eds) (1971) *The Sociology of Crime and Delinquency in Britain*. London: Martin Robertson.

Cernkovich, S. A. and Giordano, P. C. (1979) 'A comparative analysis of male and female delinquency', *Sociological Quarterly*, 20: 131–45.

Cernkovich, S. A., Giordano, P. C. and Pugh, M. D. (1985) 'Chronic offenders: the missing cases in self-report delinquency research', *Journal of Criminal Law and Criminology*, 76: 705–32.

Chambliss, W. J. (ed.) (1969) *Crime and the Legal Process*. New York: McGraw-Hill.

Chambliss, W. J. and Nagasawa, R. H. (1969) 'On the validity of official statistics: a comparison of white, black and Japanese high school boys', *Journal of Research in Crime and Delinquency*, 6: 71–7.

Chiricos, T. G. (1987) 'Rates of crime and unemployment: an analysis of aggregate research evidence', *Social Problems*, 34: 187–212.

Christie, N., Andenaes, J. and Skirbekk, K. (1965) 'A study of self-reported crime', in K. O. Christiansen (ed.) *Scandinavian Studies in Criminology*. London: Tavistock.

Cicourel, A. V. (1976) *The Social Organisation of Juvenile Justice*. London: Heinemann.

Clark, J. and Wenninger, E. (1962) 'Socio-economic class and area as correlates of illegal behaviour among juveniles', *American Sociological Review*, 27: 826–34.

Clark, J. P. and Tifft, L. L. (1966) 'Polygraph and interview validation of self-reported behaviour', *American Sociological Review*, 31: 516–23.

Clarke, R. V. G. (1980) 'Situational crime prevention: theory and practice', *British Journal of Criminology*, 20: 136–47.

Clarke, R. V. and Cornish, D. B. (1985) 'Modelling offenders' decisions: a framework for research and policy', in M. Tonry and N. Morris (eds) *Crime and Justice*, Vol. 6. Chicago: University of Chicago Press.

Clelland, D. and Carter, T. J. (1980) 'The new myth of class and crime', *Criminology*, 18: 319–336.

Cloward, R. and Ohlin, L. (1960) *Delinquency and Opportunity*. New York: Free Press.

Cohen, A. K. (1955) *Delinquent Boys*. New York: Free Press.

Cohen, S. (1973) *Folk Devils and Moral Panics: The Creation of the Mods and Rockers*. London: Paladin.

Cohen, S. (1980) *Folk Devils and Moral Panics: The Creation of the Mods and Rockers*, 2nd edn. Oxford: Basil Blackwell.

Cohen, S. (1981) 'Footprints in the sand: a further report on criminology and the sociology of deviance in Britain', in M. Fitzgerald, G. McLennan and J. Pawson (eds) *Crime and Society*. London: Routledge & Kegan Paul.

Cohen, S. (1985) *Visions of Social Control*. Oxford: Polity Press.

Commission for Racial Equality (1992) *Juvenile Cautioning: Ethnic Monitoring in Practice*. London: CRE.

Cook, D. (1989) *Rich Law, Poor Law: Differential Responses to Tax and Supplementary Benefit Fraud*. Milton Keynes: Open University Press.

Cornish, D. B. and Clarke, R. V. G. (eds) (1986) *The Reasoning Criminal*. New York: Springer-Verlag.

Crawford, A., Jones, T., Woodhouse, T. and Young, J. (1990) *The Second Islington Crime Survey*. London: Centre for Criminology, Middlesex Polytechnic.

Croall, H. (1992) *White Collar Crime*. Buckingham: Open University Press.

Crow, I. and Simon, F. (1987) *Unemployment and Magistrates Courts*. London: NACRO.

Crow, I., Richardson, P., Riddington, C. and Simon, F. (1989) *Unemployment, Crime and Offenders*. London: Routledge.

Cusson, M. and Pinsonneault, P. (1986) 'The decision to give up crime', in D. B. Cornish and R. V. G. Clarke (eds) *The Reasoning Criminal*. New York: Springer-Verlag.

Dentler, R. A. and Monroe, L. J. (1961) 'Social correlates of early adolescent theft', *American Sociological Review*, 26: 733–43.

Dickinson, D. (1993) *Crime and Unemployment*. Cambridge: Institute of Criminology.

Ditton, J. (1979) *Controlology*. London: Macmillan.

Dixon, D. (1991) *From Prohibition to Regulation*. Oxford: Clarendon Press.

Dorn, N., Murji, K. and South, N. (1992) *Traffickers: Drug Markets and Law Enforcement*. London: Routledge.

Douglas, J. (1967) *The Social Meanings of Suicide*. Princeton, NJ: Princeton University Press.

Dowds, L. and Mayhew, P. (1994) *Participation in Neighbourhood Watch: Findings from the 1992 British Crime Survey*, Home Office Research Findings No. 11. London: HMSO.

Durant, M., Thomas, M. and Willcock, H. (1972) *Crime, Criminals and the Law*. London: Office of Population Censuses and Surveys.

Durkheim, E. (1952) *Suicide: A Study in Sociology*. London: Routledge & Kegan Paul.

Dylan, B. (1988) 'Hurricane', *Lyrics: 1962–1985*. London: Paladin.

Elliott, D. S. and Ageton, S. S. (1980) 'Reconciling race and class differences in self-reported and official estimates of delinquency', *American Sociological Review*, 45: 95–110.

Elliott, D. S. and Huizinga, D. (1989) 'Improving self-reported measures of delinquency', in M. W. Klein (ed.) *Cross-National Research in Self-Reported Crime and Delinquency*. Dordrecht: Kluwer.

Elliott, D. S., Huizinga, D. and Ageton, S. S. (1985) *Explaining Delinquency and Drug Use*. Beverly Hills, CA: Sage.

Empey, L. T. and Erickson, M. L. (1966) 'Hidden delinquency and social status', *Social Forces*, 44: 546–54.

Erickson, M. and Empey, L. T. (1963) 'Court records, undetected delinquency and decision making', *Journal of Criminal Law, Criminology and Police Science*, 54: 456–69.

Farnworth, M., Thornberry, T. P., Krohn, M. D. and Lizotte, A. J. (1994) 'Measurement in the study of class and delinquency: integrating theory and research', *Journal of Research in Crime and Delinquency*, 31: 32–61.

Farrington, D. P. (1973) 'Self-reports of deviant behaviour: predictive and stable?', *Journal of Criminal Law and Criminology*, 64: 99–110.

Farrington, D. P. (1979) 'Longitudinal research on crime and delinquency', in N. Morris and M. Tonry (eds) *Crime and Justice*, Vol. 1. Chicago: University of Chicago Press.

Farrington, D. P. (1986) 'Age and crime', in M. Tonry and N. Morris (eds) *Crime and Justice*, Vol. 7. Chicago: University of Chicago Press.

Farrington, D. P. (1989) 'Self-reported and official offending from adolescence to adulthood', in M. W. Klein (ed.) *Cross-National Research in Self-reported Crime and Delinquency*. Dordrecht: Kluwer.

Farrington, D. P. (1994) 'Human development and criminal careers', in M. Maguire, R. Morgan and R. Reiner (eds) *The Oxford Handbook of Criminology*. Oxford: Clarendon.

Farrington, D. P and Burrows, J. N. (1993) 'Did shoplifting really decrease?', *British Journal of Criminology*, 33: 57–69.

Farrington, D. P. and Dowds, E. (1985) 'Disentangling criminal behaviour and police reaction', in D. Farrington and J. Gunn (eds) *Reactions to Crime: The Public, the Police, Courts and Prisons*. Chichester: John Wiley.

Farrington, D. P., Gallagher, B., Morley, L., St Ledger, R. J. and West, D. J. (1986a) 'Unemployment, school leaving and crime', *British Journal of Criminology*, 26: 335–56.

Farrington, D. P., Ohlin, L. E. and Wilson, J. Q. (1986b) *Understanding and Controlling Crime: Towards a New Research Strategy*. New York: Springer-Verlag.

Felson, M. (1994) *Crime and Everyday Life: Insights and Implications for Society*. London: Pine Forge Press.

Field, S. (1990) *Trends in Crime and their Interpretation: A Study of Recorded Crime in Post-War England and Wales*, Home Office Research Study No. 119. London: HMSO.

Fitzgerald, M. (1993a) *Ethnic Minorities and the Criminal Justice System*, The Royal Commission on Criminal Justice: Research Study No. 20. London: HMSO.

Fitzgerald, M. (1993b) ' "Racism": establishing the phenomenon', in D. Cook and B. Hudson (eds) *Racism and Criminology*. London: Sage.

Fitzgerald, M. (1995) 'Ethnic differences', in M. A. Walker (ed.) *Interpreting Crime Statistics*. Oxford: Clarendon Press.

Forslund, M. (1975) 'A self-report comparison of Indian and Anglo delinquents in Wyoming', *Criminology*, 13: 193–7.

Foster, J. (1990) *Villains: Crime and Community in the Inner City*. London: Routledge.

Foster, J. and Hope, T. (1993) *Housing, Community and Crime: The Impact of the Priority Estates Project*, Home Office Research Study No. 131. London: HMSO.

Fowles, T. (1993) 'Crown Prosecution Service: issues of implementation', paper presented to British Criminology Conference, Cardiff.

Gardiner, S. (1995) 'Criminal Justice Act 1991: management of the underclass and the potentiality of community', in L. Noaks, M. Levi and M. Maguire (eds) *Contemporary Issues in Criminology*. Cardiff: University of Wales Press.

Garland, D. (1985) 'The criminal and his science', *British Journal of Criminology*, 25: 109–37.

Garland, D. (1994) 'Of crimes and criminals: the development of criminology in Britain', in M. Maguire, R. Morgan and R. Reiner (eds) *The Oxford Handbook of Criminology*. Oxford: Clarendon.

Genn, H. (1988) 'Multiple victimisation', in M. Maguire and J. Pointing (eds) *Victims of Crime: A New Deal?* Milton Keynes: Open University Press.

George, V. and Howards, I. (1991) *Poverty amidst Affluence*. Cheltenham: Edward Elgar.

Giddens, A. (ed.) (1974) *Positivism and Sociology*. London: Heinemann.

Gilroy, P. (1982) 'The myth of black criminality', *The Socialist Register*, 47–56.

Gladstone, F. J. (1978) 'Vandalism among adolescent schoolboys', in R. V. G. Clarke (ed.) *Tackling Vandalism*, Home Office Research Study No. 47. London: HMSO.

Gold, M. (1966) 'Undetected delinquent behaviour', *Journal of Research in Crime and Delinquency*, 3: 27–46.

Gold, M. (1970) *Delinquent Behaviour in an American City*. Belmont, CA: Brooks/Cole.

Goring, C. (1913) *The English Convict*. London: HMSO.

Gormally, B., Lyner, O., Mulligan, G. and Worden, M. (1981) *Unemployment and Young Offenders in Northern Ireland*. Belfast: Northern Ireland Association for the Care and Resettlement of Offenders.

Gottfredson, M. and Hirschi, T. (1987) 'The methodological adequacy of longitudinal research on crime', *Criminology*, 25: 581–614.

Gottfredson, M. and Hirschi, T. (1990) *A General Theory of Crime*. Stanford, CA: Stanford University Press.

Gove, W. R., Hughes, M. and Geerken, M. (1985) 'Are Uniform Crime Reports a valid indicator of the index crimes? An affirmative answer with minor qualifications', *Criminology*, 23: 451–501.

Grace, S., Lloyd, C. and Smith, L. (1992) *Rape: From Recording to Conviction*, Research and Planning Unit Paper No. 17. London: Home Office.

Graham, J. and Bowling, B. (1995) *Young People and Crime*, Home Office Research Study No. 145. London: Home Office.

Gurr, T. (1976) *Rogues, Rebels and Reformers: A Political History of Urban Crime and Conflict*. London: Sage.

Gutzmore, C. (1983) 'Capital, "black youth" and crime', *Race and Class*, 25: 2.

Hagell, A. and Newburn, T. (1994) *Persistent Young Offenders*. London: Policy Studies Institute.

Hale, C. and Sabbagh, D. (1991) 'Testing the relationship between unemployment and crime: a methodological comment and empirical analysis using time series data from England and Wales', *Journal of Research in Crime and Delinquency*, 28: 400–417.

Hall, S., Critcher, C., Clarke, J., Jefferson, T. and Roberts, B. (1978) *Policing the Crisis*. London: Macmillan.

Haney, C., Banks, C. and Zimbardo, P. (1981) 'A study of prisoners and guards in a simulated prison', in D. Potter, J. Anderson, J. Clarke and P. Coombes (eds) *Society and the Social Sciences: An Introduction*. London: Routledge & Kegan Paul.

Hardt, R. G. and Peterson-Hardt, S. (1977) 'On determining the quality of the delinquency self-report method', *Journal of Research in Crime and Delinquency*, 14: 247–61.

Harris, R. and Webb, D. (1987) *Welfare, Power and Juvenile Justice*. London: Tavistock.

Hartless, J., Ditton, J., Nair, G. and Phillips, S. (1995) 'More sinned against than sinning: a study of young teenagers' experience of crime', *British Journal of Criminology*, 35: 114–33.

Harvey, L., Burnham, R. W., Kendall, K. and Pease, K. (1992) 'Gender differences in criminal justice: an international comparison', *British Journal of Criminology*, 32: 208–17.

Hedderman, C. (1995) 'Gender, crime and the criminal justice system', in M. A. Walker (ed.) *Interpreting Crime Statistics*. Oxford: Clarendon Press.

Heidensohn, F. (1989) *Crime and Society*. London: Macmillan.

Hill, M. (1990) *Social Security Policy in Britain*. Aldershot: Edward Elgar.

Hindelang, M. (1976) *Criminal Victimization in Eight American Cities: A Descriptive Analysis of Common Theft and Assault*. Cambridge, MA: Ballinger.

Hindelang, M. J., Hirschi, T. and Weis, J. G. (1979) 'Correlates of delinquency: the illusion of discrepancy between self-report and official measures', *American Sociological Review*, 44: 995–1014.

Hindelang, M., Hirschi, T. and Weis, J. G. (1981) *Measuring Delinquency*, Beverly Hills, CA: Sage.

Hindess, B. (1973) *The Use of Official Statistics in Sociology*. London: Macmillan.

Hirschi, T. (1969) *Causes of Delinquency*. Beverly Hills, CA: University of California Press.

Hirschi, T. and Gottfredson, M. (1983) 'Age and the explanation of crime', *American Journal of Sociology*, 89: 552–84.

Hobbs, D. (1988) *Doing the Business: Entrepreneurship, The Working Class and Detectives in the East End of London*. Oxford: Oxford University Press.

Hobbs, D. (1994) 'Professional and organized crime in Britain', in M. Maguire, R. Morgan and R. Reiner (eds) *The Oxford Handbook of Criminology*. Oxford: Clarendon.

Home Office (1989) *Criminal Statistics England and Wales*. London: HMSO.

Home Office (1993) *Criminal Statistics England and Wales*. London: HMSO.

Home Office (1994a) *Criminal Statistics England and Wales*. London: HMSO.

Home Office (1994b) *Race and the Criminal Justice System 1994*. London: HMSO.

Hood, R. (1992) *Race and Sentencing*. Oxford: Clarendon Press.

Hough, M. (1986) 'Victims of violent crime: findings from the first British Crime Survey', in E. Fattah (ed.) *From Crime Policy to Victim Policy*. London: Macmillan.

Hough, M. and Mayhew, P. (1983) *The British Crime Survey: First Report*. London: HMSO.

Hudson, B. (1989) 'Discrimination and disparity: the influence of race on sentencing', *New Community*, 16: 23–34.

Huizinga, D. and Elliott, D. S. (1986) 'Reassessing the reliability and validity of self-report delinquency measures', *Journal of Quantitative Criminology*, 2: 293–327.

Jefferson, T. (1993) 'The racism of criminalization: police and the production of the criminal other', in L. Gelsthorpe (ed.) *Minority Ethnic Groups in the Criminal Justice System*, Cropwood Conference Series No. 21. Cambridge: The Institute of Criminology, University of Cambridge.

Jefferson, T. and Walker, M. A. (1990) 'Ethnic minorities in the criminal justice system', *Criminal Law Review*, 83–95.

Jensen, G. F. and Eve, R. (1976) 'Sex differences in delinquency: an examination of popular sociological explanations', *Criminology*, 13: 427–48.

Johnson, R. E. (1979) *Juvenile Delinquency and its Origins*. London: Cambridge University Press.

Jones, T., McLean, B. and Young, J. (1986) *The Islington Crime Survey*. Aldershot: Gower.

Joseph Rowntree Foundation (1995) *Inquiry into Income and Wealth*. York: Joseph Rowntree Foundation.

Junger, M. (1989) 'Discrepancies between police and self-report data for Dutch racial minorities', *British Journal of Criminology*, 29: 273–84.

Junger-Tas, J. (1989) 'Self-report delinquency research in Holland with a perspective on international comparison', in M. W. Klein (ed.) *Cross-National Research in Self-Reported Crime and Delinquency*. Dordrecht: Kluwer.

Junger-Tas, J., Terlouw, G. J. and Klein, M. (eds) (1994) *Delinquent Behaviour among Young People in the Western World: First Results of the International Self-Report Delinquency Study*. Amsterdam: Kugler.

Jupp, V. (1989) *Methods of Criminological Research*. London: Unwin Hyman.

Kelman, H. C. (1978) 'Human use of human subjects: the problem of deception in social psychological experiments', in J. Bynner and K. M. Stribley (eds) *Social Research: Principles and Procedures*. Harlow: Longman.

Kinsey, R. (1984) *Merseyside Crime Survey*. Edinburgh: Centre for Criminology, University of Edinburgh.

Kitsuse, J. and Cicourel, A. (1963) 'A note on the uses of official statistics', *Social Problems*, 11: 131–9.

Klein, M. W. (ed.) (1989) *Cross-National Research in Self-Reported Crime and Delinquency*. Dordrecht: Kluwer.

Lambert, J. R. (1970) *Crime, Police and Race Relations*. London: Oxford University Press.

Landau, S. and Nathan, G. (1983) 'Selecting delinquents for cautioning in the London metropolitan area', *British Journal of Criminology*, 23: 128–48.

Lea, J. and Young, J. (1993) *What Is to Be Done about Law and Order?* 2nd edn. London: Pluto Press.

Levi, M. (1993) *The Investigation, Prosecution and Trial of Serious Fraud*, Royal Commission on Criminal Justice Research Study No. 14. London: HMSO

Levi, M. (1994) 'Violent crime', in M. Maguire, R. Morgan and R. Reiner (eds) *The Oxford Handbook of Criminology*. Oxford: Clarendon.

Levine, J. (1976) 'The potential for overreporting in victimization surveys', *Criminology*, 14: 307–27.

MacLean, B. (1991) 'In partial defence of socialist realism: some theoretical and methodological concerns of the local crime survey', *Crime, Law and Social Change*, 15: 213–54.

McCabe, S. and Sutcliffe, F. (1978) *Defining Crime: A Study of Police Decisions*. Oxford: Blackwell.

McClintock, F. H. and Avison, N. H. (1968) *Crime in England and Wales*. London: Heinemann.

McConville, M., Sanders, A. and Leng, R. (1991) *The Case for the Prosecution: Police Suspects and the Construction of Criminality*. London: Routledge.

McDonald, L. (1969) *Social Class and Delinquency*. London: Faber.

McLeary, R., Nienstedt, B. C. and Erven, J. M. (1982) 'Uniform Crime Reports as organizational outcomes: three time series experiments', *Social Problems*, 29: 361–72.

Maguire, M. (1994) Crime statistics, patterns and trends: changing perceptions and their implications, in M. Maguire, R. Morgan and R. Reiner (eds) *The Oxford Handbook of Criminology*. Oxford: Clarendon.

Maguire, M. and Corbett, C. (1987) *The Effects of Crime and the Work of Victim Support Schemes*. Aldershot: Gower.

Maguire, M. and Pointing, J. (eds) (1988) *Victims of Crime: A New Deal?* Milton Keynes: Open University Press.

Matza, D. (1969) *Becoming Deviant*. Englewood Cliffs, NJ: Prentice Hall.

Mawby, R. (1979) *Policing the City*. Farnborough: Saxon House.

Mawby, R., McCulloch, J. W. and Batta, I. D. (1979) 'Crime amongst Asian juveniles in Bradford', *International Journal of the Sociology of Law*, 7: 297–306.

Maxfield, M. T., Lewis, D. A. and Szoc, R. (1980) 'Producing official crimes: verified crime reports as measures of police output', *Social Science Quarterly*, 61: 221–36.

May, C. (1990) *Household Fires: Findings from the British Crime Survey 1988*, Research and Planning Unit Paper No. 57. London: HMSO.

Mayhew, P. and Elliot, D. P. (1990) 'Self-reported offending, victimization and the British Crime Survey', *Victims and Violence*, 5: 83–96.

Mayhew, P. and Hough, M. (1988) 'The British Crime Survey: origins and impact', in M. Maguire and J. Pointing (eds) *Victims of Crime: A New Deal?* Milton Keynes: Open University Press.

Mayhew, P., Clarke, R. V. G., Sturman, A. and Hough, J. M. (1976) *Crime as Opportunity*, Home Office Research Study No. 34. London: HMSO.

Mayhew, P., Elliott, D. and Dowds, L. (1989) *The 1988 British Crime Survey*, Home Office Research Study No. 111. London: HMSO.

Mayhew, P., Aye Maung, N. and Mirrlees-Black, C. (1993) *The 1992 British Crime Survey*, Home Office Research Study No. 132. London: HMSO.

Mayhew, P., Mirrlees-Black, C. and Aye Maung, N. (1994) *Trends in Crime: Findings from the 1994 British Crime Survey*, Home Office Research Findings No. 14. London: HMSO.

Mays, J. B. (1963) *Crime and the Social Structure*. London: Faber.

Mays, J. B. (1967) *Crime and the Social Structure*, 2nd edn. London: Faber.

Merton, R. (1956) 'The social-cultural environment and anomie', in H. Witmer and R. Kotinsky (eds) *New Perspectives for Research on Juvenile Delinquency*. Washington DC: US Government Printing Office.

Merton, R. (1957) *Social Theory and Social Structure*. New York: Free Press.

Miller, F., Court, S., Knox, E. and Brandon, S. (1974) *The School Years in Newcastle-upon-Tyne*. London: Oxford University Press.

Mirrlees-Black, C. and Aye Maung, N. (1994) *Fear of Crime: Findings from the 1992 British Crime Survey*, Home Office Research Findings No. 9. London: HMSO.

Mirrless-Black, C. (1995) 'Estimating the extent of domestic violence: findings from the 1992 British Crime Survey', *Research Bulletin* No. 37: 1–9. London: Home Office Research and Planning Unit.

Moffitt, T. E. (1989) 'Accommodating self-report methods to a low-delinquency culture: a longitudinal study from New Zealand', in M. W. Klein (ed.) *Cross-National Research in Self-Reported Crime and Delinquency*. Dordrecht: Kluwer.

Morris, A. (1987) *Women, Crime and Criminal Justice*. Oxford: Basil Blackwell.

Morris, N. and Hawkins, G. (1970) *The Honest Politician's Guide to Crime Control*. London: University of Chicago Press.

Morris, P. and Heal, K. (1981) *Crime Control and the Police*. London: Home Office Research Unit.

Morris, T. (1957) *The Criminal Area: A Study in Social Ecology*. London: Routledge & Kegan Paul.

Morris, T. (1989) *Crime and Criminal Justice since 1945*. Oxford: Basil Blackwell.

Mott, J. (1985) *Adult Prisons and Prisoners in England and Wales 1970–1982*, Home Office Research Study No. 84. London: HMSO.

Mott, J. and Mirrlees-Black, C. (1993) *Self-Reported Drug Misuse in England and Wales: Main Findings from the 1992 British Crime Survey*, Research Findings No. 7. London: Home Office Research and Statistics Department.

Murphy, F., Shirley, M. and Witmer, H. (1946) 'The incidence of hidden delinquency', *American Journal of Orthopsychiatry*, 16: 686–96.

Myrdal, G. (1962) *Challenge to Affluence*. London: Victor Gollancz.

Nelken, D. (1994) 'White-collar crime', in M. Maguire, R. Morgan and R. Reiner (eds) *The Oxford Handbook of Criminology*. Oxford: Clarendon.

Norris, C., Fielding, N., Kemp, C. and Fielding, J. (1992) 'Black and blue: an analysis of the influence of race on being stopped by the police', *British Journal of Sociology*, 43: 207–24.

Northumbria Police (1980) *Annual Report of the Chief Constable*. Ponteland: Northumbria Police.

Nye, F. I. (1958) *Family Relationships and Delinquent Behaviour*. New York: Wiley.

Nye, F. I. and Short, J. F. (1957) 'Scaling delinquent behaviour', *American Sociological Review*, 22: 326–31.

Nye, F. I., Short, J. F. and Olson, V. J. (1958) 'Socio-economic status and delinquent behaviour', *American Journal of Sociology*, 63: 381–9.

O'Brien, R. (1985) *Crime and Victimization Data*. London: Sage.

Orme, J. (1994) *A Study of the Relationship between Unemployment and Recorded Crime*, Home Office Statistical Findings No.1. London: Home Office Research and Statistics Department.

Ouston, J. (1984) 'Delinquency, family background and educational attainment', *British Journal of Criminology*, 24: 2–26.

Painter, K. (1991) *Wife Rape, Marriage and the Law: Survey Report*. Manchester: Faculty of Economic and Social Studies, University of Manchester.

Pearce, F. and Tombs, S. (1992) 'Realism and corporate crime', in R. Matthews and J. Young (eds) *Issues in Realist Criminology*. London: Sage.

Pearson, G. (1983) *Hooligan: A History of Respectable Fears*. London: Macmillan.

Pearson, G. (1994) 'Youth, crime and society', in M. Maguire, R. Morgan and R. Reiner (eds) *The Oxford Handbook of Criminology*. Oxford: Clarendon.

Pease, K. (1988) *Judgments of Crime Seriousness: Evidence from the 1984 British Crime Survey*, Research and Planning Unit Paper No. 44. London: HMSO.

Pepinsky, H. (1976) 'Police patrolmen's offence reporting behaviour', *Journal of Research in Crime and Delinquency*, 13: 33–47.

Pick, D. (1989) *Faces of Degeneration*. Cambridge: Cambridge University Press.

Plummer, K. (1979) 'Misunderstanding labelling perspectives', in D. Downes and P. Rock (eds) *Deviant Interpretations*. Oxford: Martin Robertson.

Pollak, O. (1961) *The Criminality of Women*. New York: A. S. Barnes.

Porterfield, A. L. (1946) *Youth in Trouble*. Fort Worth, TX: Leo Potishman Foundation.

Pyle, D. J. and Deadman, D. F. (1994) 'Crime and the business cycle in post-war Britain', *British Journal of Criminology*, 34: 339–57.

Quinney, R. (1970) *The Social Reality of Crime*. Boston: Little, Brown.

Reilly, B. and Witt, R. (1992) 'Crime and unemployment in Scotland', *Scottish Journal of Political Economy*, 39: 213–28.

Reiner, R. (1993) 'Race, crime and justice: models of interpretation', in L. Gelsthorpe (ed.) *Minority Ethnic Groups in the Criminal Justice System*, Cropwood Conference Series No. 21. Cambridge: The Institute of Criminology, University of Cambridge.

Reiss, A. J. and Rhodes. A. L. (1961) 'The distribution of juvenile delinquency in the social class structure', *American Sociological Review*, 26: 720–32.

Reuband, K. (1989) 'On the use of self-reports in measuring crime among adults: methodological problems and prospects', in M. W. Klein (ed.) *Cross-National Research in Self-Reported Crime and Delinquency*. Dordrecht: Kluwer.

Riley, D. (1984) 'Drivers' beliefs about alcohol and the law', *Research Bulletin* No. 17: 32–5. London: Home Office Research and Planning Unit.

Riley, D. (1985) 'Drinking drivers: the limits to deterrence', *The Howard Journal of Criminal Justice*, 24: 241–56.

Riley, D. and Shaw, M. (1985) *Parental Supervision and Juvenile Delinquency*, Home Office Research Study No. 83. London: HMSO.

Ringen, S. (1989) *The Possibility of Politics*. Oxford: Clarendon Press.

Robinson, W. S. (1950) 'Ecological correlations and the behaviour of individuals', *American Sociological Review*, 15: 351–7.

Rosenfeld, R. and Messner, S. (1995) 'Crime and the American dream: an institutional analysis', in F. Adler and W. S. Laufer (eds) *The Legacy of Anomie Theory*. London: Transaction Publishers.

Runciman, W. G. (1972) *Relative Deprivation and Social Justice*. Harmondsworth: Penguin.

Rutter, M. and Giller, H. (1983) *Juvenile Delinquency: Trends and Perspectives*. London: Penguin.

Sarnecki, J. (1989) 'Self-reported and recorded data on drug abuse and delinquency on 287 men in Stockholm', in M. W. Klein (ed.) *Cross-National Research in Self-Reported Crime and Delinquency*. Dordrecht: Kluwer.

Schur, E. M. (1965) *Crimes without Victims: Deviant Behaviour and Public Policy*. Englewood Cliffs, NJ: Prentice Hall.

Sellin, T. (1938) *Culture Conflict and Crime*. New York: Social Science Research Council.

Sellin, T. (1951) 'The significance of records of crime', *The Law Quarterly Review*, 67: 489–504.

Sellin, T. and Wolfgang, M. (1968) *The Measurement of Delinquency*. New York: Wiley.

Shah, R. and Pease, K. (1992) 'Crime, race and reporting to the police', *The Howard Journal*, 31: 192–9.

Shallice, A. and Gordon, P. (1990) *Black People, White Justice? Race and the Criminal Justice System*. London: Runnymede Trust.

Shaw, C. R. and McKay, H. D. (1942) *Juvenile Delinquency and Urban Areas*. Chicago: University of Chicago Press.

Short, J. F. and Nye, F. I. (1957) 'Reported behaviour as a criterion of deviant behaviour', *Social Problems*, 5: 207–13.

Simon, R. (1975) *Women and Crime*. Toronto/London: Lexington Books.

Skogan, W. (1976) 'Crime and crime rates', in W. G. Skogan (ed.) *Sample Surveys of the Victims of Crime*. Cambridge, MA: Ballinger.

Skogan, W. (1978) *Victimization Surveys and Criminal Justice Planning*, Law Enforcement Assistance Administration. Washington DC: US Government Printing Office.

Skogan, W. (1986) 'Methodological issues in the study of victimization', in E. Fattah (ed.) *From Crime Policy to Victim Policy*. London: Macmillan.

Smart, C. (1976) *Women, Crime and Criminology*. London: Routledge & Kegan Paul.

Smart, C. (1979) 'The new female criminal: reality or myth?', *British Journal of Criminology*, 19: 50–61.

Smith, D. A. and Visher, C. A. (1981) 'Street-level justice: situational determinants of police arrest decisions', *Social Problems*, 29: 167–77.

Smith, D. J. (1983) *Police and People in London: A Survey of Londoners*. London: Policy Studies Institute.

Smith, D. J. and Gray, J. (1985) *Police and People in London*. Aldershot: Gower.

Smith, L. (1989a) *Concerns about Rape*, Home Office Research Study No. 106. London: HMSO.

Smith, L. (1989b) *Domestic Violence*. London: HMSO.

Smithies, E. (1982) *Crime in Wartime: A Social History of Crime in World War II*. London: George Allen & Unwin.

South, N. (1994) 'Drugs: control, crime, and criminological studies', in M. Maguire, R. Morgan and R. Reiner (eds) *The Oxford Handbook of Criminology*. Oxford: Clarendon.

Sparks, R. (1981) 'Surveys of victimization: an optimistic assessment', in M. Tonry and N. Morris (eds) *Crime and Justice: An Annual Review of Research*, Vol. 3. London: University of Chicago Press.

Sparks, R., Genn, H. and Dodd, D. (1977) *Surveying Victims*. Chichester: Wiley.

Stanko, E. (1988) 'Hidden violence against women', in M. Maguire and J. Pointing (eds) *Victims of Crime: A New Deal?* Milton Keynes: Open University Press.

Steffensmeier, D. and Allan, E. (1995) 'Age-inequality and property crime', in J.

Hagan and R. Peterson (eds) *Crime and Inequality*. Stanford, CA: Stanford University Press.

Steffensmeier, D. and Harer, M. (1991) 'Did crime rise or fall during the Reagan presidency? The effects of an "aging" population on the nation's crime rate', *Journal of Research in Crime and Delinquency*, 28: 330–59.

Stinchcombe, A. (1963) 'Institutions of privacy in the determination of police administrative practice', *American Journal of Sociology*, 69: 150–60.

Sutherland, E. (1940) 'White collar criminality', *American Sociological Review*, 5: 1–12.

Sutherland, E. H. (1949) *White Collar Crime*. New York: Dryden.

Sutherland, E. and Cressey, D. (1960) *Principles of Criminology*, 6th edn. Chicago: Lippincott.

Tarling, R. (1982) 'Crime and unemployment', *Research Bulletin* No. 12. London: Home Office Research and Planning Unit.

Tarling, R. (1993) *Analysing Offending: Data, Models and Interpretation*. London: HMSO.

Taylor, I. (1994) 'The political economy of crime', in M. Maguire, R. Morgan and R. Reiner (eds) *The Oxford Handbook of Criminology*. Oxford: Clarendon.

Taylor, I., Walton, P. and Young, J. (1973) *The New Criminology*. London: Routledge & Kegan Paul.

Taylor, I., Walton, P. and Young, J. (eds) (1975) *Critical Criminology*. London: Routledge & Kegan Paul.

Thomas, C. W. and Hyman, J. M. (1978) 'Compliance theory, control theory and juvenile delinquency', in M. D. Krohn and R. L. Akers (eds) *Crime, Law and Sanctions*. London: Sage.

Thornberry, T. P. (1989) 'Panel effects and the use of self-reported measures of delinquency in longitudinal studies', in M. W. Klein (ed.) *Cross-National Research in Self-Reported Crime and Delinquency*. Dordrecht: Kluwer.

Thornberry, T. P. and Farnworth, M. (1982) 'Social correlates of criminal involvement: further evidence on the relationship between social status and criminal behaviour', *American Sociological Review*, 47: 505–18.

Tittle, C. R. and Villemez, W. (1977) 'Social class and criminality', *Social Forces*, 56: 474–503.

Tittle, C. R., Villemez, W. J. and Smith, D. A. (1978) 'The myth of social class and criminality: an empirical assessment of the empirical evidence', *American Sociological Review*, 43: 643–56.

Townsend, P. (1979) *Poverty in the United Kingdom: A Survey of Household Resources and Standards of Living*. Harmondsworth: Penguin.

Van Dijk, J, and Mayhew, P. (1992) *Criminal Victimisation in the Industrialised World: Key Findings of the 1989 and 1992 International Crime Surveys*. The Hague, Netherlands: Directorate for Crime Prevention.

Van Dijk, J., Mayhew, P. and Killias, M. (1990) *Experiences of Crime across the World: Key Findings of the 1989 International Crime Survey*. Boston: Kluwer.

Voss, H. L. (1966) 'Socio-economic status and reported delinquent behaviour', *Social Problems*, 13: 314–24.

Waddington, P. A. J. (1986) 'Mugging as a moral panic', *British Journal of Sociology*, 37: 245–59.

Wadsworth, M. (1979) *Roots of Delinquency*. Oxford: Martin Robertson.

Walker, M. A. (1981) *Crime: Reviews of United Kingdom Statistical Sources*, Vol. XV. Oxford: Pergamon Press.

Walker, M. A. (1989) 'The court disposal and remands of white, Afro-Caribbean, and Asian men 1983', *British Journal of Criminology*, 29: 353–67.

Walker, M. A. (1992) 'Do we need a clear-up rate?', *Policing and Society*, 2: 293–306.

Walker, M. A. (ed.) (1995) *Interpreting Crime Statistics*. Oxford: Clarendon Press.

Walker, M. A., Jefferson, T. and Seneviratne, M. (1990) *Ethnic Minorities, Young People and the Criminal Justice System: Main Report*. Sheffield: Centre for Criminological and Socio-Legal Studies, University of Sheffield.

Walker, N. (1971) *Crimes, Courts and Figures: An Introduction to Criminal Statistics*. Harmondsworth: Penguin.

Walklate, S. (1989) *Victimology: The Victim and the Criminal Justice Process*. London: Unwin Hyman.

Wallerstein, J. and Wyle, C. (1947) 'Our law abiding law-breakers', *Probation*, 25: 107–12.

Walmsley, R., Howard, L. and White, S. (1992) *The National Prison Survey 1991: Main Findings*, Home Office Research Study No. 128. London: HMSO.

Weiss, J. (1976) 'Liberation and crime: the invention of the new female criminal', *Crime and Social Justice*, 6: 17–27.

Weitekamp, E. (1989) 'Some problems with the use of self-reports in longitudinal research', in M. W. Klein (ed.) *Cross-National Research in Self-Reported Crime and Delinquency*. Dordrecht: Kluwer.

Wells, J. (1995) *Crime and Unemployment*, Economic Report Vol. 9. London: Employment Policy Institute.

West, D. J. (1969) *Present Conduct and Future Delinquency*. London: Heinemann.

West, D. J. (1982) *Delinquency: Its Roots, Careers and Prospects*. London: Heinemann.

West, D. J. and Farrington, D. P. (1973) *Who Becomes Delinquent?* London: Heinemann.

West, D. J. and Farrington, D. P. (1977) *The Delinquent Way of Life*. London: Heinemann.

Wheeler, S. (1967) 'Criminal statistics: a reformulation of the problem', *Journal of Criminal Law, Criminology and Police Science*, 56: 277–84.

Wiles, P. (1971) 'Criminal statistics and sociological explanations of crime', in W. Carson and P. Wiles (eds) *The Sociology of Crime and Delinquency in Britain: The British Tradition*. Oxford: Martin Robertson.

Wilkins, L. (1960) *Delinquent Generations*. London: Home Office Research Unit.

Wilkins, L. (1964) *Social Deviance: Social Policy, Action and Research*. London: Tavistock.

Williams, J. R. and Gold, M. (1972) 'From delinquent behaviour to official delinquency', *Social Problems*, 20: 209–29.

Willis, C. F. (1983) *The Use, Effectiveness and Impact of Police Stop and Search Powers*, Home Office Research and Planning Unit Paper No. 15. London: HMSO.

Wilson, J. Q. and Herrnstein, R. J. (1985) *Crime and Human Nature*. New York: Simon & Schuster.

Wise, N. B. (1967) 'Juvenile delinquency among middle class girls', in E. W. Vaz (ed.) *Middle Class Juvenile Delinquency*. New York: Harper and Row.

Wolfgang, M. E., Figlio, R. M. and Sellin, T. (1972) *Delinquency in a Birth Cohort*. Chicago: Chicago University Press.

Wolfgang, M. E., Thornberry, T. P. and Figlio, R. M. (1987) *From Boy to Man, From Delinquency to Crime*. Chicago: University of Chicago Press.

Young, J. (1971) *The Drugtakers*. London: Paladin.

Young, J. (1986) 'The failure of criminology', in R. Matthews and J. Young (eds) *Confronting Crime*. London: Sage.

Young, J. (1988a) 'Radical criminology in Britain: the emergence of a competing paradigm', in P. Rock (ed.) *A History of British Criminology*. Oxford: Clarendon Press.

Young, J. (1988b) 'Risk of crime and fear of crime: a realist based critique of survey-based assumptions', in M. Maguire and J. Pointing (eds) *Victims of Crime: A New Deal?* Milton Keynes: Open University Press.

Young, J. (1992) 'Ten points of realism', in J. Young and R. Matthews (eds) *Rethinking Criminology: The Realist Debate*. London: Sage.

Young, J. (1994) 'Incessant chatter: current paradigms in criminology', in M. Maguire, R. Morgan and R. Reiner (eds) *The Oxford Handbook of Criminology*. Oxford: Clarendon.

Young, J. and Matthews, R. (1992) 'Questioning left realism', in R. Matthews and J. Young (eds) *Issues in Realist Criminology*. London: Sage.

Young, M. (1991) *An Inside Job*. Oxford: Clarendon Press.

Zedner, L. (1994) 'Victims', in M. Maguire, R. Morgan and R. Reiner (eds) *The Oxford Handbook of Criminology*. Oxford: Clarendon.

Index